Digital Content Ma

Digital Content Marketing: Creating Value in Practice introduces the principles of the content marketing discipline and serves as a guide to any professional or student who wants to learn how to successfully plan and implement digital content marketing strategies and tactics.

Filled with contemporary examples of the most successful creative content marketing practices, case studies, and professional advice from subject experts, this text offers an in-depth view of the world of content marketing from a value-based perspective. The textbook also includes practical advice on content marketing ideation, content management, and content curation, as well as offering recommendations for the best content marketing software.

The textbook offers a good balance of both theory and practice and is suitable for advanced undergraduate students and postgraduate students studying content marketing, digital marketing or social media marketing. Support material includes an instructor manual, chapter-by-chapter PowerPoint slides and a test bank of exam questions.

Dr Agata Krowinska is a Lecturer in Digital Marketing at The Business School at Edinburgh Napier University.

Prof Christof Backhaus is Professor of Marketing and Head of Research at The Business School at Edinburgh Napier University.

Benjamin Becker has been working for Omnicom Media Group Germany for 10 years. As Managing Partner, he is responsible for the group's new business and corporate communications as well as business transformation.

Fabian Bosser works at Omnicom Media Group Germany, with the team responsible for the development of new products, content strategies, and customised models in an international context.

Digital Content Marketing

Creating Value in Practice

Edited by Agata Krowinska, Christof Backhaus, Benjamin Becker, and Fabian Bosser

Routledge
Taylor & Francis Group

LONDON AND NEW YORK

Designed cover image: smartboy10

First published 2024
by Routledge
4 Park Square, Milton Park, Abingdon, Oxon OX14 4RN

and by Routledge
605 Third Avenue, New York, NY 10158

Routledge is an imprint of the Taylor & Francis Group, an informa business

British Library Cataloguing-in-Publication Data
A catalogue record for this book is available from the British Library

Library of Congress Cataloging-in-Publication Data
Names: Krowinska, Agata, editor. | Backhaus, Christof, editor.
Title: Digital content marketing : creating value in practice / edited by Agata Krowinska, Christof Backhaus, Benjamin Becker and Fabian Bosser.
Description: First Edition. | New York, NY : Routledge, 2024. |
Includes bibliographical references and index. |
Identifiers: LCCN 2023023320 (print) | LCCN 2023023321 (ebook) |
ISBN 9781032387376 (hardback) | ISBN 9781032346793 (paperback) |
ISBN 9781003346500 (ebook)
Subjects: LCSH: Internet marketing. | Strategic planning. | Value added.
Classification: LCC HF5415.1265 D53853 2024 (print) |
LCC HF5415.1265 (ebook) | DDC 658.8/72--dc23/eng/20230713
LC record available at https://lccn.loc.gov/2023023320
LC ebook record available at https://lccn.loc.gov/2023023321

ISBN: 978-1-032-38737-6 (hbk)
ISBN: 978-1-032-34679-3 (pbk)
ISBN: 978-1-003-34650-0 (ebk)

DOI: 10.4324/9781003346500

Typeset in Times New Roman
by MPS Limited, Dehradun

Access the Support Material: www.routledge.com/9781032346793

Contents

List of contributors

Dr Agata Krowinska is a lecturer in digital marketing at Edinburgh Napier University. She leads a variety of digital marketing modules at both postgraduate and undergraduate levels. Agata is an engaging educator passionate about helping her students develop practical digital skills and in-depth knowledge about the ever-changing digital marketing environment. Her main research interests lie in content marketing, social media engagement behaviours, and use of artificial intelligence. Agata is also a Programme Leader for MSc International Marketing programme suite and UG dissertation co-ordinator for Marketing subject group.

Prof Christof Backhaus is Professor of Marketing and Head of Research at The Business School at ENU. Following completion of his PhD at the University of Muenster, he worked as an Assistant Professor at the Universities of Dortmund, Bochum, and Braunschweig in Germany, and as a Professor of Marketing at Newcastle University Business School and at Aston Business School. Christof's research interest lies primarily in the field of Retail and Services Marketing and Management. His work has been published in international marketing journals such as the *Journal of Business Research, Journal of Marketing, Journal of Retailing, Journal of the Academy of Marketing Science, Journal of Small Business Management, Industrial Marketing Management*, and *Psychology & Marketing*. To ensure that his research activities are of practical relevance, he regularly collaborates with companies and industry associations to help resolve issues in the areas of service innovation, customer and partner relationship management, marketing control and monitoring, and sponsorship management.

Benjamin Becker has been working for Omnicom Media Group Germany for ten years. As Managing Partner he is responsible for the group's new business, corporate communications and marketing as well as identifying and driving new business areas, e.g., driving the digital transformation of sports institutions as well as rights holders and supporting clients in identifying suitable content-/Sponsoring partners for consumer activation. He and his team recently celebrated the 50th episode of the corporate podcast 'Let's Make Lemonade'. As host, Benjamin is happy to have been ranked in the top ten on Spotify Business & Technology. For the past years, Benjamin has been the Board Member at Marketing Club Düsseldorf. Before Omnicom Media Group, Benjamin worked for about ten years in management consulting. Benjamin is married, father of two sons, lives in Düsseldorf and is an avid tennis player and sports fan.

Fabian Bosser is Group Manager at Omnicom Media Group Germany and responsible for the development of new products, content strategies and customised models in an international context. He has experience in business development from previous positions at various startups and companies. The focus of his work is on transforming and building new models and products for customers and potential customers.

He is a Member of the Advisory Board in the Marketing Club Düsseldorf and believes in strong partnerships and collaboration with communities, startups and universities.

Dr Jackie Cameron is a digital media and content marketing specialist, who has worked on strategies and conceptualised, developed, and delivered an extensive range of tactical assets for local, national, and global companies. She has worked for content marketing, advertising and PR agencies as well as in-house marketing communications teams in roles ranging from copywriter and content curator to account director. Project management experience includes researching, planning, and launching titles (print and digital) for media companies. As digital marketing lecturer, at the Edinburgh Napier University Dr Cameron has supervised dozens of students in the UK and elsewhere on their final-year research projects and has delivered bespoke content marketing training to London-listed companies.

Lucas Petermeier is Managing Director at FUSE, which is part of Omnicom Group. FUSE is an agency for popcultural marketing, delivering impactful brand communication through the perfect match between data, insights, strategy, creativity, and consultancy. Besides social media, e-sports and gaming, sports and entertainment are also part of FUSE's core services. Lucas Petermeier was previously responsible for live communications, sponsorships, and brand cooperations across all locations and clients. Before joining FUSE, the sports and business administration graduate was, among other things, responsible for brand experience and brand cooperations at Porsche and also headed the Motorsport and Business Development department at Volkswagen Group China.

Dr Denitsa Dineva joined Cardiff Business School in 2020 as a lecturer in Marketing and Strategy. Denitsa has a degree in Business and Management, a specialist MSc degree in Marketing, and a PhD in Business and Management (Digital Marketing). Denitsa's work has been published in inter-disciplinary outlets including marketing, information technology, social psychology, and hospitality. Denitsa acts as an ad hoc reviewer for a number of internationally recognised journals. At present, Denitsa sits on the grant review panel for the College of Arts, Humanities and Social Sciences and is a member of Cardiff Business School's Ethics Committee.

Dr Clidna Soraghan is a lecturer in marketing at Edinburgh Napier University. Her main research interests include critical marketing, social marketing, and behaviour change. Clidna is particularly interested in examining societal issues and the impact of marketing on society. She has published in international, peer-reviewed journals and presented at several international conferences. Clidna is a Fellow of the Higher Education Academy and a Member of the Chartered Institute of Marketing.

Dr Elaine Mercer-Jones has taught business and marketing ethics at Edinburgh Napier University for 25 years. She has a PhD in the History of Medicine from Edinburgh University and, as 'Elaine Thomson', is the author of numerous journal articles on history and sociology. Her current research interests include the impact of social media marketing on Gen Z girls' self-esteem, and the role of archives as a source of advertising and other ephemera for historical marketing research. She is also working on an analysis of how the UK Atomic Energy Authority used marketing and public relations at Dounreay Nuclear Power Development Establishment visitors' centre between c.1960 and 2000. As E. S. Thomson she is a best-selling author of historical crime fiction.

Dr Simone Kurtzke is a former digital industry professional turned lecturer, and the Deputy Head for Global Online at Edinburgh Napier University. She ran early social media campaigns at a London digital agency in 2007, before becoming the Scottish Tourist Board's first Social Media Manager in 2011. She has also worked at Google's Digital Garage in Edinburgh and as a freelancer for various agencies. Simone considers herself half academic/half practitioner, and her goal is to bridge the gap between marketing theory and practice, to ensure marketing education is aligned with the needs of industry and business. Simone's research interests are marketing education, small business marketing, and digital marketing. Originally from Germany, Simone moved to the UK in 2000 and has lived and worked in London, Aberdeen, and Edinburgh. She loves teaching herself new things and feels very lucky that in digital this comes with the territory.

Dr Ashleigh Logan-McFarlane is a lecturer in marketing at Edinburgh Napier University. Ashleigh's research predominantly explores societal issues related to consumer behaviour and marketing. Her expertise in digital ethnographic methods reveals how emerging behaviours in digital spaces are shaping marketplace behaviours with a focus on influencers, market dynamics, labour, fashion marketing, and visual methodologies. Ashleigh's recent research is published in the *European Journal of Marketing* and the *Journal of Fashion Marketing and Management*.

Dr Kat Rezai is a lecturer in marketing at Edinburgh Napier University, specialising in market research, marketing communications, and marketing ethics. Kat's research predominantly explores the uneasy relationships between social media content, consumer wellbeing, self-image and body image. Her latest research explores the impact of social media content on teenage girls' consumer wellbeing and is leading a team on building social media literacy workshops to help empower young consumers.

Dr Fan Lu obtained her PhD in Operations Management from Northumbria University in 2021, after completing her MSc in Marketing and Management at Loughborough University in 2014. She joined Edinburgh Napier University the same year and has since been teaching marketing-related modules to both undergraduate and postgraduate students. Her research interests currently revolve around the impact of Metaverse implementations on customer engagement within the retail sector.

Jasmiina Milne is a PhD candidate in marketing at Edinburgh Napier University. Her research interests lie in contemporary societal issues related to consumer behaviour and marketing. Her current research focuses on consumer behaviour, social media, body image and beauty culture, as she explores how Instagram influences women's cosmetic surgery and non-surgical procedure consumption decision-making. Jasmina specialises in qualitative research methods, including digital and novel visual research methods, which reveal how emerging behaviours in digital spaces are shaping marketplace behaviours.

1 Introduction to Digital Content Marketing

By Dr Agata Krowinska and Prof Christof Backhaus

Learning Outcomes

- To gain an in-depth understanding of content marketing and its history.
- To identify the main differences between advertising and content marketing.
- To understand the role that value plays in content marketing.
- To acknowledge the benefits of content marketing, alongside the main challenges that content creators face in modern marketing practice.

The Prevalence of Digital Content

In today's marketplace the success of a company's digital marketing communications largely depends on the quality of its content marketing (Balteş, 2015). With the growing number of content-sharing platforms, the phrase 'Content is King', coined by Bill Gates 27 years ago, has never been more relevant (Gates, 1996, cited in Evans, 2017). New developments in digital technology and the emergence of Web 2.0 have given consumers and companies an active voice in the market, which is expressed via different forms of digital content. Every day, internet users are exposed to a significant volume of online material that comes from brands, social media influencers, third party endorsements, and other users. Recent statistics show that over 3.96 billion people worldwide consume content on social media and that, on average, they spend more than two hours a day using different platforms (Broadband Search, 2023). The new social media sensation TikTok has recently reached one billion users, and according to the latest research, short videos have developed into the most widespread trend amongst marketers (HubSpot, 2023). Digital marketers have quickly become aware of the benefits of content marketing. This, in turn, has led to the emergence of a content marketing industry that achieved an estimated revenue of $63 billion in 2022 alone, with industry revenues predicted to reach $72 billion in 2023 and $107 billion by the end of 2026 (Statista, 2023).

DOI: 10.4324/9781003346500-1

What is Content Marketing?

To understand what content marketing is, we must first explain what we mean by 'content'. According to Handley and Chapman (2011, p. 21) content is 'anything created and uploaded to a website: the words, images or other things that resides here'. As such, content can be seen as everything that users consume whilst utilising digital platforms (Syrdal & Briggs, 2018). However, simply distributing any type of digital material to online users is not enough to achieve marketing success (Lopes & Casais, 2022). The content that companies share with their audiences must be created and delivered strategically, as an integrated part of the marketing mix. This is reflected in the Content Marketing Institute's definition, which refers to content marketing as:

> A strategic marketing approach focused on creating and distributing valuable, relevant, and consistent content to attract and retain a clearly defined audience – and, ultimately, to drive profitable customer action.
>
> (Content Marketing Institute, 2016)

Based on the above definition, content that is distributed to consumers must be perceived by them to be of value. In contrast to traditional advertising approaches, where the marketing message focuses on promoting a product or a service, content marketing focuses on generating value to consumers by delivering a specific piece of content (Lopes & Casais, 2022). As pointed out by Hollebeek and Macky (2019), digital content marketing is 'designed to build and maintain consumers' long-term engagement, trust, and relationships, rather than attempt to convince prospects to purchase the firm's offerings directly' (Hollebeek & Macky 2019, p. 21). In content marketing practice, a company is only mentioned indirectly, as the primary focus of the content is to attract users (Stürmer & Einwiller, 2022). This represents a paradigm shift and highlights the consumer-centric approach that is at the core of content marketing (Holliman & Rowley, 2014; Terho et al., 2022). As such, one of the key takeaways this book communicates is that content marketing can only be effective if the content is in some way of **value** to the consumer.

So, how can we create and deliver content that provides value to the customer or user? Importantly:

It is the recipient who determines whether content is of value or not.

Even if an organisation puts a tremendous effort into developing a state-of-the-art content marketing campaign, this does not automatically mean that the target audience will see it as valuable. Of course, this begs the question 'what is value?' and in what sense might we use the term in a content marketing context?

The creation of customer value is at the heart of any business (Kumar & Reinartz, 2016). Not being able to create value, in some form, for one's customers means that one will be navigating the business out of the market: perceived value is the precondition that elicits a willingness to pay a price so that a business can generate revenues and profits. Profits, as a share of revenues generated, then represent value as seen from the perspective of the firm (Kumar & Reinartz 2016).

With purchasing situations following a 'give' and 'get' logic, value derives from comparing the 'give' with the 'get'. Perceived customer value results from the perceived benefits ('get') of a purchase exceeding what we need to sacrifice ('give') to achieve those benefits. Both perceived benefits and sacrifices can result from various attributes and sources, and what constitutes a benefit and sacrifice differs across consumers (Zeithaml, 1988). Summarising four perspectives on consumer-perceived value, Zeithaml defines perceived value as 'the consumer's overall assessment of the utility of a product based on perceptions of what is received and what is given' (Zeithaml, 1998, p. 14).

This idea of 'get' and 'give' also applies in content marketing. Regarding the 'get' element, the benefits of content consumption might appear in several different forms. Referring to some of the main forms, content can include *information benefits*, where users learn something that they perceive to be useful (De Vries et al., 2012). Content consumption can also have *social benefits*, where users are able to feel connected to the brand or the brand community(Dolan et al., 2015). Furthermore, content can provide some form of enjoyment to users through the *entertainment benefits* it delivers (Muntinga, 2011). There is also a 'give' element involved in content consumption. Specifically, consuming content means sacrificing time and attention. But there are other sacrifices too: importantly, the business model used by content marketers relies on generating data. Consuming content leaves digital traces – data that is consciously or unconsciously left behind, (or 'given') by users. Providers, and others, then work with such data, often with unlooked-for consequences. In the following chapters, when speaking of information value, social value, and entertainment value, we refer to value with a focus on benefits, bearing in mind that these are benefits rather than representing the overall trade-off of the 'give' and 'get' components of content consumption.

To be valuable, content must be relevant to the consumer and the brand which shares the content. Every day, in both online and offline environments, we 'scroll through' large amounts of content that we deem of little or no relevance – in the news, on social media channels, when streaming music, or on YouTube or TV. The more relevant a piece of content is, the more likely it is that we interact with it. This triggers network effects, so that the more users interact with branded content, the more visible the content becomes. Thus, for content marketing to work effectively, the audience must be clearly defined, the content produced matching the interests of the chosen target market. As with other marketing methods, delivering content to the appropriate audience at the appropriate time is vital (Lopes & Casais, 2022).

Content must also be consistent across different social media channels. Just like human beings, brands have an active voice in the marketplace, and this voice is reflected in the content they share with users and with their brand communities. The content that an organisation shares online helps that organisation reflect its personality and brand values. It is crucial, therefore, that the personality that is portrayed and reflected online is consistent across all platforms and channels. Companies should create a clear branding guide for their social media employees to ensure quality and consistency of their content marketing.

A Brief History of Content Marketing Practice

Although the exact origins of content marketing are difficult to pinpoint, several milestones in the development of content marketing have been identified (Lopes & Casais, 2022; Pulizzi, 2012). *The Furrow*, a trade marketing magazine published in-house in 1895 by John Deere, a company specialising in agricultural equipment, is often considered the most notable example of early content marketing (Content Marketing Institute, 2013.) Instead of directly advertising their equipment, John Deere introduced *The Furrow* magazine to educate farmers on the latest technology and how it could improve their business operations (Pulizzi, 2012). As a result, John Deere became a credible source of information for agriculturists, leading them to turn to the company when they needed equipment, and ultimately increasing John Deere's revenue (Pulizzi, 2012). By 1912, the magazine had a readership of over four million (Gardiner, 2013). To this day, the online edition of *The Furrow* attracts its target audience using tailored, relevant, and valuable content (see also: www. deere.com/en/publications/the-furrow/).

Another example is JELL-O, the American brand that sells powdered gelatine desserts. JELL-O used a similar approach to drive growth in the early 1900s by distributing free recipe books to customers; while Sears adopted the same strategy in the 1920s by launching the World's Largest Store (WLS) Radio Show aimed at the farming community (Pulizzi, 2012).

One of the most notable examples of content marketing practice in recent years is the video series 'Will it Blend?' created by the blender manufacturer Blendtec and published on YouTube since 2006. In each episode of the series, the company's CEO blends various objects using Blendtec blenders, showcasing the product's features. Blended objects ranged from paintballs to iPads. Due to its entertainment value the series has become a huge success, and Blendtec YouTube content continues to attract regular viewership. The series marks the beginning of modern digital content marketing practice.

What are the Key Benefits of Content Marketing Practice?

Content creation has become a critical element of digital marketing practice across virtually all industries. Digital content now represents a business asset that fosters relationships with customers, facilitates the pre-sales process, and actualises the customer's purchase decision (Wall & Spinuzzi, 2018). Organisations that utilise content marketing as part of their promotional mix can achieve numerous benefits. For example, content published online can **stimulate positive customer engagement** on social media, such as likes, comments and shares (Doorn van et al., 2010). In turn, this can strengthen consumer loyalty (Fehrer et al., 2018), increase consumer satisfaction (Carvalho & Fernandes, 2018), positively influence purchase intentions (Wirtz et al., 2013) and drive electronic word of mouth (eWOM) (Islam & Rahman, 2016). High engagement rates can also make content 'go viral' and be more visible to new users. User engagement with a brand's content can be viewed as a metric of how well the message was conveyed, as it shows a post's popularity (Lopes & Casais, 2022). Content marketing practice can also **help brands develop better relationships with their customers**. By producing content that is valuable and relevant to their audience, organisations can be perceived as more credible and trustworthy (Yaghtin et al., 2020). Furthermore, sharing content that is specific to their audience helps an organisation build a community of like-minded people who share common interests. In turn, this can help consumers form deeper connections with a brand, and with other customers.

Content marketing can also help brands **achieve brand-related objectives**, for example to establish themselves as thought leaders in their industry or to become more authoritative (Du Plessis, 2017). By consistently curating high-quality content informing audiences about important and relevant topics in their industry, an organisation can position itself as an expert and a valuable resource for its target market. This can lead to increased trust which in turn can lead to more sales. Content marketing can also help **humanise a brand** (Plessis, 2017), making it more relatable and authentic to the target audience. Through content, a brand can present their digital persona, and better showcase their character, values, and views; they can tell their story in a way that resonates with their audience and generates positive engagement behaviours (van Doorn et al., 2010). Sharing authentic content on social media can add a personal touch and establish a recognisable brand voice (Lopes & Casais, 2022). Given all of the above, it is perhaps not surprising that HubSpot (2023) predicts a significant increase in the use of relatable content. In 2023, 46 per cent of social media marketers are planning to use this type of content for the first time, and of those marketers who already integrate it, 49 per cent plan to increase their investment.

Content marketing can also **add value to search engine optimisation (SEO) efforts** (Walter, 2022). One of the key factors in SEO is content that answers users' questions. Brands that produce informative content have a higher chance of increasing their ranking in search results. Also, by developing content that is centred around keywords related to their business, organisations can improve their relevance to search queries. Most importantly, high-quality content can generate backlinks from other websites sharing that content, thereby signalling to search engines that a company's website is valuable, and again improving its rankings. Finally, traffic that comes from social media can also have a positive impact on brand positioning.

Key Challenges of Content Marketing Practice

While there are several benefits to marketers of implementing content marketing into their marketing strategy, there are also some challenges. Many organisations distribute content online, which means that there is strong competition in the market (Wang et al., 2023). As such, it is becoming more difficult for an organisation to break through and develop innovative content that stimulates positive customer engagement (van Doorn et al., 2010). Furthermore, the media landscape today is much more fragmented compared to the 1950s, when a single TV commercial could reach a significant portion of the target market (Wall & Spinuzzi, 2018). In the past, it was common to spend time together in the evening watching favourite TV programmes. Nowadays, because of the high number of digital content-sharing services, we can decide individually what we would like to watch, when we would like to watch it, and on which platform. This presents a challenge to marketers as there is a need to develop much more personalised content. In addition, the digital marketing landscape is constantly growing and changing, with new platforms being developed. These new platforms might offer different functionalities and be guided by different rules. Thus, while a piece of content may be appropriate for one social media platform, it may not work on another, implying that marketers need to produce content adaptation for different digital channels. The 24/7 online environment means there is a constant need for more content to be created. Organisations need to develop new and original ideas continually, which over time can become increasingly difficult. Another challenge is that content needs to be developed for different marketing goals (Wang et al., 2023), which again requires more effort, more original thinking, and dedicated creative resources.

What This Book Offers

This book introduces the key strategic steps marketers must take to develop a successful content marketing strategy. Throughout 12 chapters you will learn how to create compelling content that resonates with audiences and drives positive consumer engagement. You will explore various digital channels and tactics for content distribution, and get to know different ways to create valuable, meaningful, and memorable content. Many of the book's chapters are supported by real case studies which illustrate how different organisations practice content marketing to achieve their marketing objectives. Selected chapters are accompanied by interviews with industry experts, who share their industry knowledge and provide you with tips and shortcuts related to various aspects of content marketing strategy. Below we provide an outline of what follows.

Chapter 2: Content Marketing Planning, Execution, and Measurement

In this chapter, Dr Fan Lu discusses the process of planning digital content marketing strategy. She addresses each step of the planning process, including situational analysis, objective setting, strategy development, tactics selection, and campaign evaluation. The final part of the chapter explores KPIs and measurement techniques. The chapter ends with an interview with Stephan Naumann who specialises in content marketing strategy planning and execution at Omnicom agency. Stephan Naumann highlights best practice and outlines the most common pitfalls of planning and implementation.

Chapter 3: Content Marketing Ideation: How to Generate and Manage Creative Concepts

In this chapter, Dr Jackie Cameron focuses on practicalities related to content development and management. The chapter offers a guide to the core elements of content marketing practice. The chapter also explores the concept of hero, hygiene, and hub content, which are an essential part of modern content strategy. The chapter concludes with an interview with Fabian Bosser that offers practical tips for developing engaging digital content.

Chapter 4: Value Creation Through Digital Content: Informative Value

Written by Dr Agata Krowinska, this chapter discusses the role that informative value plays in driving positive social media engagement behaviours. Various types of informative content such as branded educational videos, behind the scenes videos, online TV series, infographics, blogs, and branded editorials are discussed. The chapter also provides a case study from Renault ZOE E-Tech 100% electric campaign highlighting the role that educational content plays in content marketing practice.

Chapter 5: Value Creation Through Digital Content: Entertainment Value

In this chapter, Dr Agata Krowinska and Dr Clidna Soraghan discuss the role that entertainment value plays in content marketing practices. Different forms and features of online branded entertainment are introduced. Furthermore, the chapter talks about digital product placements and their unique benefits. Suggestions are offered on how marketers can use humour in their content marketing tactics to become relatable to their target market. Finally, the chapter discusses the role that content aesthetics play in stimulating user engagement.

Chapter 6: Value Creation Through Digital Content: Social Value

Written by Jasmiina Milne, this chapter centres on the role that social value plays in content marketing practice. Readers will learn about the importance of online communities and their impact on organisations. The chapter also discusses how brands use current trends and events in their content marketing practices, thereby stimulating engagement. At the end of the chapter, a case study from MAN Truck & Bus showcases how social value can be embedded within a content marketing strategy.

Chapter 7: Value Creation Through Digital Content: User Co-creation Value

In Chapter 7, Dr Denitsa Dineva discusses the fundamental principles of value co-creation and user-generated content (UGC). The chapter discusses the essential steps that organisations must take to stimulate the highest quality user-generated content, introducing and reviewing the most prominent forms of digital content co-creation. A step-by-step UGC marketing campaign process is outlined, and practical considerations for user co-created content are discussed. The chapter concludes with a case study from McDonalds that discusses their successful UGC campaign.

Chapter 8: Digital Content and Social Media Influencers

Written by Dr Ashleigh Logan-McFarlane, this chapter discusses social media influencer domains and reviews different types of influencers, such as mega, macro, micro, and nano. The chapter evaluates social media influencer partnerships and talks about important issues of trust and authenticity. A criteria checklist for selecting social media influencers for social media campaigns is also presented. The concepts of parasocial interaction and issues surrounding social media influencer gendered and exploitative labour are also addressed. The chapter also explores the concept of virtual influencers (VI).

Chapter 9: Content Curation: Best Practices and Techniques

In this chapter, Dr Jackie Cameron discusses the role that content curation plays in stimulating social media brand-related engagement. Issues related to topic selection and copyright are addressed. The chapter is supported by an interview with Raphael Fix, the Head of Innovation Management at Omnicom Media Group, Germany.

Chapter 10: Content Marketing and Sponsorship

Chapter 10, co-authored by Benjamin Becker, Lucas Petermeier, and Christof Backhaus, focuses on the role of content marketing within sponsorship and sponsorship leveraging. Following an outline of the evolution of sponsorship as a marketing instrument, the chapter discusses the relevance of content marketing in the context of sponsorship, illustrating effective content-based sponsorship leveraging with practice-based examples. Subsequently, the authors present four key principles supporting content-based leveraging, as well as a structured process to help manage sponsorship partnerships for generating value for fans and brand-related communities.

Chapter 11: The Dark Side of Marketing

In Chapter 11, Dr Elaine Mercer-Jones and Dr Kat Rezai discuss the dark side of content marketing. Important ethical considerations related to content marketing practices and more general content marketing limitations are addressed in depth. The chapter reflects on matters of responsibility, honesty, and harm, and discuss ethical approaches and ways of thinking that might offer some practical and theoretical solutions to modern marketers. The chapter also provides a set of guidelines on how to practice ethical content marketing.

Chapter 12: Contemporary and Emerging Content Marketing Trends

Written by Dr Simone Kurtzke, the final chapter of the book focuses on the latest content marketing trends. Metaverse and virtual content marketing are discussed in depth. The chapter focuses on the role of artificial intelligence in content marketing practice, addresses the differences between machine learning and generative AI, explores AI content creation in practice, and demonstrates the role and use of prompts in content creation. At the end of the chapter, readers will find a list of AI content creation tools and case study from Škoda.

The book concludes with an overall summary of the guiding principles of content marketing.

End of Chapter Exercise

1. End of Chapter Quiz – below is a set of questions based on Chapter 1

*   What is the main difference between content marketing and traditional advertising?

- What are the key criteria of a successful content marketing practice?
- What is the role of value in content marketing practice?
- What are the key benefits and challenges of modern marketing practice?
- Have a look at the online version of *The Furrow* magazine (www.deere. com/en/publications/the-furrow/). Which types of values do the particular articles feature?
- Why should modern marketers implement content marketing in their digital marketing strategy?

2. Content Creation Exercise

Fictional Brief

Ali-health is a new online company that specialises in selling healthy vegan supplements to consumers who wish to improve their general health. Their target market is focused mainly on health-conscious Gen Z and Millennials. As part of their monthly membership (£11.99 per month), customers get a 30-day personalised set of supplements. The company currently struggles to achieve its sales target and it's close to bankruptcy.

Your Task

You have been employed to help Ali-health with their content marketing efforts. In this task, you are asked to develop four Facebook posts for Ali-health that will help them develop positive relationships with their existing as well as potential new consumers. Please note that the focus of the posts should be on relationship building rather than on generating sales!

Important Considerations

It is up to you to decide on the context and type of content. Think about the target market and what they might find useful and relevant. Remember it is essential to provide users with content the target market will see value in.

The case study is fictional, and you do not have to perform any research for this task.

References

Balteș, L. P. (2015). Content marketing – the fundamental tool of digital marketing. *Bulletin of the Transilvania University of Brasov. Series V: Economic Sciences.*

Broadband Search (2023). Average daily time spent on social media.

Carvalho, A., & Fernandes, T. (2018). Understanding customer brand engagement with virtual social communities: A comprehensive model of drivers, outcomes and moderators. *Journal of Marketing Theory and Practice*, 26(1–2), 23–37. 10.1080/10696679. 2017.1389241

Content Marketing Institute (2013). What content marketing's history means for its future. https://contentmarketinginstitute.com/articles/content-marketing-history-and-future/

Content Marketing Institute (2016). *No Title.*

De Vries, L., Gensler, S., & Leeflang, P. S. H. (2012). Popularity of brand posts on brand fan pages: An investigation of the effects of social media marketing. *Journal of Interactive Marketing, 26*, 83–91. 10.1016/j.intmar.2012.01.003

Dolan, R., Conduit, J., Fahy, J., & Goodman, S. (2015). Social media engagement behaviour: A uses and gratifications perspective. *Journal of Strategic Marketing,* online (May), 1–17. 10.1080/0965254X.2015.1095222

Doorn van, J., Lemon, K. N., Mittal, V., Nass, S., Pick, D., Pirner, P., & Verhoef, P. C. (2010). Customer engagement behavior: Theoretical foundations and research directions. *Journal of Service Research, 13*(3), 253–266. 10.1177/1094670510375599

Evans, H. (2017). "Content is King" – Essay by Bill Gates 1996, by Heath Evans, Medium. https://medium.com/@HeathEvans/content-is-king-essay-by-bill-gates-1996-df74552f80d9

Fehrer, J. A., Woratschek, H., Germelmann, C. C., & Brodie, R. J. (2018). Dynamics and drivers of customer engagement: Within the dyad and beyond. *Journal of Service Management, 29*(3), 443–467. 10.1108/JOSM-08-2016-0236/FULL/XML

Gardiner, K. (2013). The story behind "The Furrow", the world's oldest content marketing [Review of the story behind "The Furrow", the world's oldest content marketing]. Contently.

Handley, A., & Chapman, C. (2011). *Content Rules,* New Jersey: Hoboken.

Hollebeek, L. D., & Macky, K. (2019). Digital content marketing's role in fostering consumer engagement, trust, and value: Framework, fundamental propositions, and implications. *Journal of Interactive Marketing.* 10.1016/j.intmar.2018.07.003

Holliman, G., & Rowley, J. (2014). Business to business digital content marketing: Marketers' perceptions of best practice. *Journal of Research in Interactive Marketing, 8*(4), 269–293. 10.1108/JRIM-02-2014-0013

How to Unite Content Marketing and SEO Strategies [Sponsored]. (n.d.). Retrieved March 30, 2023, from https://contentmarketinginstitute.com/articles/content-marketing-seo-strategies

Islam, J. U., & Rahman, Z. (2016). Linking customer engagement to trust and word-of-mouth on Facebook brand communities: An empirical study. *Journal of Internet Commerce, 15*(1), 40–58. 10.1080/15332861.2015.1124008

Kumar, V., & Reinartz, W. (2016). Creating enduring customer value. *Journal of Marketing, 80*(6), 36–68.

Lopes, A. R., & Casais, B. (2022). Digital content marketing: conceptual review and recommendations for practitioners. *Academy of Strategic Management Journal, 21*(2), 1–17. https://login.napier.idm.oclc.org/login?qurl=https%3A%2F%2Fwww.proquest.com%2Fscholarly-journals%2Fdigital-content-marketing-conceptual-review%2Fdocview%2F2726072668%2Fse-2%3Faccountid%3D16607

Muntinga, D. G. M. (2011). Introducing COBRAs. *International Journal of Advertising, 30*, 13–46.

Plessis, C. du. (2017). The role of content marketing in social media content communities. *South African Journal of Information Management, 19*(1). https://login.napier.idm.oclc.org/login?qurl=https%3A%2F%2Fwww.proquest.com%2Fscholarly-journals%2Frole-content-marketing-social-media-communities%2Fdocview%2F1950788529%2Fse-2%3Faccountid%3D16607

Pulizzi, J. (2012). The rise of storytelling as the new marketing. *Publishing Research Quarterly, 28*(2), 116–123. 10.1007/S12109-012-9264-5/FIGURES/2

Statista. (2023). *Content marketing revenue 2026 | Statista.* 2023. www.statista.com/statistics/527554/content-marketing-revenue/

Stürmer, L., & Einwiller, S. (2022). Is this advertising or not, and do I care? Perceptions of and opinions regarding hybrid forms of content. *Journal of Marketing Communications, 29*(2), 161–178. 10.1080/13527266.2022.2154065

Syrdal, H. A., & Briggs, E. (2018). Engagement with social media content: A qualitative exploration. *Journal of Marketing Theory and Practice.* 10.1080/10696679.2017.1389243

Terho, H., Mero, J., Siutla, L., & Jaakkola, E. (2022). Digital content marketing in business markets: Activities, consequences, and contingencies along the customer journey. *Industrial Marketing Management, 105,* 294–310. 10.1016/J.INDMARMAN.2022.06.006

The State of Content Marketing in 2023 [Stats & Trends to Watch]. (n.d.). Retrieved March 29, 2023, from https://blog.hubspot.com/marketing/state-of-content-marketing-infographic

Wall, A., & Spinuzzi, C. (2018). The art of selling-without-selling: Understanding the genre ecologies of content marketing: TCQ. *Technical Communication Quarterly, 27*(2), 137–160. 10.1080/10572252.2018.1425483

Walter, E. (2022) How to unite content marketing and SEO strategies [sponsored], Content Marketing Institute. Available at: https://contentmarketinginstitute.com/articles/content-marketing-seo-strategies

Wang, F., Xu, H., Hou, R., & Zhu, Z. (2023). Designing marketing content for social commerce to drive consumer purchase behaviors: A perspective from speech act theory. *Journal of Retailing and Consumer Services, 70,* 103156. 10.1016/J.JRETCONSER.2022.103156

Wirtz, J., Ambtman, A. Den, Bloemer, J., Horváth, C., Ramaseshan, B., Klundert, J. Van De, Canli, Z. G., & Kandampully, J. (2013). Managing brands and customer engagement in online brand communities. *Journal of Service Management, 24,* 223–244. 10.1108/09564231311326978

Yaghtin, S., Safarzadeh, H., & Karimi Zand, M. (2020). Planning a goal-oriented B2B content marketing strategy. *Marketing Intelligence and Planning, 38*(7), 1007–1020. 10.1108/MIP-11-2019-0559

Zeithaml, V. A. (1988). Consumer perceptions of price, quality, and value: A means-end model and synthesis of evidence. *Journal of Marketing, 52*(3), 2–22.

2 Content Marketing Planning, Execution, and Measurement

By Dr Fan Lu

Learning Outcomes

- To outline the content marketing strategy process, including situation analysis, setting objectives, identifying targeted audiences, selecting tactics, evaluation, and measurement.
- To explore frameworks and tools that can help with planning, developing, and execution of content marketing strategies.

Content Marketing Planning

Planning is an essential element of developing a content marketing strategy. Content planning helps companies break the communication silos among internal departments and external intermediaries and directs the marketing team to fulfil the overall business goal. The most common cause of unsuccessful content marketing strategies is skipping the planning process and moving right away to the stage of creating digital content (Kotler et al., 2017). Planning can be divided into multiple phases. Marketers can select a planning framework associated with their marketing objectives, processes, resources, and experiences to help develop their digital content plans effectively. Kotler et al. (2017) introduced a planning framework outlining eight steps which can be used to develop content marketing campaigns, and which provides the structure for the following paragraphs of the chapter.

Situation Analysis and Content Audit

Planning content marketing starts with an analysis of the current situation – sometimes this is also referred to as a marketing audit. The situation analysis systematically collects, reviews, and analyses relevant internal and external data to identify potential business gaps and opportunities. It can help marketers to assess the digital-marketing environment, review their current content performance, and clearly understand where the brand is positioned within the content marketing landscape. Although conducting a situation analysis can be time-consuming, it is a critical step that helps develop key marketing objectives.

DOI: 10.4324/9781003346500-2

Within content marketing, the situation analysis can take the form of a content audit. In the first step of the content audit, marketers should determine the purpose of the analysis. Setting up a clear goal can help marketers translate the data into the desired insights from the audit results and provide a rationale and benchmark in the later stage. For example, marketers can identify the content gap on TikTok to optimise their content performance, find effective keywords to optimise the website content to improve ranking on search engines, understand what content factors drive customer engagement on YouTube, and analyse why the growth rate of followers slows down on Twitter.

In the second step of the content audit, marketers need to decide what type of data needs to be collected for the purpose of the analysis. As collecting large data sets from various digital platforms can be time-consuming and costly, marketers should determine what content scope and type should be collected, and over what period. Marketers also can consider what data can be used as metrics to measure and evaluate content performance during the audit and in the later stage of content evaluation. For example, marketers might collect online traffic, traffic source, returned and new visits, average time spent, and conversion rate from the brand's own website and apps over October to January to monitor the performance of a Christmas campaign and eventually use conversion rate and returned and new visits as the main indicators to measure content performance. There are some digital tools available for marketers to collect content performance data, such as Google Analytics and SEMrush.

Then marketers can compile the collected data from step two into a template that helps them organise and clean the content data to prepare for the next step – data assessment. Marketers can select a template based on the audit purpose from step one and consider whether it suits the data scope and type and measurement metrics from step two. The data can be compiled into a simple template using Microsoft Excel Spreadsheet or third-party tools, such as Screaming Frog, HubSpot, and Curata, a content management software to help marketers to collect, compile, and assess content data under one 'roof'.

Once data is compiled into a template, marketers can assess the current content and translate the data into insights and evidence to meet the set purpose and outline the potential areas for setting objectives in the next planning stage. For example, if marketers aim to understand what content factors drive customer engagement on YouTube, then they can export rich media data from YouTube and evaluate the performance of each piece of content. Some of the metrics that content marketers may consider might include different types of user engagement behaviours such as likes, comments or shares and rank them based on the defined metrics to find top- and under-performing videos, then analyse viewers' data, e.g., traffic source and viewers' demographics, and engagement data, to create the target audience's persona. Eventually, marketers can gain insights which can help them to optimise the existing content and improve its performance.

Objective Setting

Content marketing objectives do not sit in isolation, instead they should follow from business objectives, marketing objectives and digital-marketing objectives. Brands are more likely to unlock customer opportunities to create connected, relevant content that aligns with business objectives (PWC, 2016). As with any type of objectives, content marketing objectives should also follow the SMART framework (i.e., be specific, measurable, achievable, relevant, and time-bound). To help deciding which kind of objectives to focus on, content marketers can follow the REAN (reach, engage, activate, nurture) model developed by Xavier Blanc and Leevi Kokko in 2006 (Jackson, 2009). Hanlon (2022) applied the model to the digital environment, but it can be further extended to a content marketing context, with its key components outlined below:

- **Reach** – objectives targeted at raising brand awareness by attracting traffic to the content, such as attracting online traffic from YouTube influencers to a brand's website.
- **Engage** – objectives targeted at increasing the customer-brand interaction through generating quality content, such as posting a photograph on Instagram, so followers can like, share, repost, save, download, comment, etc.
- **Activate** – objectives targeted at measuring how effective content converts traffic into actions, such as click-through rate in a promotional email.
- **Nurture** – objectives targeted at driving customer growth and customer retention, such as tracking the traffic source to identify new and returned visitors.

Strategy

Objectives focus on where marketers want to go or what they hope to achieve through content marketing. On the other hand, strategy sets the direction for businesses, like a roadmap that navigates marketers. Content marketing serves as a 'vehicle' that marketers 'drive' to follow directions to their 'destinations'. A good strategy guides businesses through an 'optimised short-cut' that delivers desired results with consistency and efficiency. A bad strategy causes confusion to target customers, wastes brands' resources, and pushes the brand further away from its objectives. Unlike tactics, strategy is more than a series of actions or practical approaches. A strategy is a plan that gives marketers consistent directions on what content activities should be undertaken to achieve the objectives with the available resources. A content marketing strategy should be customer-centric and consider 3Cs – customer persona, customer journey, and customer touchpoints.

Customer Persona

Conventional marketing segments of customers are based on their similar demographic, geographical, behavioural, or psychographic characteristics. Practitioners and academics acclimated segmentation in the digital setting (Temkin, 2010; Hendriks & Peelen, 2012). Hendriks and Peelen (2012) define customer persona as a 'representation of archetypical users' that visually and contextually portrays patterns, needs, and relevant characteristics of target customers (p. 60). Persona is based on customer insights from market research and analysis that reflect customers' needs and wants (Harris, 2022) and can be driven by digital data (Jansen et al., 2020). Chaffey and Smith (2013) and Hanlon (2022) divide digital users based on their demographics, psychographics, and webograhics (that blend digital behaviours with geographical factors).

Developing customer personas helps marketers stand in the customers' shoes, distinguish their motivations and pain points, identify cross-channel integration opportunities, and predict their responses in each stage of a customer journey, so they can create and customise the content for the target audiences.

Chaffey and Ellis-Chadwick (2022) suggest that customer persona can be categorised based on two types of variables – classification (e.g., education, employment, gender, geography, income, race, family size) and character (e.g., belief, perception, attitude, intention, and experience). Classification variables tend to be straightforward, stay consistent and stable over time. Character variables, quite the opposite, are those abstract or intangible attributes that may develop or change.

Customer Journey

A customer journey maps a customer's path to purchase, outlining all the touchpoints where a customer interacts with a brand and considers their needs. Hanlon (2022) defines the customer journey as 'the process or sequence of events' a customer goes through 'from searching for an item to concluding with a successful outcome' (p. 44). Marketers can break down each stage by identifying the main touchpoints and understanding how customers interact with brands via these touchpoints, which can be owned by brands, third-party owned, and customer-owned. Marketers can consider customer and business challenges in each stage of the journey when developing personas. This will help brands create the right content targeting customers' pain points in each stage and nurture them to move forward. For example, marketers use short videos to generate more leads and nurture them from interest to purchase.

They can produce clips with educational content and post them on TikTok to reach a wide range of viewers, then provide more detailed explanations and know-how in longer videos and post them on YouTube to nurture viewers to register and start a free trial (Mendez, 2017).

The following three stages outline the customer journey in a digital context (based on Hanlon, 2022):

Stage 1: Raise Awareness of Target Audiences

- Reach out to target audiences (e.g., traffic, views)
- Initiation of a conversation

Stage 2: Create Interest

- Drive traffic towards online resource (e.g., website, app, online shop)
- Educate and engage target audience (e.g., likes, shares, comments)

Stage 3: Conversion

- Download/install/register/subscribe
- Free trials
- Store visit
- order/purchase

Creating A Customer Persona

Marketers can follow a three-step process to create a customer persona (Figure 2.1). For example, a digital travel agency connecting travellers from homes to their desired destinations and deliver a memorable journey seamlessly. Having a diverse customer base around the world, marketers in the

Figure 2.1 Three-step process of creating a customer persona.

digital travel agency try to develop a solid digital presence to connect and inspire customers. They create a content marketing campaign to target two customer groups: Generation Z students and pensioners. Applying Step 1 of the model, marketers collect data from internal sources, such as order history, website activities and external sources, e.g., engagement data, Mintel marketing reports, online surveys, or sales data. In relation to Step 2, they find that emotional and digital behaviour elements are the most relevant to these two groups. In the final step, data from internal sales, emailing list, social media platforms are analysed to understand the target group's needs and motivations during their customer journeys.

The insights extracted in Step 3 can be translated into a template of the customer persona. Marketers developed a persona for Gen Z students (Figure 2.2), who tend to search for their next travel destinations on social media and search for budget travel due to stretched finance. They are more likely to read content that provides guidance or information about discounts, budget flights, stays or restaurants. Alternatively, pensioners receive travelling information from direct emails, promotional letters, or catalogues. They read the itinerary description and are more willing to pay for updated rooms or transport for convenience and comfort. Thus, the agency decides to embed discounts in short videos to drive Gen Z students' conversion on YouTube and use email marketing with cruise deals and taxi booking links to drive pensioners' retention.

	USER DESCRIPTION:		
	Jassie is a full-time student and enjoys travelling with friends. Jessie tends to search for their next travel destinations on social media and search for budget travel due to stretched finance. They are more likely to read content that provides guidance or information about discounts, budget flights, stays or restaurants.		
	PERSONAL CHARACTERISTICS:		**HOBBIES AND INTERESTS:**
	• Adventurous • Adaptable • Curious		• Travelling • Hiking • Gym
NAME — Jessie	**GOALS:**		**CHALLENGES:**
AGE: — 21 years old	• Find where to go for a three-day city break in May after exam		• Jessie can only take a short break during the university term
OCCUPATION: — Full-time student & part-time Retail Assistant	• Find a budget travel package to a European city • Find discounted travel information		• Holidays outside of the university term period can be costly • Stretched finance
LOCATION: — London	**NEEDS:**		**SOURCES OF INFO:**
	• Socialising with friends		• YouTube • Instagram

Figure 2.2 Persona for Gen Z students in the example.

USER DESCRIPTION:		
Heather lives near Cornwall and enjoys gardening, and her children live in the UK and Australia. She receives travelling information from direct emails, promotional letters, or catalogues. She read the itinerary description and is willing to pay more for comfort and convenience when booking rooms and transport.		
PERSONAL CHARACTERISTICS:		HOBBIES AND INTERESTS:
• Patient • Empathic • Honest		• Gardening • Reading • Baking

NAME	Heather
AGE:	65 years old
OCCUPATION:	Ex-teacher & now retired
LOCATION:	Cornwall

GOALS:	CHALLENGES:
• Find a travel package including a cruise for a return journey from the UK to Australia in April and a return transport from Cornwall to Southampton	• The cruise departs from Southampton. As Heather does not drive, taking public transport can be a hassle
NEEDS:	SOURCES OF INFO:
• Hassle-free experiences	• Email • Letter • Catalogue

Figure 2.3 Persona for pensioners in the example.

Despite customer personas being a generally helpful tool, at times it can be challenging to execute. For example, when the data used for persona creation is from unreliable sources or is stereotyped, the persona is unlikely to be able to accurately represent the target audience. Since developing a persona requires time, resources and skills, a persona can be outdated quickly in a fast-changing or highly competitive business environment.

Tactics

Once marketers know where to go (objectives), whom to target (customer personas), and the direction of getting there (strategy), they then need to work out how to get there (tactics). Specifically, they need to determine how the strategy can be implemented and what actions need to be taken to achieve the formulated objectives. Tactics are detailed actions, activities, events, people, and tools to implement the strategy. Without tactics, a content marketing strategy is just a plan. Content marketing tactics can be divided into content planning, creation, and distribution (Kotler et al., 2017), as further discussed below.

Content Planning

High-quality content starts from planning and considers three elements: themes, formats, and narratives (Kotler et al., 2017). In line with SMART marketing objectives, content themes should be relevant to the target audience's needs and pain points and reflect the brand image and characteristics. Content themes can also vary with the business event calendar or publisher's editorial calendar. After deciding the theme, marketers choose content formats that match the following factors – target audience, marketing objectives, budget, and characteristics of publication channels. Once the format is confirmed, the content narrative should tell the brand's story and build resonance with the target audience.

Content Creation

After planning, marketers can go through a process involving briefing, research, creation, testing, review, and adjustment to create content. During content creation, Hanlon (2022) suggests incorporating branding and four elements – story, storyteller, style, and publication.

Story

Content narratives can focus on three perspectives – brand attributes, inspiration, and self-identity (Zhou et al., 2021). Content can share knowledge about specific brand attributes, e.g., information or product reviews, to give customers brand or product recommendations. For example, influencers review a book on their YouTube channel. Rather than promoting the product directly, marketers can create a narrative to inspire a customer's desire or build a positive emotional connection with brands, such as sponsoring social media influencers to create 'my first' luxury bag or holiday associated with target audience's life events. Ultimately, content can create a narrative moving customers beyond primary product consumptions to explore self-identity, associating a brand with values, attitudes, beliefs, social status, lifestyle, and subcultural representations. (*Please see Chapter 3 on the process of content ideation*).

Style

Brands can select one, or use a combination of multiple formats to support their objectives. Short content is for quick viewing and circulation, which should be simple, punctuated, snackable-size, and easy to understand, like Twitter posts and TikTok clips. Most UK internet users tend to read or watch short content on their phones or tablets and through social media platforms (McGrath, 2022). Short content unlocks the opportunity to reach a broader range of audiences. Long content, on the contrary, can support brand authority and authenticity by producing in-depth content, like case studies, reports, and educational tutorial videos. Unlike conventional marketing content, digital content can be uploaded, updated, and deleted throughout the campaign. Thus, the lifecycle of some digital content is not time-restricted and can be recycled, whilst some might be temporary and need to be updated or removed in real time, such as promotional information. Also, organisations can curate content from other sources and add their perspective. This refers to the process of content curation, which Chapter 9 explores in great depth.

Publication

Marketers distribute content through various channels with distinctive characteristics. These channels can be owned, paid, and earned, which we will discuss further in the content distribution section. Creating unique content for each channel can be time-consuming and costly. Daniel Jacobson (2009), the Director of Application Development for NPR, introduced a simple philosophy – COPE: Create Once, Publish Everywhere. For example, an article could be created and adapted to different content formats, like emails, websites, blogs, paid media, etc. Marketers should consider the BEST principle proposed by Pulizzi and Barrett (2009) to ensure the content supports the marketing and business objectives (Hanlon, 2022).

Content Distribution

Following content creation, marketers need to decide where, when and how often to reach the target audience (Harris, 2021).

Where?

Kotler et al. (2017) categorised three media channels – owned, paid, and earned, and Hanlon (2022) added shared media to the mix.

Owned media is the channel assets (e.g., websites, blogs, emails, mobile apps, social media, etc.) owned, controlled, and managed directly by the brands. Brands can publish the content on the owned media as they need at any time. The pitfalls are the initial investment in development and the continuous maintenance cost. Owned media content primarily reaches the brand's current customers, who may think the content is biased and has less authenticity.

Paid media is the channel brands need to pay for posting their content, such as printed or digital newspapers and magazines, SEO-sponsored listings, social media influencers' content, digital pop-up advertisement on websites, etc. Paid media can drive online traffic to the owned media, converting online clicks into store footfalls, attracting new customers, and building brand awareness. Customers may find the content less authentic. Following legal and some platforms' regulations, brands should reveal content that includes paid promotion. For example, YouTube requests content creators to disclose paid promotions in their videos, and Instagram offers the 'paid partnership' feature. Facebook (26 per cent), Instagram (19 per cent), YouTube (18 per cent),

Twitter (13 per cent), and TikTok (11 per cent) are the top five social media platforms with the highest ROI on campaigns in 2022, and over half of businesses consider increasing their investment on TikTok (HubSpot, 2022).

Earned media is organic. Its content is created by users, customers, and followers. For example, both satisfied and unsatisfied customers can share, repost, and comment on a brand's owned and paid media, e.g., the brand's website, Twitter, Google Review, or TripAdvisor. Earned media can enhance a brand's reputation and influence, but not by itself. It is the joint effort of brand exposure generated by the owned and paid media, public relations management, and eventually, the amplification of word of mouth (Kotler et al., 2017).

Hanlon (2022) defines *shared media* as being developed and owned by third parties, such as YouTube, but a brand shares the social media account ownership with the platform. Hence, a brand can share content generated by others on its third-party platforms.

When?

A content calendar is a sharable planning tool to help marketers manage when to plan, create, and distribute content to support overall marketing communication. It helps schedule key promotional events, track publication deadlines, identify content gaps and opportunities, prepare content in advance, allocate marketing resources, and liaise across different teams with transparency. The content calendar should consider some elements – holidays, festivals, seasonal promotions, products, services, project launches, timelines, other marketing campaigns, customer journeys, content creation, publication channels, and resources. For example, customers can register on a brand's website to download a PowerPoint presentation. Their information will then be sent to the Customer Relationship Management (CRM) database, so marketers can create a personalised email calendar for the customer. The CRM system can email customers automatically according to the calendar and streamline the workflow of email communication to a large scale, so marketers can focus on content creation, determining the calendar, and reaching the target audience effectively. Many online tools or templates help marketers organise content calendars, such as Microsoft Excel or Project, Monday, Asana, and Smartsheet.

How Often?

Content can be created in advance or timely. Marketers can publish content immediately, daily, weekly, fortnightly, monthly, quarterly, and annually, and the frequency can depend on the target audience, publication platforms, resources, competition, and industry. According to HubSpot (2022), the best time to post content on social media platforms, e.g., Facebook, YouTube, Twitter, LinkedIn and TikTok, is between 6 p.m. and 9 p.m. The best posting days for Twitter, YouTube, and Facebook throughout the week are Tuesday, Wednesday, and Thursday. A common posting frequency is between four and six times per week.

Budget

Creating and distributing content can be costly, whether managed in-house or by outsourced professionals or marketing agencies. When determining the content distribution, businesses can adopt three pricing models when out-sourcing marketing professionals – they may be charged at an hourly rate (e.g., marketing freelancers), a flat monthly fee (e.g., such as Canva) or based on a project itself (e.g., marketing agencies). The estimated cost can be for-mulated using an hourly rate:

cost = content volume x time needed for creating the content x hourly rate

The project-based pricing can vary hugely based on what the marketing brief requires. According to a growing digital-marketing agency – WebFx (n.d.), the estimated cost for creating marketing content depends on the size of the target audience (e.g., number of current email subscribers), content origi-nality, format, design, volume, quality, frequency, functionality, whether integrated with other technologies (such as social media, databases systems), industry, experience, timeline, and locations.

Budgeting is allocating available resources for the best return opportunities for investment (Chaffey & Smith, 2013). Content marketing budget can be spent on generating leads, email marketing that targets specific segments, marketing tools (such as software, subscription, maintenance), or outsourcing skills (Hanlon, 2022). Creating content requires dedicated commitment in skills, time, and budget (Kotler et al., 2017), yet 38 per cent of marketers find it challenging to reach targeted audiences through content marketing (CMI, 2022). Agius (2021) suggested that content marketing should account for 25 per cent and 30 per cent of the marketing budget. Businesses with less experience investing in content marketing can start from the lower end of the range. However, over 30 per cent of organisations spent less than 10 per cent of their marketing budget on content marketing. Marketers should determine a budget when setting SMART objectives in a content marketing plan. As such, mar-keters can prioritise the objectives and implementation options to ensure resources allocated to the content source with a satisfied return on investment (ROI) – the ratio of content marketing cost to sales (Chaffey & Smith, 2017).

Evaluation and Measurement

According to Kotler et al., (2017), after publishing the content, marketers should use metrics to track content performance and review whether it achieves the marketing objectives. Farris et al. (2010, p. 1) defined a metric as 'a measuring system that quantifies a trend, dynamic, or characteristics', and data-based metrics are crucial to business success. Hence, metrics can be measured as 'a percentage, number, or volume' (Hanlon, 2022, p. 375). In practice, the metrics can also vary with the customer journey, content formats, media platforms, and analytic tools. Bendle et al. (2010) conducted a survey of senior managers, and the popular advertising and web metrics are reach (42 per cent), impressions (41 per cent), frequency (37 per cent), visitors (37 per cent), CTR (35 per cent), cost per customer acquired (32 per cent), etc. Marketers should consider what metrics are relevant to the set objectives, whether the metrics data is available, how the metrics data should be analysed, and how the analysis results can be embedded into the decision-making process (Hanlon, 2022). The common metrics to measure content performance include the following: *visibility* which is focused on measuring brand awareness, *relatability* that measures attention that a given piece of content generates, *search* which measures how easy it is to find content on search engines, action that measure the effectiveness of calls to action embedded in different types of content, and *share* which measures content shares (Kotler et al., 2017).

Referring to the digital measurement metrics proposed by Kotler et al. (2017), Chaffey and Ellis-Chadwick (2022) and Hanlon (2022), as well as considering the business practices outlined by Leibtag (2019).

Metrics Category	Effectiveness	Metrics	Tools	Content Checklist
Finance	Strong	• Conversion rates: ratio of people who complete specific actions over total visitors for the content, such as registration rate from the whitepaper and subscription rate from trial. • Number of qualified leads generated. • Revenue per visit: the ratio of total sales generated on site over the total visitors. • Costper visitor/lead/acquisition or per thousand people reached. • Cost per action (CPA): the average cost of each converted action.	Social media platform, Google Analytics, HubSpot, Salesforce	☐ Add call-to-action link
Engagement	Strong	• Share ratio: percentage of shares over total views. • Click-through rate (CTR): the ratio of visitors who click on the link over the total visitors who view the content. • Engagement rate: ratio of total interaction (sum of shares, likes, reposts, replies, mentions, and comments) over total views.	Social media platforms	☐ Allow comments ☐ Add live chat ☐ Add an invitation to share ☐ Add hashtag
Traffic	Weak	• Unique views: how many people viewed the content. • Total views: how many times the content is viewed. For example, a video attracts 10,000 views in a month. • Search engine referrals: how many referred visitors from the search engine results.	Google Analytics, Bing Analytics, Qunitly	☐ Select appropriate media channels
Exposure	Weak	• Search-engine rank: what is the position on a search engine when searching specific keywords?	Google Webmaster	☐ Include tags/keywords ☐ Include backlinks ☐ Include metadata, e.g., title, descriptions, tags ☐ Add tags/keywords for images, graphics, and videos
Quality	Strong	• Unsubscribe rate. • Bounce rate: the percentage of visitors who leave just after landing. A high bounce rate indicates poor-quality content. • Duration: how much time visitors spend on the site. • Page views per visitor: how many pages visitor view on the same site. • Repeat visitors.	Social media platforms, Google Analytics, Buffer	☐ Match the customer persona ☐ Consider the customer journey ☐ Create appropriate content theme, format, and length ☐ Publish 4–6 times per week

Figure 2.4 Content metrics, tools, and checklist.

Marketers can use the proposed set of metrics to measure, track, and analyse whether the performance achieves the marketing objectives within a specific time frame and identify opportunities for improving the content and metrics. Unlike traditional marketing, digital content is dynamic and flexible regarding 'themes, format, and distribution channels' (Kotler et al., 2017, p. 134). The performance insight from analysing metrics data can help marketers make decisions timely and continuously.

Interview with Stephan Naumann

Stephan Naumann

Stephan Naumann is Managing Partner at OMD Germany and responsible for the Brand OMD Create. He is an expert on social media listening (Brandwatch and others), ratings and reviews (Bazaarvoice), social media management in a multi-brand environment (Sprinklr) and influencer analytics (Traackr and others), and content creation. He also loves to follow consumer trends within digital and explore new platforms as podcasts, TikTok, LinkedIn or Google MyBusiness.

Please outline the key steps you take when developing a content marketing plan.
Our creative work is based on so-called mindful content strategy. That means after a (re-) brief from our client we start the creative process with listening to consumers. Besides traditional research sources, such as market media studies, we deploy social listening across TikTok, Instagram, LinkedIn, Pinterest, YouTube or any other social channel to understand needs, desires as well as likes and dislikes of consumers. In the next step we run a collaborative ideation session together with media teams – and sometimes clients or content creators – to generate first ideas, followed by the phasis of developing a creative concept, which includes not only the creative idea but also strategies for channels, budgets and paid-owned-earned formats across the channels.

How important is the pre-planning stage?
Following the proverb 'garbage in – garbage out', we dedicate a lot of time to the pre-planning stage by closely listening and understanding pain points and passion points of consumers. Hereby, identifying the relevant trigger for engagement is key to create concepts that involve the communities on social media.

What information do you collect or analyse prior to the planning of content marketing strategy?
Within the media and creative brief, we initially collect all relevant information as insights about the target audience, budgets, campaign duration, channel

strategy or creative key beliefs and more. It is key to understand consumers, channel, and category: what are the interests of the audience, what media channels and platforms show a high usage and affinity for our audience, what are the best formats for storytelling and performance, what are relevant insights about the category and market that might help to develop a creative idea.

What is the role of setting campaign objectives?
All stakeholders within a content marketing campaign have to work towards the same goal – setting campaign objectives helps to align all marketing activities and to define the dedicated budgets for media and content. Furthermore, campaign objectives help us to evaluate the success of a campaign. If the overall campaign objective is to create brand awareness it makes sense to makes sense to measure awareness key performance indicators (KPIs) and not performance KPIs.

What makes a good content marketing objective?
Content marketing objectives have to be crisp and contribute to the overall business objectives of a brand – no matter if they are short- or long-term objectives. This helps to create a meaningful and efficient content marketing strategy. Hereby, we pay a lot of attention to interlink content and media objectives to generate the highest impact for our clients.

What typical objectives does OMD Create try to achieve through a content marketing plan?
Brand or product awareness are among the most popular objectives of our clients, followed by (positive) engagement. But also leads, as clicks to websites or app registrations, are often requested. For example, for one of our FMCG clients the role of traditional media is to create brand awareness whereas the role of content marketing, e.g., via influencers, is to create deeper involvement with the brand through engagement. In traditional media the brand gets prompted to the audience for a few seconds, followed by a deeper phasis with a higher watch time on social content.

What content does OMD Create develop to achieve the planned objectives? What are the criteria for determining the right ones?
Empathy plays a crucial role within our content marketing process. We create mindful content strategies. That means insights on the behaviours of audiences on digital and/or traditional channels lead the planning of objectives. Insights tell us, what are the most relevant content formats for a brand within a specific category. On top we always strive for innovations – new channels, fresh formats or trending topics.

How does OMD Create choose the right tactics for achieving campaign objectives?
Marketing tactics follow on marketing strategy. For example, if the strategy of our client is to optimise the brand image by sports sponsoring, within our

campaign tactics we decide which sports team, platform or event we will pick for the client's sponsoring. The details of campaign tactics are part of the content marketing concept and include formats, flightings, and budgets for the respective channels.

What role do personas play in your content marketing planning and development? How many personas do you usually develop?
Personas can play an important role in understanding the audience and creating a concept that triggers their emotions and engagement. With personas we can bring rather rational data about interests and usage of our audiences to life and enrich data with insights from real life behaviour, e.g., with social media insights. However, personas are a rather old-fashioned methodology within research. Today we have tons of personalised data and can address consumers almost one by one – the need for personas is decreasing. And creating several personas takes time, which slows down the marketing process. Often, we have the task to create ideas within a very short time as content marketing plays with fast-moving social trends. That means personas are not mandatory for our teams.

After the planning, how does OMD Create create the marketing content? What is the process of producing various types of content?
Our clients love lean processes between media and content production because in the modern digital-marketing world, media and content have to go hand in hand. Just think about a paid social expert who has to set up and run a performance campaign on Instagram but lacks creative assets for best performing formats. Only a good creative can create outstanding performance: we call our approach the symbiosis of media and content to create marketing impact.

Within our team, we not only have paid social experts, but also community managers, art directors, and multimedia designers who produce most of the creative assets in-house. That means we own the whole process from media planning to content production. In addition, we collaborate with content creators as they are experts on specific channels and formats, e.g., there are content creators who know best how to shoot a car porn for Instagram Reels and there are other content creators who know best how to shoot and cut TikTok videos within the health segment. Content production is always a process which involves various experts across the field – collaboration is key.

What department or roles are involved in creating the marketing content?
Within OMD Germany, our OMD Create team is the key player when it comes to content creation. Along the content creation process we also involve our OMD client service teams, activation teams as well as clients. Furthermore, we work with external partners as content producers and platforms, e.g. Meta, Twitch, YouTube or TikTok. Within our team, creative managers take the lead on a project and together with creative directors, art

directors, and multimedia designers they are responsible to create the planned creative assets.

What KPIs/metrics do you use to measure the performance of content marketing strategy?

Measurement closes the loop and provides valuable feedback to optimise the running campaign as well as future campaigns. As content marketing often takes place on digital channels, it's obvious that we use clickstream data as views, clicks and engagements to keep track of the performance of content pieces on digital channels. Hereby, it's key to measure the right metrics for the right campaign objectives – on social media of course we measure organic and paid impressions or video views as well as frequency when it comes to awareness KPIs. On top of – often short-term – clickstream data from tools such as Google Analytics, YouTube Analytics, Instagram Insights or TikTok Insights we also keep track of – often more long-term – marketing KPIs as brand perception, purchase intent or others by running brand lift studies and even deeper consumer insights studies.

On top of the standards, we recommend measuring the digital share of voice of a brand; as the goal of content marketing is often to create buzz and drive branding – only if people talk positively about a brand, it will win the hearts of the communities online.

How do you test and evaluate the performance of marketing content?

For measurement and analysis of visual media attention we partner with an AI tech provider from Finland. The technology enables us to forecast audience attention on creative content within a panel of the specific audience. The methodology is based on eye-tracking and inventory data streams of real online usage. This helps us to gain insights as the Attention Score is almost in real time to provide visual content with the highest ad impact.

Do you have any recommendations for content marketing monitoring?

Social listening is a great tool to understand if the audience likes or dislikes a brand's content once the campaign is live. Here we monitor tweets, comments or posts across the social web with technology of providers, such as Brandwatch Analytics. Social listening data is unfiltered and authentic in real time – a great source for short-term optimisation of the content.

What are the most common pitfalls of planning and implementation of Content Marketing Strategies. Could you describe them? And how do you tackle them?

During the last years we have seen many content marketing campaigns with great content but poor reach – for example video content series on YouTube brand channels with only a few hundreds of video views. This is a mismatch between content creation and media execution that needs to be avoided. Content marketing is not an end in itself but has to drive business KPIs.

Another pitfall is the so-called content dilemma – more digital channels with more formats create the need for more and more format-specific content on the side of marketing. This causes higher costs during the content production phasis. At OMD Create we avoid the content dilemma by offering our clients a content-first production – a single or two-day content production in which our team not only creates a hero content piece as a long-form video asset but also hundreds of other content pieces as short videos, images or audios that we use for content distribution on paid, organic, and earned social. This makes content production more effective.

Do you have any recommendations for making an effective content marketing plan? We truly believe in eye-level communication between an audience and a brand. Authenticity of the content and emotions are key for positive engagement. Last but not least a marketer has to regard communication as a system, everything is connected and content pieces on different channels have an impact on each other, and a sustainable relationship between a brand and the audience. It's key to find the sweet spot between relevance, reach, and surprise.

References

Agius, A. (2021, Jan). How much should your company budget for content marketing? Forbes. Retrieved December 21, 2022, from www.forbes.com/sites/forbesagencycouncil/2021/01/20/how-much-should-your-company-budget-for-content-marketing/

Bendle, N., Farris, P., Pfeifer, P., & Reibstein, D. (2010). Metrics that matter – to marketing managers. *Marketing Zfp, 32(JRM 1)*, 18–23.

Chaffey, D., & Ellis-Chadwick, F. (2022). *Digital Marketing: Strategy, Implementation and Practice* (8th edn). Pearson Education.

Chaffey, D., & Smith, P. R. (2013). *eMarketing eXcellence: Planning and Optimizing Your Digital Marketing.* Routledge.

Chaffey, D., & Smith, P. R. (2017) *Digital Marketing Excellence, Planning, Optimising and Integrating Digital Marketing*, 5th edn, Taylor & Francis

CMI. (2022). *Content marketing: benchmarks, budgets, and trends.* CMI. Retrieved December 26, 2022, from https://contentmarketinginstitute.com/wp-content/uploads/2022/03/Tech_2022_Research-FINAL-3-17-22.pdf

Farris, P. W., Bendle, N., Pfeifer, P. E., & Reibstein, D. (2010). *Marketing Metrics: The Definitive Guide To Measuring Marketing Performance.* Pearson Education.

Harris, J. (2021, February). *Social media content plan: Take control of your strategy.* CMI. Retrieved December 20, 2022, from https://contentmarketinginstitute.com/articles/control-social-media-success-plan/

Hanlon, A. (2022). *Digital Marketing: Strategic Planning & Integration* (2nd edn). Sage.

Harris, J. (2022, October). *How to build a better audience persona (Choose a detailed or quick method).* CMI. Retrieved December 26, 2022, from https://contentmarketinginstitute.com/articles/build-better-audience-persona

Hendriks, M., & Peelen, E. (2013). Personas in action: Linking event participation motivation to charitable giving and sports. *International Journal of Nonprofit and Voluntary Sector Marketing, 18*(1), 60–72.

HubSpot. (2022). *State of inbound marketing trends 2022.* HubSpot. Retrieved December 27, 2022, from www.hubspot.com/hubfs/2022_State-of-Inbound-Marketing-Trends_V08122022.pdff

Jackson, S. (2009). *Cult of Analytics: Driving Online Marketing Strategies Using Web Analytics*. Routledge.

Jacobson, D. (2009, October). *COPE: Create Once, Publish Everywhere*. ProgrammableWeb. Retrieved December 20, 2022, from www.programmableweb.com/news/cope-create-once-publish-everywhere/2009/10/13

Jansen, B. J., Salminen, J. O., & Jung, S. G. (2020). Data-driven personas for enhanced user understanding: Combining empathy with rationality for better insights to analytics. *Data and Information Management*, *4*(1), 1–17.

Kotler, P., Kartajaya, H., & Setiawan, I. (2017). *Marketing 4.0: Moving from Traditional to Digital*. John Wiley & Sons, Inc., Cop.

Leibtag, A. (2019, June). *Must-have checklist to creating valuable content*. CMI. Retrieved December 28, 2022, from https://contentmarketinginstitute.com/articles/creating-valuable-content-checklist/

McGrath, R. (2022). *UK social media: Sharing & socialising Market Report 2022*. Mintel. Retrieved December 30, 2022, from https://store.mintel.com/

Mendez, Juan. (2017, March). *5 types of video content perfect for each stage of the customer journey*. CMI. Retrieved December 28, 2022, from https://contentmarketinginstitute.com/articles/video-content-customer-journey/

Pulizzi, J., & Barrett, N. (2009). Get content get customers – turn prospects into buyers with content marketing. *Saxena NSB Management Review*, *2*(2), 98–100.

PWC. (2016, January). *Leading with customer-focused content: Driving growth through personalized experiences*. PWC. Retrieved December 23, 2022, from https://www.pwc.nl/nl/assets/documents/pwc-leading-with-customer-focused-content.pdf

Temkin, B. D. (2010). *Mapping the customer journey*. Forrester Research, *3*, 20. From www.arataumodular.com/app/wp-content/uploads/2022/09/Mapping-The-Customer-Journey.pdf

WebFX. (n.d.). *The cost of marketing — A complex marketing budget breakdown*. WebFX. Retrieved December 21, 2022, from www.webfx.com/digital-marketing/pricing/cost-of-marketing/

Zhou, S., Blazquez, M., McCormick, H., & Barnes, L. (2021). How social media influencers' narrative strategies benefit cultivating influencer marketing: Tackling issues of cultural barriers, commercialised content, and sponsorship disclosure. *Journal of Business Research*, *134*, 122–142.

3 Content Marketing Ideation: How to Generate and Manage Creative Concepts

By Dr Jackie Cameron

Learning Outcomes

- To develop an in-depth understanding of how content marketers generate creative ideas and apply key theories and concepts in practice.
- To identify the characteristics and benefits of hero, hub, and hygiene content.
- To acknowledge the role of journalism practices and processes in content marketing ideation.
- To recognise, and explain, practical ways to conceptualise and manage content, from the idea stage to the promotion of creative campaigns.

Introduction

Creativity is the lifeblood of content marketing, just as it is for other subdisciplines of marketing. Compelling concepts that underlie creative assets can serve as intellectual and emotional hooks to attract customers. The polished execution of these powerful ideas can ensure marketers attract, retain, and cross-sell to customers. However, there is no shortage of exciting, engaging content in the public domain, which means that content marketers have a huge challenge in tapping into creativity that can get their clients, brands, products, and services noticed in a vast ocean of excellence. There are also many examples of mediocre and even poor content marketing, which underscores how hard it can be for practitioners to come up with the right ideas and follow through with high-quality production. Creative teams are often disappointed when award-winning tactical assets and campaigns fail to break through this bombardment of content, leaving their clever – and often expensive – work unnoticed. This in turn means practitioners don't end up delivering the metrics that signal their work has succeeded in its marketing intentions. This chapter is aimed at equipping you with the foundation knowledge to succeed as a content marketer.

DOI: 10.4324/9781003346500-3

Ideation Defined: Developing Stories That Sell

The term 'ideation' is commonly used by marketers to refer to the early process for creativity that generates new concepts. Dictionaries define ideation simply as the formation or conception of ideas (Collins, 2023) and/or images (Oxford, 2023). Industry practitioners highlight that the objectives of ideation are to identify, produce, and source relevant topics for future use in marketing content (Chen, 2020), and to optimise your marketing efforts (Pascual, 2020).

Scholars understand idea generation as the creative foundation of the innovation process, which in turn involves the synthesis and implementation of ideas in a new way (Titus, 2018; McAdam & McClelland, 2002; Herring et al., 2009). Ideas generated at this early stage are used throughout the execution and rollout of marketing tactics to deliver on the marketing strategy. Coming up with the right concepts at the start of the creative journey is therefore crucial to marketing success (Herring et al., 2009).

Marketing concepts are typically generated by combining two or more ideas into 'an output that is novel/original' (Miceli & Raimondo, 2020, pp. 90–91). Characteristics of ideas considered to have the potential to be successful as marketing concepts include rarity, feasibility, plausibility, and usefulness (Meslec et al., 2020, p. 2). These thoughts must be imaginative, new-to-the-world, refined, personally relevant to target audiences, and marketing focused (see Titus, 2018, pp. 237–238).

As content marketing is also known as story marketing, with customers seeking facts delivered in a compelling way to guide them in the decision-making process, the art lies in sharing valuable information (Kee & Yazdanifard, 2015, p. 1055) in a format and style that promotes higher visibility for a brand (Vinerean, 2017, p. 95). These interpretations can range from words and micro-blogs to videos and infographics, or a combination of tactical assets, and are explored at the ideation stage.

There is a broad cultural context to this flow of imagination of which the creative team must be mindful at the start of the ideation process. Creativity is socially constructed, and content marketers therefore need to take into consideration social nuances, including potential pitfalls in the messages conveyed to specific groups. There are many examples of cultural misunderstandings by global marketing teams. As Kee and Yadzanifard (2015, p. 1057) emphasise, 'Apart from getting the right words, right placement and right timing must also exist, within a culture'.

It is critical at the ideation stage to understand the behaviour of consumers across distribution channels in different markets. Creative teams can, and do, harness peer-reviewed research in academic journals and industry analysis during the ideation process to understand how specific ideas might be interpreted and distributed. Content marketers also develop their own intelligence. This underlying research can range from the development of personas, or detailed sketches of potential customers, to macro-economic and social trends, such as which types of social media channels are popular among demographically and geographically defined groups.

Collective and Individual Marketing Ideation: Key Factors for Success

Idea generation is at the start of the creativity life cycle. It is the activity most frequently associated with creative problem solving and is also the process many practitioners find most challenging (Herring et al., 2009, p. 2). Individuals who work at the ideation stage include account directors, copywriters, and designers, and teamwork often benefits from the combination of ideas from people with different skill sets and knowledge of the client as well as trends and technologies in content production. Content marketers work individually and in groups and use a variety of techniques to stimulate creativity. These include, to name a few examples: brainstorming; mind-mapping; stripping complex structures into simplified graphics; imagining themselves into the minds and situations of their ideal customers to hone a creative solution or narrative that will address a problem.

People tend to have their favourite ways to generate ideas, which might not be effective for everyone else in a team. For example, one individual might use diagrams to distil concepts; another may find their best ideas come out while walking and talking with a colleague. Marketing companies and consultants often have proprietary, or in-house, methods to structure this first step of the creative process. Ideation techniques are not always based on an in-depth understanding of how to get the best out of the people working on these tasks, and instead are often based on gut feel or what appears to have worked well in the past. This can help explain why ideation can have uneven outcomes, with exciting concepts often seeming like the result of serendipity rather than hard work.

However, there is a vast body of research on creativity for that content marketing practitioners can tap. This ranges from finding ways to identify people who have the best personalities and skills for jobs that require innovation, to how to stimulate effective teamworking. There are also many studies on consumer behaviour with a view to developing insights into how to get audiences to respond positively to marketing activities.

Research into the psychology of creativity, leadership and creativity, the creative process, collaborative creativity, and artificial intelligence (AI) in creativity continues to mushroom, and it is beyond the scope of this book to cover the vast field of theoretical, experimental, and empirical studies on creativity. However, there are key concepts and foundational theories that endure and can be useful for practitioners in content marketing who are considering a more methodical, evidence-based approach to ideation.

Creative Marketing Thought Generation Processes: Divergent Marketing Thought Model

Titus (2018) developed a model on creative marketing thought, referred to as the Divergent Marketing Thought Model (DMTM). This framework sets out key characteristics of the individuals typically involved in marketing ideation. The DMTM also attempts to explain how practitioners draw on tangible and intangible stimuli to deconstruct and then reconstruct concepts into new forms that are meaningful from a marketing perspective.

The term 'divergent thinking' refers to the ability to generate a large, varied range of creative marketing structures and interpretations as well as transformations of information and facts in concert with a specified marketing problem and objective. Convergent thinking entails sorting out and synthesising information in a different way from divergent thought by paring down ideas instead of expanding the range of concepts. More typical of the evaluation stage of idea generation and development, convergent thought is also seen as an important ideation skill and integral to creative success.

The process set out in the DMTM reflects real-world practice whereby individuals and teams undertake research to understand the problem, then generate several ideas appropriate to the brief. Thus, concepts are continually evaluated for their use in addressing key objectives, with many rejected or refined and more ideas added to the pool of possibilities.

Here are some of the key features of the Divergent Marketing Thought Model (Titus, 2018) commonly found in the marketing industry:

- It is **multidimensional** yet highly **focused** on solving a specific marketing problem, for example positioning.
- It requires the involvement of individuals with a propensity to be creative.
- **Creative provocations**, or thought-provoking triggers, are required to initiate ideation activity. These can be tangible, such as specific artefacts or places, or intangible, for example emotions or facts. Provocations should disrupt routine thought to activate the deconstruction process (ibid, p. 239).
- There are three main modes of ideation. These include: *creative synthesis*, which involves 'making new connections or relationships between seemingly unrelated concepts or ideas' (p. 242); *creative abstraction*, which entails the discovery of unusual patterns or simplifying the complex; and *vicarious imagery*, the attempt by practitioners to enter the minds and worlds of their target audiences.
- Considerable research is typically undertaken in a **pre-ideation**, or preparation, stage (ibid, p. 245).
- While ideation is purposeful, there is also some element of chance and trial-and-error apparent in much divergent transformation – successful and unsuccessful.

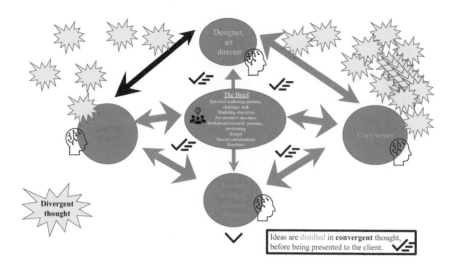

Figure 3.1 Content marketing ideation: divergent thought, convergent thought.

Content marketing creativity in action: Creative individuals expand their minds to generate a large volume of ideas, with the brief at the centre of ideation activities.

Sources include: Titus, 2018; Finke, Ward and Smith, 2006; Frich et al., 2021.

Divergent thought has been conceptualised as distinct, and very different, from convergent thought. This is because multiple ideas and combinations are the product of divergent thought, while narrowing down and refining these into a workable, appropriate concept are the result of convergent thinking. Frich et al. (2021, p. 3) posit that creative processes must naturally go through a cycle of moving through divergent and convergent thinking, usually repeatedly. They observe that: 'Whereas divergent thinking is producing a diverse collection of ideas as the response to a question or a task, convergent thinking concentrates on narrowing down a collection of ideas to a single solution' (ibid). This is what is referred to as the iterative creative process, with content marketing practitioners reflecting on earlier creative efforts to refine and develop new ideas long after the foundational phase of concept development. This ideation can even take place after a campaign has finished, during a 'wash up' or post-mortem of what worked well and what didn't.

An example of the way thinking moves between convergent and divergent, or iterative creativity, is illustrated by the Design Council UK. Its Double Diamond model is a simplified, memorable way to explain the process and is based on four phases (Ball, 2019, n.p., 'The Double Diamond: A universally accepted depiction of the design process'):

1   **Discover**. Practitioners in the creative department start by questioning the brief, instead of assuming what the problem is. This step involves

research, including trying to accurately understand the challenge from the perspective of those affected by the issues. This phase entails divergent thought.

2   **Define**. The second phase is where insights developed in phase one are used to redraft the challenge in a different way, with the fine-tuning typical of convergent thought.

3   **Develop**. Practitioners look for answers to the clearly defined problem and may collaborate with others as they look for inspiration. Divergent thought, with an emphasis on generating a depth and breadth of ideas to solve the problem, characterises this stage.

4   **Deliver**. The final phase involves selecting a single solution that works and preparing it for launch, in a convergent thought process.

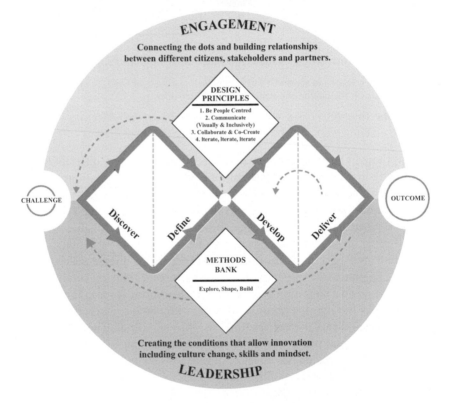

Figure 3.2 The Double Diamond of Ideation.

Iterative creativity cycle: This diagram encapsulates the open-ended, multifaceted, collective nature of concept development which repeats as new facts come to light, and as practitioners continually re-evaluate assets.

Source: Design Council UK ©

Key Creativity Concepts, Theories That Underpin Ideation in Marketing

Teamwork is a significant feature of the marketing industry (Meslec et al., 2020). A breadth and diversity of concepts is regarded as an indicator of effective team ideation, with the proviso that the volume of ideas should be appropriate to marketing objectives. There is an industry-wide assumption that teams are likely to generate a higher number of great marketing ideas, because each individual can contribute to the collective effort. Research suggests that there is a direct relationship between the number of initial ideas produced and the quality of the final idea (Herring et al., 2009).

However, studies also show that in practice the group situation is complicated, with many obstacles in the way of effective teamworking in generating creative marketing thought. Amabile (1950) underscores that creativity is fragile and that sharing ideas is risky and can only flourish in a supportive environment (Berg, 2020, p. 2). This links to studies on the importance of establishing the right working environment. Meslac et al. (2020, p. 2) highlight how the following social and cognitive factors can get in the way of high-quality team ideation:

- **Social loafing**: a reluctance to put forward ideas in front of others.
- **Social matching**: a self-censored approach to limiting ideas to the same number as those advanced by others in the group.
- **Production blocking**: where individuals are unable to generate and/or share ideas because they must conform to group norms and listen to other group members at the expense of undertaking mental work.
- **Fixation**: a situation where team members must conform to categories proposed by other members and subsequently fail to explore imaginative ideas beyond imposed conceptual boxes.

Looking for solutions to these challenges, Menold and Jablokow (2009) suggest that teams made up of cognitively diverse individuals are more effective at coming up with creative ideas. Communication tools such as visualisations, narratives, metaphors, and analogies can have significant effects on getting individuals to understand the cognitive perspectives of other team members (Herring et al., 2009). Underscoring that the ideation process requires divergent and convergent thinking, Knoll and Horton (2011) and Szopinski, (2019) identify three mental activities that support idea generation:

- **Jumping**, which entails using information from other situations to explore fresh angles, in a typical divergent thinking process. For example, practitioners may ask: 'What would the competitor do?'

- **Dumping**, or discarding an assumption about the creative brief in order to leave well-trodden thought paths and generate a change of perspective, in a convergent process. For example, you may look at an assumption about a product feature, then decide another feature may be more powerful as the focus of ideation.
- **Pumping**, commonly known as brainstorming, is where individuals are encouraged to come up with a volume of ideas (divergent thought) before these are narrowed down (convergent).

Meanwhile, as the digital economy has continued to evolve, creativity has been stimulated using sophisticated tools and applications that can generate insights based on data. Marketers have access to objective ways to measure and assess creativity. Analytics tools such as Google Trends and Google Analytics (and there are many others), can provide inspiration by helping marketers identify topics and themes that are of proven interest to consumers or clients. Practitioners can execute ideas suggested by algorithms in new, engaging ways. These same tools can help marketers keep tabs on the performance of creative assets, allowing them to adapt or change these as metrics dictate.

Artificial intelligence (AI) has added concerns, and opportunities, for marketers, with machines successfully generating and executing creative ideas. AI can, for example, write excellent poems based on style requests, for example whether you'd like to read a Shakespearean or Burnsian version, produce portraits that look like they have been painted by masters and even develop original tracks in the same style as music artists. However, Ameen et al. (2022) found that humans have been harnessing the automation benefits of AI, rather than AI doing all the creative work for them. This echoes comments in *The Economist* (2021), which predicted that AI is more likely to emerge as collaborator than competitor for workers in the creative industries (for more, watch this video: https://youtu.be/cgYpMYMhzXI; also see Chapter 12).

Another feature of ideation in the digital era is the involvement of the target customer in the process. User-generated content (UGC) has become ubiquitous along with the adoption of the smartphone (Melumad, 2019). As Vinerean (2017, p. 92) points out:

> The interactivity dimension of the internet has allowed the customer to be a part of the marketing of any brand, product, services, or other entity. To this extent, digital inbound marketing encourages a customer-centric perspective in which organisations have to focus on helping consumers and involving them in the value-delivering process.

Consequently, marketers use social listening through social media channels to draw inspiration from their customers' conversations. These digital tools and techniques are used in conjunction with other methods to generate fresh ideas, and can be used as provocations, or stimuli, by individuals or in group ideation meetings.

The Kano Model: How to Unearth the Best Marketing Angles in Your Content

The earlier part of this chapter dealt with individual and group processes in ideation. This section looks at identifying a story hook to engage a customer or client and ultimately get them to respond positively towards a product. It explores the theory of Attraction Quality, developed by Japanese scholars led by Dr Noriaki Kano (1984), that can help marketing practitioners excavate the right types of information around which to develop creative ideas. Furthermore, it can help you think about which facts and figures to prioritise, or even omit, as you aim to use your content to get a product or service to stand out from its competitors.

The theory of Attraction Quality, also known colloquially as the Customer Delight or Customer Satisfaction model, gives fresh perspective on the product or service lifecycle. It can help you to excavate specific information that can serve as a useful focal point for idea generation. Kano (1984 and 2001) provides a guide to identify which aspects of an offering you might want emphasise, downplay or ignore altogether as you come up with story angles and shape narratives that resonate deeply, and in a positive way, with specific groups of customers.

Kano and his collaborators (see Kano, 2001; Sauerwein et al., 1996) developed a structured approach to help identify which objective and subjective attributes are most relevant for a target market. Each question is asked twice about a product feature, in a positive (functional) and negative (dysfunctional) way. Answers are plotted on a grid with a view to ascertaining whether customers: desire and want more of a specific feature; expect a certain feature and will not be satisfied by more of it, yet will be dissatisfied if it is missing; are neutral if a feature is missing but delighted if it is included; indifferent about a feature; dislike a specific feature and will be dissatisfied if it is present. These findings are then illustrated in a graph that helps to clearly illustrate which features should be emphasised, with the horizontal axis showing the physical (objective) qualities and the vertical axis indicating degrees of satisfaction (subjective). Variations of this questionnaire are used across the global marketing industry to undertake customer research on specific products and services ahead of the development of content (see Paul et al., 2022). Marketing practitioners can prioritise and highlight specific features in content, based on what the findings of this research reveal.

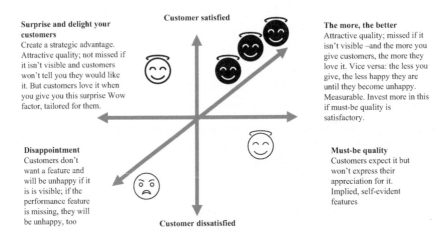

Figure 3.3 Key concepts developed by Kano.

Knowing which features will sell: This grid summarises the key concepts developed by Kano et al. (1984). There are variations of this research in practice. It complements other research that lays the groundwork for ideation.

Here are the key tenets of the theory of Attraction Quality and what they imply for content marketers:

- **Quality has two sides: objective and subjective**, with the latter most relevant for content marketers, who need to understand what this subjectivity looks like for target markets at different stages of the product or service lifecycle. Then, using this knowledge, the content needs to be crafted to make the facts, figures, and narrative relevant for specific audiences. Personas can be used to help map subjective quality elements with customer need states, pain points, and other characteristics.
- **The relationship between product quality and customer satisfaction is not linear or one-dimensional**. It is not true that the higher the perceived quality of this feature of a product, the higher the customer satisfaction. This in turn means that a greater focus on quality does not necessarily translate into a higher return on investment in content. Marketers therefore need to look for a feature or attribute that can be made to stand out.
- **Customers are attracted to different features over a product or service lifecycle**. Content marketers should understand how customers respond emotionally to various product or service attributes over time and in relation to the buyer journey. In the light of these insights, they can adjust positioning, and the types of information to elevate, in tactical assets.
- **Features change in their appeal to customers**, moving from attractive to must-have as shiny new characteristics come into view or as a competitor puts a product or service under pressure. The environment can also

change, making a once-appealing feature suddenly unattractive. Some features may appeal differently to various target groups.

- **Some features are only noticed when they are missing**. Customers take some features for granted, including those characteristics that were originally shiny and new (e.g., mobile phones: the screen sensitivity to touch is something we take for granted, though this feature was initially the distinctive one. If we are not able to use this feature, we will complain). From a content perspective, we expect to find certain information on a website and if it is not there, we complain. For example, you may need to see an 'about us' page for a charity looking for donations, or an easy-to-see return address and form for a product supplier.
- **Spend resources on features that will have the greatest appeal**. Content marketing campaigns take time and money, and you will need to demonstrate a return on this investment. Develop a narrative around the feature that is most likely to strike a chord with your target audiences and you will increase your chances of getting your audience to respond in a way that meets your marketing objectives.

Hygiene, Hub, and Hero Content

Marketers used to often speak about unique selling points (USPs), or those attributes that are original to one product or service. However, with the global economy at such an advanced stage, and very few offerings entirely unique, the shift has been to differentiators. Kano et al. (1984), for example, identified another way to view product attributes and then highlight these in specific ways to customers. Their ideas about attraction quality have infused content marketing practice.

Hygiene Content

This content is based on product/service/client attributes that are expected, assumed, or given – and are core needs. These are also known as hygiene factors because we miss them if they are not evident. Their absence will cause dissatisfaction; but no amount of execution will lead to positive satisfaction in a survey.

Take the example of the number of toilet rolls required in the bathroom: one toilet roll is essential, but 15 will make no difference to your experience. Customers won't tell you about what they think about the number of toilet rolls in your bathroom, unless there aren't any. You need to figure out what the content equivalent of the toilet roll is for your marketing campaign or objective.

Make sure you have taken consideration of this hygiene content in your overall content marketing strategy by looking for articles, web pages and information that fall into this must-have, or expected, category and making sure they are included. If you don't, you can expect complaints or dis-satisfaction to register in client feedback. Types of hygiene content vary, depending on what type of brand, product or service is being marketed. Hygiene content can be as basic as directions to an office or may include: frequently asked questions (FAQs), 'how to' guides, product fact sheets, and case studies.

Hub Content

Clients or customers seek out hub content and actively evaluate it. The more they get, the more satisfied they are – provided it is quality content. Hub content could be a suite of foundation videos that cover all the other important – albeit often less interesting – aspects of your brand. Often at the heart of the content marketing plan, this is the type of information that is useful, interesting, and can keep customers hooked and engaging with your brand.

Hub content is usually published regularly. For example, if you are marketing pet food, you may want to develop regular articles that provide pet owners with scientific advances in veterinary health. This type of content is often distributed using links in email newsletters and on social media feeds.

Hero Content

This is the main piece of content that attracts attention to your brand, so there is less of it as it tends to be more expensive to produce. If you are developing a campaign, this is the content that makes a big splash or is also referred to as a lead magnet. www.thinkwithgoogle.com suggests you ask yourself the following questions to ascertain whether you have written hero content: Would people bother to share this on social media? Would this make a good newspaper headline? Can you imagine your audience paying for this content?

Hero content may be centred around a piece of research, for example a commissioned survey, that has surprising findings of relevance to customers of the brand you are marketing. A series of GIFs, aimed at amusing customers while delivering helpful tips, could represent hero content for a brand.

The main idea with hero content is that it is surprising, remarkable, unique, or unusual, and the target audience for whom it is developed will want to consume it and share it. It may not have a long shelf life, like hygiene content, and is likely to be of higher impact than hub content. Hero content is where you can let your concepts sparkle, so play with different formats and interpretations at the ideation stage.

Over time, excitement needs (hero content) evolve into performance needs (hub content), and finally into core needs (hygiene content). There is no point having hero content, however, unless your hygiene content and hub content are in place because you will waste resources attracting customers who won't return.

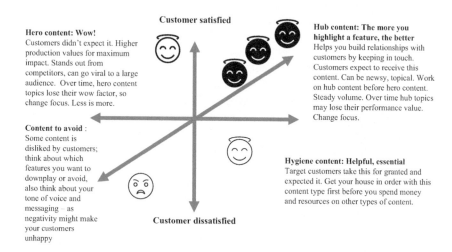

Customer satisfied

Hero content: Wow!
Customers didn't expect it. Higher production values for maximum impact. Stands out from competitors, can go viral to a large audience. Over time, hero content topics lose their wow factor, so change focus. Less is more.

Hub content: The more you highlight a feature, the better
Helps you build relationships with customers by keeping in touch. Customers expect to receive this content. Can be newsy, topical. Work on hub content before hero content. Steady volume. Over time hub topics may lose their performance value. Change focus.

Content to avoid :
Some content is disliked by customers; think about which features you want to downplay or avoid, also think about your tone of voice and messaging – as negativity might make your customers unhappy

Hygiene content: Helpful, essential
Target customers take this for granted and expected it. Get your house in order with this content type first before you spend money and resources on other types of content.

Customer dissatisfied

Figure 3.4 Applying Kano's attractive quality theory: Hero, hub, hygiene.

Hero, hub and hygiene content: This analysis, based on work started by Kano et al. (1984) on product development and built on by other scholars, is very useful for understanding how topics and formats should be used as you roll out a content marketing strategy.

How Content Marketers Marry Marketing with Journalism

As content marketing practitioners are effectively in the business of publishing (Baer, 2022), they often rely on newsroom processes and practices for developing specific types of assets. Media businesses are specialists in the craft of non-fiction storytelling – which, in essence, is what content marketing is, with the added requirement that the narrative must fit a specific marketing objective. Marketers consider the styles, structures, themes, and topics of content created by media businesses as they develop ideas for their own campaigns. To a large extent, content marketers must think like journalists. This starts with ideation, by coming up with specific angles on topics so that marketing narratives can compete for a place among the media-produced stories that are well-read and being shared widely.

Journalists begin their daily routine by scanning headlines. Also, for content marketers, it is helpful to do so, getting up to date with the news, including in the sectors and niche areas of relevance to the target audiences. The better one's knowledge about what is happening in the public domain on issues that affect clients and the products and services they are selling, the easier it will be to identify appropriate hooks and develop story lines.

Public relations (PR) practitioners have been using their operational understanding of how journalists work for decades. This is because outputs that look like journalism are effective tools for communicating with target audiences. Often, journalists draw heavily on press or media releases that are produced by PRs where the content is seen to be valuable and in so doing are manipulated to publish information that fits the agenda of whoever has paid for the work. PRs use these publications to demonstrate their success to their paying clients. Infographics, videos, social media posts, and other content formats are also often distributed this way for free use, with the final pieces looking similar to those produced by professional journalists.

Content marketers use the same tools and techniques, publishing content that looks like journalism on corporate websites or submitting it to media companies for use as native content (paid for or sponsored, but blending in with the journalistic content), thought leadership, a column or blog – with the latter used for free by media companies. If links to owned media, such as a website, are included in content distributed to media companies, this can help with search engine optimisation and help to boost traffic, with those metrics included to gauge the success of content marketing activities. The main difference between content produced, distributed, and published by PRs and content marketers is that the former tends to be earned media, while the latter is owned or paid for by a corporate or business client or sponsor.

It is worth noting that there is a blur between the work of PRs, content marketers and journalists, with PRs and content marketers often crossing paths in their content activities – and journalists often moonlighting or freelancing to do the work of PRs and content marketers. Accordingly, many former journalists are now working in the fields of PR and content marketing.

Journalists focus on developing creative ideas. This early idea generation process entails a search for topics that can be developed into narratives. A key feature of these stories is that they must be newsworthy and of interest to target audiences; in other words, they are telling us something new and reflect real-life activities and discoveries. Content marketers use the same skills and techniques to produce and distribute content, with website articles a prime example of how the outputs can look the same. Content marketing and journalism stories are characterised by engaging headlines, subheadings that keep the reader hooked, a strong introductory paragraph, and a series of paragraphs that flow in a logical narrative order.

Deciding What Works to Attract, Engage Audiences: News Values

Journalists are specialists in identifying specific topics and themes that are likely to be interesting to their audiences. While many have an intuitive sense, also called a 'nose for news', there are also certain characteristics of news – or news values – that make it likely to gain traction. Theorists have examined what news values are common in news articles and in social media content that has gained traction or gone 'viral'.

Harcup and O'Neill (2017, 2001) identified a series of news values that are present in content that makes the headlines. Trying to understand why some events become news and others don't, they have responded to the question of 'What is news?' by developing a taxonomy of news values. These include:

1 **Power elite**. Stories are more likely to make it onto the news diary if they are about powerful people, individuals, organisations, and countries.
2 **Celebrity**. Similar to the power elite category, that builds on the seminal work of Galtung and Ruge (1968; see Galtung & Ruge, 1973), people who are already famous do not need to do extreme things to appear on the news agenda. This is why influencers who don't seem to do much are often paid to promote brands, as their celebrity status can help to create a halo effect around a product or service without them doing anything exciting connected to the offering.
3 **Entertainment**. There is a popular saying that 'sex' sells, which is why the media often opts for photographs of attractive people. Also in this category of entertainment are animals, hence the many dog and cat memes and viral videos. Stories that have a drama unfolding like a television soap opera are also newsworthy, appealing to the appetite audiences have to be entertained.
4 **Surprise**. Stories must give you information that is new, or 'surprise' audiences by serving up this information in a fresh way. It is worth noting at the ideation phase that you can be successful at reworking news or developing the surprise element for a piece of content that did not work the first time.
5 **Bad news**. Negativity sells. Stories about events in which people die or have something bad happening to them are more likely to make the major headlines. This is a challenging news value for content marketers whose job it is to nurture a positive image for their clients.
6 **Good news**. Sometimes positivity is newsworthy. But many positive events are regarded as boring and to be expected, so they don't make the news agenda.
7 **Magnitude**. Size counts. The number of people that are affected by an event plays a role in newsworthiness. You are more likely to see a headline about an event attended by many people than one involving a small group, for example.
8 **Relevance**. News that is about your target audience or information that affects them directly or people close to them is more likely to be newsworthy. Focusing on people in this way can help you connect with individuals in your target market.
9 **Follow-up**. Once an event or person is in the news, they are likely to stay in the news for some time. Stories about a subject already in the news are more likely to be of interest. This means you should look for new angles or fresh perspective to add to a topic or theme that is hitting the right notes with audiences. For example, if you are producing a series of website articles for an investment firm, you may notice that technology shares are in the news – and so you come up with specific angles on tech stocks,

drawing on research by the company's analysts. In the social media world, an easy way of hitching a ride on a news wave is by looking at which hash tags are popular and finding an angle that is relevant to your customer to join the hash tag momentum.

A question often asked by journalists and content marketers is: 'What works best on Facebook?' (Harcup & O'Neill, 2017, p. 1475). Making content shareable is the Holy Grail for many in marketing and journalism. Journalists will also tell you that there are some obvious devices to help your story garner attention, including:

- **Images**. Always think of visuals to go with your stories to complement what you are saying as these help capture the attention of your audience. These visuals could be photographs, charts, infographics, videos, embedded social media activity, GIFs.
- **People**. It is always more interesting to read about people than general statistics or developments. For example, instead of writing a story that a disease is killing trees, craft an angle about what the death of these trees means for the people who rely on them. When we read about climate change, we are more captivated by stories about the activists – such as Greta Thunberg – than the scientific discussions about melting ice caps. Case studies, where the focus is on a specific customer, are more effective than generic facts and figures about what a product or service can do for an audience.
- **Audiences care about themselves first**. Above all, and in the sense of value-oriented content marketing, audiences care about themselves and their own pockets. Think about the 'what's in it for them?' when you develop a story hook, so focus on how to solve their problem or address their need rather than selling your product or service directly as you develop your concept.

Website Content: Getting the Right Hooks

The headline is a critically important aspect of an article, so spend time crafting these few words for maximum impact. A good headline gets attention while also implying a value benefit for the reader – so a reason to keep reading. A similar principle applies to videos and other visual formats: The images and words need to work together quickly, or you will lose your audience.

Make sure your message is clear, as you do not want your reader to do any work figuring out what you are trying to say. Short headlines of about six words work best, though there are exceptions.

It's a good idea to start playing with headline possibilities at the ideation stage, as this can help you identify your content angle for development. Aim for three different headlines to get your creative engine started if you are struggling to find a way into a narrative.

Deciding What Works to Attract, Engage Audiences: Digital Tools

Content marketers have a wealth of digital tools available to help with ideation. There are many apps that are designed to assist with providing useful statistics for marketers, and many have built-in metrics. The usual starting point is to analyse any data connected to the offering you must market, looking at what content has worked, and what has not. You can also look at competitors' data for clues on where the gaps and opportunities might lie. In the digital environment, you can aim to create more content on themes or topics that are working well so that you can ride a wave of popularity. Pay attention to how you position your content so that it stands out from the mass of information.

Google Analytics is commonly used to keep track of audience activity, but there are many other packages. An analytics tool will help you see which content is popular, whether people are reading to the end and if they are moving to another piece of content on your site – to name just a few of many features you can assess.

Keyword research is a staple for content marketers. This entails identifying the search terms that your target audience are likely to use while trying to find your information and using these tactically in your text, or copy. The idea is that the more effectively you use keywords, in conjunction with other search engine optimisation techniques, the more likely your content will rise to the top of the search rankings. However, there is a caveat here: while keywords are useful, it is important to prioritise the overall quality of your content. In addition, search engines can penalise your content if it is deemed to be gaming the system by, for example, keyword stuffing. Nevertheless, keywords can provide useful prompts to generate ideas for specific pieces of content and even campaigns. In addition, keywords can help you keep your content focused on a specific theme or topic throughout your text.

Identifying the Right Angles: Keyword Tools

Here is a small selection of keyword tools that you can use to kickstart your idea generation. Many have free trials, so you can play around with keywords to see what might work for your specific campaign:

- **Google Ads Keyword Planner**. You need a credit card/account.
- **Answerthepublic**. This one provides questions that people have been asking. You could structure your content around answering these.
- **Similarweb**. Also helps you get insights into which keywords your competitors are using successfully.
- **Semrush, Moz Keyword Explorer, Ahrefs** and Neil Patel's **Ubersuggest** are similar, with data that helps with identifying top-performing content.

Listening on the web and social media can also be a useful way to identify topics, themes, and specific angles to develop in your content:

- **Google Trends**. You can look up which stories are popular and can fine-tune keyword selection by comparing choices.
- Hashtag campaigns can give you a flavour of what's working, including volume of reach, sentiment analysis, and the number of mentions. You can also discover which hashtags are waxing and waning in popularity. Tools include: **Keyhole, Hashtagify, Brand24**.
- Social media management tools like Hootsuite include analytics that can give you ideas on the best times to post as well as what to post and can include suggestions for reaching out to specific social media accounts.

Ideation: Identify What You Want to Achieve with Your Content

There is more to great marketing content than its creative appeal. Marketers need to elicit a response from consumers that benefits their business. This reaction is often linked to where the consumer is in the buying journey, and ranges from generating awareness of a business or product to purchase, repurchase and championing a brand.

Think about what you want to achieve with your content as you generate and evaluate ideas at the ideation stage. There is no point pouring time and resources into creative assets that do not achieve marketing objectives. Hub content, hygiene content and hero content can all be linked to stages in the buying journey, as shown in Figure 3.5.

Marketing Ideation: The Starting Point – The Brief

Content ideation does not happen in a vacuum. The ideation process for content typically starts after the development of a brief. This is a summary of the requirements of the job. It will include the name of the client (internal contacts or external to the business, and usually both), the marketing objectives, and deliverables. A good brief will usually include:

- Relevant background information about the business, brand or service that is being marketed.
- What the content needs to achieve, also referred to as marketing objectives, and often explicitly stipulated as calls to action (CTAs).
- The budget, or cost estimate for producing the content.
- Project timelines, including deadlines and sign-off procedures so that the stakeholders, including the client, give formal approval for activities.

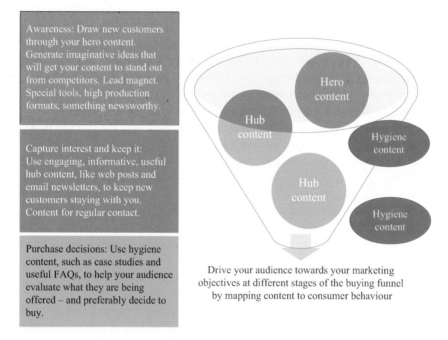

Awareness: Draw new customers through your hero content. Generate imaginative ideas that will get your content to stand out from competitors. Lead magnet. Special tools, high production formats, something newsworthy.

Capture interest and keep it: Use engaging, informative, useful hub content, like web posts and email newsletters, to keep new customers staying with you. Content for regular contact.

Purchase decisions: Use hygiene content, such as case studies and useful FAQs, to help your audience evaluate what they are being offered – and preferably decide to buy.

Drive your audience towards your marketing objectives at different stages of the buying funnel by mapping content to consumer behaviour

Figure 3.5 Mapping content to the buyers' funnel – from creating awareness to driving purchase.

At the end of the ideation process, you will be expected to distil ideas to pitch to a client or stakeholders in the business.

Marketing Ideation: Personas, Pain Points, Need States, Positioning

Just as ideation should not start without a clear brief, the process is also most effective when underpinned by marketing research. Much of the work of the marketing strategist focuses on understanding the behaviour of consumers and clients, and then feeding this intelligence into the inception, production, and delivery of marketing communications. As digital marketing strategy expert P. R. Smith (2021, p. 27) states:

> If you can't define exactly who is your ideal customer, how can you ever find them? It's like looking for a needle in a haystack, except you don't know what you are looking for since you don't have a clear customer description or profile.

Here are some tools and concepts to help shine a light on appropriate ideas so that your content can stand out and connect with individuals in your target audience:

- **Personas**. This is detailed research that helps you excavate the various characteristics about specific types of individuals in your target audience.
- **Pain points**. These are the questions that keep your potential clients or customers awake at night. If you identify what these are, you can structure content to address these issues and help them solve problems.
- **Need states**. This is what motivates your customer to buy something. This similarly applies to wants, which are aspirational but not essential.
- **Customer journeys and touch points**. There are different theories on how a customer moves in stages from awareness to purchase to repurchase. Your choices of content will depend on where your customer is in this journey, so it is useful to factor these details into your ideation activities from the start.
- **Customer feedback**. You can learn a lot about what your customers do and don't want to hear about by paying close attention to what they have said or are saying. Use this intelligence to your advantage at the ideation stage.
- **Competitor analysis**. Keeping a close eye on the strengths and weaknesses of competitors can help you identify ideas for development.
- **Positioning**. Your content proposition aims to own a unique, valuable gap in the market where you meet the most pressing needs of your audiences.

Presenting Your Ideas

Content marketers often pitch ideas at three levels, for different budgets – for example bronze, the lower end of the price range; gold, more expensive with the pricing linked to a more elaborate execution; platinum, very expensive but highly distinctive. These budgets must be within range of the figure presented to you in your initial brief.

One of the reasons you may include three ideas with different budgets is so that you can impress your client with your ideas. You may also find that the client is willing to stretch the budget. Remember you want your client to opt for at least one and pay you for the execution of this creative work. Too many ideas can also confuse the client.

You are being paid for your expertise so, as the expert, you should make considered recommendations, and your rationale with each idea. This is important to remember, as you will need to constantly think about the relevance of your ideas as you originate and develop them. Every word, image, sound, representation should have a reason for existing in your creative asset.

An important part of ideation is fine-tuning a broad concept so that you can present a clear plan for how you will develop a concept into a piece of marketing collateral that achieves predetermined objectives and fits specific considerations and a budget. You should consider these types of details at the ideation stage. As you explore the creative possibilities, bear in mind that you will have to explain and justify your recommendations to whoever controls the budget. Have a rationale for every artistic execution.

Content Calendars

A content calendar is a project management tool that indicates what type of content you plan to publish, and when and where you would like it to appear. It is a similar tool to an editorial calendar, which is used in the media sector. It can help you visualise what an overall campaign will look like so that you can make sure you have important dates covered and that there are no gaps or overlap in content. The content calendar also makes it easy for teams to collaborate because the information is all in one place.

This tool, which is a spreadsheet, enables you to create a clear timeline for sharing and promoting content so that it has the best chance of being effective in meeting your marketing objectives. You can use the calendar to plot all your content types so that you can have a holistic picture of your content marketing activities.

While the calendar details will vary between marketing teams, they mostly contain the following information:

- Topics.
- Publication channels.
- Dates and times of publication.
- Reposting dates and times.
- Key stakeholders and content responsibilities, so it is clear who is doing what.

Often the content calendar is the starting point of ideation or forms part of this process. For example, you may know you need a certain amount of hub and hygiene content so you can figure out from the times you want to publish what types of concepts might work. If, for example, you have a retail business, you may decide to publish content ahead of key dates in the calendar, such as Valentine's Day, Easter, Mother's Day, Father's Day and so on to tap into the need among consumers to buy certain items.

The content calendar is a living document. You can make adjustments to creative assets and the way you promote these throughout the duration of a marketing plan. You can also use it for the hero, hub, and hygiene content that is pre-planned, while being aware of gaps where you may want to be reactive and quickly develop content to take advantage of hashtag trends or news.

Remember, creativity and the execution of ideas in content marketing deliverables are iterative. Where a starting point is suggested, note that ideas are generated and interpreted by creative teams and audiences in many different ways. Practitioners are routinely testing their ideas, revising them, retesting, reworking creative assets, and also throwing these out and starting again.

Content marketing is, like other forms of marketing, part art and part science. This means we can be guided by qualitative and quantitative techniques and tools like the content calendar but must be mindful that there are multiple influences over what works – and these factors can change, sometimes rapidly.

How to Develop a Creative Habit – Reflective Diaries

Creativity can be nurtured. The more creative you are, the more creative you get. It starts with developing the habit of generating excellent creative marketing ideas: those that capture the attention of your target audiences while also achieving marketing objectives. A reflective diary, encourages you **observe** (take note of a campaign), **reflect** (evaluate the campaign), and then **recommend** ways to improve it (make adjustments, refine ideas, using your imagination, and with reference to evidence, concepts, and theories). This gets your creative engine started and working. As Biz Stone (2015, p. 23), founder of Twitter has famously noted:

> Creativity is a renewable resource. Challenge yourself every day. Be as creative as you like, as often as you want, because you can never run out. Experience and curiosity drive us to make unexpected, offbeat connections. It is these nonlinear steps that often lead to the greatest work.

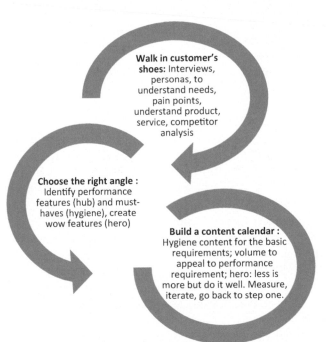

Figure 3.6 Content ideation cycle: Iterative, research-based.

Ideation rooted in insights: As this diagram illustrates, ideation is integrated with other content marketing processes and practices and is iterative.

In this chapter you have learned:

- How content marketers generate creative ideas, and you developed insights into key theories and concepts about creative processes, and how practitioners can become more effective at ideation.
- How to develop hero, hub, and hygiene content.
- Ways in which journalism practices influence ideation in content marketing.
- To recognise and explain practical ways to conceptualise and manage content, from planning and the idea stage to the promotion of creative campaigns.
- Practical skills in content marketing ideation.

Interview with Fabian Bosser

Fabian Bosser

Where do you start with the ideation process?

When starting the ideation process, it's important to first understand the goals and objectives of the content marketing campaign. This includes understanding the target audience and the message that needs to be conveyed. From there, it's helpful to brainstorm and generate as many ideas as possible, even if they seem far-fetched or impractical at first.

Some people have specific places or techniques for sparking ideas. Do you?

It is helpful to spark ideas by looking at industry news and trends, conducting market research, or even just taking a walk to clear your mind. Personally, I find it helpful to set aside dedicated time for ideation and to try to come up with as many ideas as possible, even if they seem crazy or unrealistic at first. In addition, it helps a lot to put together an interdisciplinary team and to generate ideas at regular intervals using various creative techniques. Classic techniques like brainwriting or the Walt Disney method.

Do you have a set process for developing ideas? If so, please explain, step-by-step, how you come up with concepts?
My process for developing ideas typically includes:

- Understanding the goals and objectives of the content marketing campaign.
- Refining and prioritising the ideas based on feasibility, relevance, and potential impact.
- Developing a content calendar or editorial plan to organise and schedule the ideas.
- Collaborating with a team to bring the ideas to life.

Do you draw on theories, consumer behaviour research to develop your ideas? If so, please give an example of a theory that underpins one of your successful concepts.
Yes, I often draw on theories and consumer behaviour research to develop my ideas. For example, I might use Maslow's Hierarchy of Needs to understand what motivates a particular target audience, or I might use the AIDA model to structure the content in a way that captures attention, interests the audience, and inspires action.

How important is teamwork in generating award-winning ideas?
Teamwork is often crucial in generating award-winning ideas, as different team members bring their own perspectives and expertise to the table. To inspire creativity in my colleagues, I try to foster an open and collaborative work environment where everyone feels comfortable sharing their ideas and feedback. I also encourage team members to take breaks and try new things to keep their minds fresh and open to new ideas.

What do you do if you have a creative block? Please set out some of your best suggestions for getting your creative juices flowing.
If I'm experiencing a creative block, I try to take a break and do something different to get my mind off the task at hand. This might include going for a walk, trying a new hobby, or just taking some time to relax and clear my mind. I also find it helpful to seek out inspiration from other sources, such as industry news, social media, or even just conversations with friends and colleagues.

How did you develop your creative thinking abilities? And what do you do to keep taking your creativity to the next level?
I developed my creative thinking abilities through a combination of education and experience. As an Innovation Coach I know various creative theories and techniques, and I have also gained a lot of knowledge and skills through hands-on experience working on various content marketing campaigns. To continue to take my creativity to the next level, I try to stay up to date with

industry trends and best practices, and I also try to expose myself to new and diverse experiences that can help me see things from different perspectives.

There are many concepts that are entertaining, but they do not necessarily contribute to the bottom line. How do you gauge whether a creative concept will work before you go too far in the production process with a dud idea?
To gauge whether a creative concept will work before going too far in the production process, I try to consider factors such as the target audience, the message being conveyed, the overall goals and objectives of the campaign, and the budget. I also try to get feedback from colleagues and, if possible, conduct market research to see how the idea resonates with potential customers.

What should students, who want to emulate your successes, be doing now to nurture their creativity?
Students who want to nurture their creativity should try to expose themselves to new and diverse experiences, stay up to date with industry trends and best practices, and practice brainstorming and idea generation on a regular basis. It can also be helpful to seek out educational opportunities, such as courses or workshops, that can help develop creative thinking skills.

How important is the budget in the ideation process? Do you factor in the financial considerations at the beginning of the process or at the end?
The budget can be an important consideration in the ideation process, as it may impact the feasibility and scope of certain ideas. I generally try to consider budget constraints at the beginning of the process, but I also try to be flexible and open to adjusting my ideas as needed to fit within the available budget.

Are there topics or ideas that you stay away from because they can be detrimental to a brand? Or do you embrace controversy and sensitive topics? Why? Please elaborate on some successes and failures you have seen in your career.
There may be certain topics or ideas that a brand may choose to avoid for various reasons, such as if they could be perceived as controversial or offensive to certain audiences. Ultimately, the decision to embrace or avoid sensitive topics will depend on the brand's values and goals, as well as the potential risks and benefits of addressing such topics. It's important to carefully consider the potential consequences of addressing controversial or sensitive topics, and to be prepared for a range of possible reactions. In my experience, brands that handle such topics with sensitivity and authenticity tend to be more successful in engaging their audiences and building trust.

How do you get your creative ideas to stand out from the many other excellent creative assets competing for attention?
To make creative ideas stand out, it can be helpful to focus on creating unique and memorable content that resonates with the target audience. This might

involve using compelling visuals, telling a compelling story, or using a unique perspective or tone. It can also be helpful to stay up to date with industry trends and to conduct market research to understand what types of content are most likely to capture the attention of the target audience.

Do you develop more than one idea for presentation to a client? Please elaborate on what you consider to be best practice?

It's generally best practice to develop more than one idea for presentation to a client, as this allows the client to have more options to choose from and helps to ensure that the final content aligns with their goals and objectives. When developing multiple ideas, it's important to ensure that they are diverse and offer a range of options for the client to consider.

How do you get clients to buy into good ideas? Have you ever had to fight to get a great idea over the line – and what was your negotiating strategy?

To get clients to buy into good ideas, it can be helpful to present a well-researched and thoughtfully crafted pitch that clearly explains the benefits of the idea and how it aligns with the client's goals and objectives. It can also be helpful to provide data and examples to support the idea, and to be flexible and open to feedback and revisions as needed.

How do you avoid the dilution of ideas when they are passed to a team for final sign-off?

To avoid the dilution of ideas when they are passed to a team for final sign-off, it can be helpful to clearly communicate the vision and goals of the idea, and to establish clear roles and responsibilities for team members to ensure that everyone is working towards the same objectives. It can also be helpful to periodically review and assess the progress of the idea to ensure that it is on track and aligned with the original vision.

There is a lot of 'me too' creativity out there, which suggests that copying others can work. Do you agree? Why? How have you harnessed other people's ideas? And what have you done when others have stolen or drawn heavily on your ideas?

Copying others can sometimes work, but it's generally more effective to strive for originality and to find ways to differentiate oneself from competitors. It's important to be mindful of copyright and intellectual property laws, and to respect the ideas and creations of others. If someone has stolen or heavily drawn on your ideas, it may be necessary to seek legal recourse or to have a conversation with the offending party to address the issue.

Do you use any technology or tools in the ideation process? Some people use sticky notes and discovery workshops; others use brainstorming software. Please elaborate on your favourite apps/techniques/tools.

There are many technologies and tools that can be helpful in the ideation process, such as brainstorming software, project management tools, and collaboration platforms. Some people also find it helpful to use sticky notes or to conduct discovery workshops to generate ideas and gather feedback. It's important to find the tools and techniques that work best for your team and your workflow.

What metrics do you use to gauge success? Please elaborate on how you use analytics. Are there some metrics that are a waste of time but are used widely? The metrics I use to gauge success will depend on the goals and objectives of the content marketing campaign. Some common metrics that may be used to evaluate the success of a campaign include engagement metrics (e.g., likes, comments, shares), reach (e.g., number of impressions), website traffic, and conversions (e.g., sales, sign-ups). It's important to select the metrics that are most relevant to the specific campaign and to use them to inform future strategy and decision-making.

What interview questions would you ask a young graduate who has aspirations to join a creative team to ascertain whether they have the ability to generate award-winning ideas?

1   How do you stay up to date with industry trends and best practices?
2   How do you come up with new and original ideas? What techniques or processes do you use to generate ideas?
3   How do you approach brainstorming sessions? Do you have any techniques or strategies for contributing ideas and fostering collaboration within a team?
4   Can you share an example of a time when you had to persuade someone to adopt your idea? What was your approach, and how did you ultimately succeed in getting your idea approved?
5   How do you handle feedback and criticism on your ideas? Can you give an example of a time when you had to revise or adapt an idea based on feedback?
6   Can you share an example of a time when you had to work within constraints or limitations (e.g., budget, time, resources)? How did you approach the challenge, and what was the outcome?
7   How do you stay motivated and inspired to come up with new ideas? What do you do when you experience a creative block?
8   Do you have any examples of successful ideas that you have generated in the past?

End of Chapter Exercise

Tutorial Task 1: Nurturing Creative Content Ideas – Reflective Diary

Start a reflective diary. Identify a content marketing campaign. Observe the key creative features about the campaign: describe it in detail, including who it is aimed at, and which product or service attributes are being highlighted. Then, reflect on the campaign: What works? What doesn't work? What could they do better? Where are the risks for the brand? Where are the opportunities for a competitor?

Make a list of three to five recommendations for a rival brand.

Weekly Tutorial Task

Bring a reflection about a content marketing campaign, or piece of content, to your class. Be prepared to describe your case study and take your peers through the steps you took, as recorded in your diary, to observe, reflect and recommend improvements to the campaign. Ask for feedback from your peers about your reflection on a content marketing campaign.

Tutorial 2: Building a Creative Team

Group work: You are a marketing consultancy that has been hired to improve the creativity outputs of a corporation's marketing division. With reference to theories and concepts covered in this chapter, discuss the following:

• What would you look at in the current working environment to assess whether the organisational culture and processes are conducive to effective content marketing ideation?
• If you were hiring new staff, what characteristics would help demonstrate that individuals are likely to be creative as content marketers?
• How would you motivate individuals to be creative (and what is likely to demotivate them)? Use theories and concepts covered earlier in this chapter to back your points.
• Would you encourage individual or group ideation, or both? Why?
• How would you get the most out of group ideation activities?
• Think of a time when you participated in creative group work and explore whether you succumbed to social loafing.
• How do you think you can improve your own creativity in a group situation? Discuss with the group and share your feedback on how others can do the same.

References

Ameen, N., Sharma, G. D., Tarba, S., Rao, A., & Chopra, R. (2022). Toward advancing theory on creativity in marketing and artificial intelligence. *Psychology & Marketing*.
Baer, J. (2022, August 26). Why you need to turn your content marketing upside down. Convince & Convert. Retrieved January 30, 2023, from www.convinceandconvert.com/content-marketing/why-you-need-to-turn-your-content-marketing-upside-down/

Ball, J. (2022). The Double Diamond: A universally accepted depiction of the design process, Design Council – Design for Planet. Design Council. Available at: www. designcouncil.org.uk/our-work/news-opinion/double-diamond-universally-accepted-depiction-design-process/ (Accessed: January 30, 2023).

Berg, J. M. (2009). Brilliant and benevolent: The optimism of Teresa Amabile's legacy for creativity in organizations. *Creativity at Work: A Festschrift in Honor of Teresa Amabile*, 1–8.

Chen, J. (2022). A guide to content ideation & development, *Sprout Social*. Available at: https://sproutsocial.com/insights/content-ideation-development/ (Accessed: January 30, 2023).

Collins. (n.d.). Ideation. In Collins.com dictionary. Retrieved January 30, 2023, from www. collinsdictionary.com/dictionary/english/ideation

Finke, R. A., Ward, T. B., & Smith, S. M. (1996). *Creative Cognition: Theory, Research, and Applications*. MIT press.

Frich, J., Nouwens, M., Halskov, K., & Dalsgaard, P. (2021, May). How digital tools impact convergent and divergent thinking in design ideation. In *Proceedings of the 2021 CHI Conference on Human Factors in Computing Systems* (pp. 1–11).

Galtung, J., & Ruge, M. (1973). Structuring and selecting news. The manufacture of news: Social problems, deviance and the mass media, *1*(62), 62–72.

Harcup, T., & O'Neill, D. (2017). What is news? News values revisited (again). *Journalism Studies*, *1*(12), 1470–1488.

Harcup, T., & O'Neill, D. (2001). What is news? Galtung and Ruge revisited. *Journalism Studies*, *2*(2), 261–280.

Herring, S. R., Jones, B. R., & Bailey, B. P. (2009, January). *Idea generation techniques among creative professionals*. In 2009 42nd Hawaii International Conference on System Sciences (pp. 1–10). IEEE.

Kano, N. (2001, September). *Life cycle and creation of attractive quality*. In Proceedings of the 4th QMOD Conference, Linkoping, Sweden (pp. 12–14).

Kano, N., Seraku, N., Takahashi, F., & Tsuji, S. (1984). Attractive quality and must-be quality. *Journal of Japan Society for Quality Control*, *14*, 39–48.

Kee, A. W. A., & Yazdanifard, R. (2015). The review of content marketing as a new trend in marketing practices. *International Journal of Management, Accounting and Economics*, *2*(9), 1055–1064.

Knoll, S. W., & Horton, G. (2011). Changing the perspective: Using a cognitive model to improve thinklets for ideation. *Journal of Management Information Systems*, *28*(1), 85–114.

McAdam, R., & McClelland, J. (2002). Individual and team-based idea generation within innovation management: Organisational and research agendas. *European Journal of Innovation Management*.

Melumad, S., Inman, J. J., & Pham, M. T. (2019). Selectively emotional: How smartphone use changes user-generated content. *Journal of Marketing Research*, *56*(2), 259–275.

Menold, J., & Jablokow, K. (2019). Exploring the effects of cognitive style diversity and self-efficacy beliefs on final design attributes in student design teams. *Design Studies*, *60*, 71–102.

Meslec, N., Graff, D., & Clark, M. A. (2020). Increasing team ideation by sequencing the task type and content. *Design Studies*, *70*, 100947.

Miceli, G., & Raimondo, M. A. (2020). Creativity in the marketing and consumer behavior literature: A structured review and a research agenda. *Italian Journal of Marketing*, 2020. *1*, 85–124.

Oxford. (n.d.). Ideation. In Oxford.com dictionary. Retrieved January 30, 2023, from www. oxfordlearnersdictionaries.com/definition/english/ideation?q=ideation

Pascual, G. (2020). What is content ideation? A friendly guide for beginners, *Hightail Blog*. Available at: https://blog.hightail.com/what-is-content-ideation-a-friendly-guide-for-beginners/ (Accessed: January 30, 2023).

Paul, P., Giri, S., Mitra, P., & Haque, M. M. (2022). Analysing the Customer Satisfaction Index of E-banking using Kano (1984) Model Framework. *Global Business Review*, 09721509221093892.

Sauerwein, E., Bailom, F., Matzler, K., & Hinterhuber, H. H. (1996, February). The Kano model: How to delight your customers. In *International working seminar on production economics* (Vol. 1, No. 4, pp. 313–327).

Stone, B. (2015). *Things a Little Bird Told Me*. Pan Macmillan.

Szopinski, D. (2019). Jumping, dumping, and pumping: Three mental principles for idea generation to activate software-based tools in business model innovation. Conference: *Proceedings of the Thirty-Second Bled eConference*.

The Economist Newspaper. (2021, April 7). How ai is transforming the creative industries. *The Economist*. Retrieved January 30, 2023, from https://www.economist.com/films/2021/04/07/how-ai-is-transforming-the-creative-industries?utm_medium=cpc.adword.pd&utm_source=google&ppccampaignID=18156330227&ppcadID=&utm_campaign=a.22brand_pmax&utm_content=conversion.direct-response.anonymous&gclid=CjwKCAiAk--dBhAB EiwAchIwkRvOvjRBHYqfaovO8DZGEyhIcmV0T

Titus, P. A. (2018). Exploring creative marketing thought: Divergent ideation processes and outcomes. *Psychology & Marketing*, *35*(3), 237–248.

Vinerean, S. (2017). Importance of strategic social media marketing. In *Expert Journal of Marketing*, *5*(1), 28–35, Vinerean, Simona.

4 Value Creation Through Digital Content: Informative Value

By Dr Agata Krowinska

Learning Outcomes

- To develop an understanding of what informative value is and how it can be embedded within branded content.
- To recognise the main benefits of educational branded content and its use in content marketing practice.
- To identify the most popular formats of educational branded content and its characteristics.

Informative Value

The number of digital channels through which internet users and brands can access and share information is constantly growing. Internet users are frequently presented with different forms of digital communications (Lou et al., 2019). The way in which consumers search for information has been revolutionised, allowing online users to instantly review multiple digital sources to find topics of interest. Studies conducted on virtual environments have revealed that informative value is an important reason for consumers to use social media (Lin & Lu, 2011), participate in a virtual community (Dholakia et al., 2004) as well as consume brand-related information (Muntinga, 2011).

'Informativeness' relates to the extent to which a message includes an informative content (Aaker & Norris, 1982). The information gratification has been extensively examined by scholars and has been mentioned in relation to information seeking and self-education (Whiting & Williams, 2013) as well as information exchange (Ridings & Gefen, 2004).

It is important to acknowledge that consumers may be interested in information directly from brands as well as from the other consumers who share their views via different forms of user-generated content (UGC). In Chapter 7, Dr Denitsa Dineva takes a thorough look at UGC, examining its various features and implications. The focus of Chapter 4, is solely on the educational content that is marketer-generated (Yang et al., 2022).

DOI: 10.4324/9781003346500-4

The Emergence of Informative Branded Content

Providing social media users with added informational value can offer a lot of benefits to the overall content marketing strategy. De Vries et al., (2012) found that consumers have more positive attitudes towards informative brand posts compared to non-informative brand content. This type of content can not only stimulate customer engagement with specific posts (Dolan et al., 2019; Kujur & Singh, 2020), but it can also have a positive impact on brand perception, reputation, and overall brand health. For example, if the brand creates educational content that demonstrates a lot of knowledge on a relevant topic this can help the brand to be perceived as more authoritative and knowledgeable to its target audience. Lou et al., (2019, p. 783) found that 'informative content can satisfy consumers' informative needs and facilitate their learning, which in turn accelerates their value acquisition and subsequent brand attachment'. Further, this type of content can even appeal to consumers who were previously unaware of a brand, subsequently resulting in increased brand awareness.

Informative branded content can be viewed as any type of content that is related to a specific brand or industry and offers educational value to the consumer. In academic literature this type of content is sometimes also referred to as rational content (Dolan et al., 2015; Shahbaznezhad et al., 2021). Branded content can be viewed as informative when it contains information about the company, brand, products, or industry (Davis et al., 2014) but to offer true value the information that is placed in the content must be useful to the consumer (Naseri & Noruzi, 2018). As such content creators should always closely evaluate the information value of the content that they share with their online audiences, as providing consumers with content that is solely focused on the brand's product or services is unlikely to stimulate a lot of interactions.

Furthermore, when developing educational content, it is important to remember that the content's main topic must be related to the brand's core values. For example, if a brand focuses in its mission statement on environmental issues or other important societal issues it is then advised that part of the educational contents posted on social should be dedicated to educating users about these issues. There are many formats of educational content that content creators can use as part of the content marketing strategy. In the sections below, some of the most popular types of educational content are outlined.

Educational Email Newsletters

Over 360 billion emails are sent every day (Statista, 2021) and many of these are marketing efforts A newsletter is an email that is sent out on a regular basis and updates your audience on the newest information about your goods or services (Campaign Monitor, 2023), For a newsletter to be successful it must include information that is relevant and interesting to the end user. It is crucial for marketers to avoid putting information into their newsletters that sounds like an ad (Sutter, 2016). Newsletters should only be sent to users who have genuine interest in the content included in the newsletter. One of the most successful newsletters ever made was created by Gwyneth Paltrow. In 2008, the actress has developed Goop's newsletter (Goop, n.d.). The newsletter was focused on topics related to everyday life and wellness. The content of the newsletter included recipes for healthy foods, articles about unconventional medical practices, fashion tips, and relationships advice. The success of the newsletter was largely since the shared content was relevant and interesting to Goop's target market, and she viewed her audience as friends (GEO Magazine, 2021). Over time, the newsletter has turned into a multimillion-dollar wellness empire but for the brand the principles of their content marketing stayed the same. To this day Goop focuses mostly on content and the content distributed to users has informative value (e.g., raises awareness about important issues, saves time, improves health) and the consumer is seen as a friend which makes the content feel more authentic and relevant. Goop can be seen as a pioneer of modern content marketing practice and to this day can be used as an inspiration by the marketer interested in content creation.

Branded Educational Videos

Over the past few years video content has become the one of the most consumed forms of online content. The preference for video content extends beyond entertaining the users as brands can also benefit from the video content by educating their audience. According to research, 54 per cent of customers want to see more video content from brands or companies they like (HubSpot, 2018, cited in ADSCHOLARS, 2022). Many brands are now actively creating various sorts of video content in response to the growing demand. Recent studies have shown that branded video content is more popular among the brands because viewers are more likely to pay attention to it (Oberlo, 2023). There are many types of educational branded videos that marketers can use in their content marketing strategy and below we outline the most effective formats.

• **Product demos and how-to videos** are a fantastic way of showcasing branded products and demonstrating to users how the products can be used. How-to videos can reduce and simplify the shopping and decision-making activities of online shoppers (Al-Gasawneh & Al-Adamat, 2020). Therefore, this type of educational content is especially useful at the decision-making stage of the sales funnel as it can help the users to make the final choice whether to purchase a product. When developing product demos or how-to videos it is crucial to make sure that the content has some utilitarian benefits to the users.

- Behind-the-scenes videos are a great way of educating users about how the products are being made and showcasing the real people behind the brand (see Chapter 6). This type of educational content can help the consumers to feel closer to the brand as it shows a more authentic and unpolished version of the brand. Further providing behind-the-scenes content can not only drive brand-related customer engagement behaviours on social media but it can also strengthen the emotional bond between a consumer and a brand. As such, when creating behind-the-scenes video, the marketer should try to incorporate customers, vendors, or employees. A good example of the brand that effectively uses behind-the-scenes content is car brand, Honda. On their YouTube page the brand showcases videos about how the cars are being manufactured and it also introduces and interview their employees – please see the following video as one of the great examples of Honda's well-executed educational videos: www.youtube.com/watch?v=xgMuJIu3RnA. Similarly, the fashion giant Vogue is another brand that successfully implements behind-the-scenes footage on a regular basis as part of their content strategy.

Podcasts and Interviews

In recent years branded podcasts have gained increased popularity among consumers around the world. A study by the BBC (2019) has discovered that brand references in branded podcasts tend to stand out from the background material, generating 16 per cent more engagement and 12 per cent more memory encoding. It is 5 per cent more than radio. Additionally, they outperformed TV benchmarks in terms of engagement, emotional intensity, and memory encoding related to brand references by 22 per cent. The same study discovered that this type of content promotes better brand growth in listeners' eyes. Some other benefits included: greater awareness by 89 per cent, greater brand consideration by 57 per cent, greater brand favourability by 24 per cent and 14 per cent more inclination to buy.

When developing branded educational podcasts, the marketers must remember that podcasts should not be focused on advertising brand product and services. As stated by Lex Friedman, the CRO of Midroll:

> No one wants to listen to a 10-episode podcast about how great ZipRecruiter is at finding a job or helping hire the right applicant. But if we can create a show with someone like entrepreneur and author Seth Godin about what it means to be successful and being the most productive person around, that's going to appeal to exactly the kind of people that ZipRecruiter wants to reach.
>
> (cited in Locker, 2018: online)

A good example of a well-executed branded podcast is a Sephora podcast called #LIPSTORIES. The brand produces stories about prominent female thinkers, inventors, and entrepreneurs. Despite the fact that Sephora is a beauty brand, the programme emphasises the creativity, resourcefulness, and business inspiration for women rather than being focused just on beauty products. This podcast provides the listeners with a lot of valuable insights and each episodes offers clear educational value. For Sephora the branded podcast allows the brand to connect with its audience and improve brand perceptions. The example of Sephora yet again demonstrates that brands do not have to only provide informative value directly connected to its products, and they can also provide educational branded content that is relevant to their brand values.

Blogs and Branded Editorials

Blogs are a fantastic content type that can help brands share knowledge with their target audience (Hetler, 2022). Blogs are one of the least expensive and easiest educational branded content to make. They are a low-cost and a simple way to produce educational content that can either function independently or as part of a brand's website. Brands can benefit greatly from blogs, but many e-commerce sites struggle with blogging since it requires time, consideration, and work to do it well. Consistency is extremely important here. However, when done well blogs can become a learning channel for the target audience.

One of the best examples of companies that have used blogs effectively is River Pools. In 2008, River Pools, a fibreglass pool company from the Virginia-Maryland area, was experiencing financial difficulties due to the recession (Hayden, 2013). At that time, pool purchases have significantly declined, and the company was heading towards bankruptcy. The founder of the company Marcus Sheridan had decided to close the retail stores and move to manufacturing. After some reflection he realised that he and his team possessed extensive knowledge about making pools. In this video clip from The Story of Content Marketing documentary, Marcus Sheridan shared how River Pools utilised content to become not only the number one seller of fibreglass pools in their area, but the entire country, and are now, not just selling, but also manufacturing their own pools. Marcus Sheridan, the director of the company stated:

> The moment we stop saying we are the pool builders and started saying we are the best teachers in world about the fibre glass pools and we happen to install them as well, that was one of the most prosperous days of our lives.

The brand has proclaimed themselves as Wikipedia for pools. Their blog has generated significant levels of customer engagement and most importantly the educational content has help them to survive a recession. To watch a video discussing the success of River Pools access: www.youtube.com/watch?v=fgSxWDSkWT4

Infographics

Infographics can be defined as a chart, diagram, or illustration (as in a book or magazine or on a website) that uses graphic elements to present information in a visually striking way (Merriam Webster Dictionary, n.d.). Data visualisation is a fantastic method for brands to attract customers and establish trust. Infographics are excellent for educational content, especially for marketers who aim to convince users. Content creators can easily turn their own surveys, user information, or statistics from outside sources into content that their audience would find interesting and useful. According to the Institute of Content Marketing (2022) a good infographic should align with the following principles:

- Provide a title that gives the primary finding.
- Include a clear subhead that explains the question being visualised.
- Captions with highly detailed clarifying information.
- Provide source credits.

Flourish as well as Cava are great starting software that can simplify the visual work for unexperienced creators.

This chapter has discussed some of the most effective formats of educational branded content. However, the list presented here is not exclusive, and as more digital channels emerge new formats are being introduced.

End of Chapter Questions

- What are the main benefits of informative value?
- What should content creators focus on when developing branded educational content?
- What are the key types of educational videos?
- What is the main benefit of infographics?

Case Study – The Renault ZOE EV Campaign

Background and Challenge

In recent years interest in electric vehicles (EVs) has significantly increased. In response to looming threats posed by the climate change, organisations such as Fridays For Future call for more sustainable forms of transportation. Furthermore, the German government's introduction of an electric car bonus scheme during the COVID-19 pandemic has further fuelled interest in EVs. As a result, potential car buyers are now considering whether an EV is the right choice for them and are looking for some credible sources of information that can help them to make an educated purchase decision.

The Renault ZOE E-Tech 100% electric has been a leading player in the EV market in Germany, but as competition from brands like VW with their ID3 model increases, it was important for Renault to continue to appeal to potential buyers and maintain its position as the best-selling EV in the country. However, functional questions about EVs such as range, charging, and safety were often unanswered, creating scepticism that can prevent a purchase.

Campaign Objectives

Goal #1: Consideration (measured by watch time and cost per hour watch time)

The performance-driven client Renault wanted to combine two campaigns' goals as efficiently as possible. The task of the campaign was to actively anchor the ZOE E-Tech 100% electric in the relevant set of Renault's target audience. Consumers should deal intensively with the Renault ZOE E-Tech 100% electric, and above all, get answers to their so far unanswered questions – to address and overcome their scepticism before buying an electric car.

KPIs fitted to measure our target audience's interest were watch time and cost per hour watch time: the benchmark – as defined by an A/B test – for a 20-second video ad is €3.60.

Goal #2: Purchases (measured by units sold)

The Renault ZOE E-Tech 100% electric should remain the most sold e-car in Germany in 2020, so the 2nd goal was to increase the number of units sold. In 2019, the target was only just achieved (plus four per cent) with 9,431 cars sold ahead of the BMW i3 (9,117) and the Tesla Model 3 (9,013). In 2020, the result was required to be more significant: taking the successful year 2017 as benchmark, the goal was to restore the 44 per cent leads for ZOE E-Tech 100% electric compared to its nearest competitor.

Overview of the Campaign

To address these unanswered questions regarding e.g., range, charging, and safety, and to guide potential buyers through the purchase process, Renault decided to take a bold approach with its campaign for the Renault ZOE E-Tech 100% electric. Rather than relying on traditional forms of advertising that might be seen as outdated, the company decided to switch to a more zeitgeisty approach and deliver infotainment – a combination of entertainment and information. To do this, Renault teamed up with famous German YouTuber Alex Bangula and Google to investigate and define the most relevant and interesting questions that potential buyers had about EVs. Alex, who has been testing a variety of products related to electromobility for years, was given a Renault ZOE E-Tech 100% electric to test and answer these questions in a series of infotainment videos.

The infotainment videos were designed to retain the character of a classic test video while also providing engaging and entertaining content. In the hero video, Alex answered questions like 'How many hamsters does it take to charge an e-car?' and used the Renault ZOE E-Tech 100% electric to show how charging works in practice. The videos also addressed more functional questions about EVs, such as range, charging, and safety, in a way that was easy for viewers to understand and relate to.

To reach potential buyers, the infotainment videos were played out programmatically using a range of targeting methods. Custom intent targeting was used to focus on individuals with an interest in EVs, as demonstrated by website visits and searches for EV-related terms. First party data was used to reach individuals who had shown an interest in the Renault ZOE E-Tech 100% electric by visiting the website or configurator. Affinity targeting was used to reach individuals with an interest in EV-mobility and small cars.

The Results

The results of the campaign were highly positive. The infotainment videos achieved a higher level of engagement and a lower cost per completed view compared to previous campaigns that employed more traditional forms of advertising. This shows that the format of the content must be tailored to the needs and preferences of the consumer, rather than following established rules or best practices. By providing in-depth information about the Renault ZOE E-Tech 100% electric in a format that was both engaging and entertaining, Renault was able to guide potential buyers through the purchase process and ultimately drive sales of the EV.

Takeaways From This Campaign

The success of the Renault ZOE E-Tech 100% electric campaign highlights the importance of adapting to the needs and preferences of the consumers and delivering content in a way that resonates with them. It also demonstrates the effectiveness of using YouTube influencers and experts as a credible and engaging way to reach potential buyers. By following these strategies, Renault was able to maintain its position as the best-selling EV in Germany and tap into yet untapped market potential.

References

Aaker, D. A., & Norris, D. (1982). Characteristics of TV commercials perceived as informative. *Journal of Advertising Research*, *22*(2), 61–70.

Aaker, J. L. (1997). Dimensions of Brand Personality. *Journal of Marketing Research*, *34*, 347.

ADSCHOLARS (2022). *Video marketing statistics you can't ignore in 2022*. https:// adscholars.com/video-marketing-statistics-you-cant-ignore/

Al-Gasawneh, J., & Al-Adamat, A. (2020). The mediating role of e-word of mouth on the relationship between content marketing and green purchase intention. *Management Science Letters*, *10*, 1701–1708. 10.5267/j.msl.2020.1.010

BBC (2019). *Audio: Activated – new BBC Global News study reveals unique effectiveness of branded podcasts – Media Centre*. 2019. www.bbc.co.uk/mediacentre/worldnews/2019/ audio-activated

Campaign Monitor (2023). What is an email newsletter, and why is it so important for your business? *Campaign Monitor*. www.campaignmonitor.com/resources/knowledge-base/ what-is-an-email-newsletter/

Davis, R., Piven, I., & Breazeale, M. (2014). Conceptualizing the brand in social media community: The five sources model. *Journal of Retailing and Consumer Services*, *21*(4), 468–481. 10.1016/j.jretconser.2014.03.006

De Vries, L., Gensler, S., & Leeflang, P. S. H. (2012). Popularity of brand posts on brand fan pages: An investigation of the effects of social media marketing. *Journal of Interactive Marketing*, *26*, 83–91. 10.1016/j.intmar.2012.01.003

Dholakia, U., Bagozzi, R., & Pearo, L. (2004). A social influence model of consumer participation in network- and small-group-based virtual communities. *International Journal of Research in Marketing*, *21*(3), 241–263. 10.1016/j.ijresmar.2003.12.004

Dolan, R., Conduit, J., Fahy, J., & Goodman, S. (2015). Social media engagement behaviour: A uses and gratifications perspective. *Journal of Strategic Marketing*, online (May), 1–17. 10.1080/0965254X.2015.1095222

Dolan, R., Conduit, J., Frethey-Bentham, C., Fahy, J., & Goodman, S. (2019). Social media engagement behavior. *European Journal of Marketing*, *53*(10), 2213–2243. 10.11 08/EJM-03-2017-0182

GEO Magazine (2021). How Gwyneth Paltrow created her Goop empire worth US$250 million. www.theceomagazine.com/business/health-wellbeing/gwyneth-paltrow-goop/

Goop (n.d.). What's goop?: The story behind the brand goop. Retrieved April 20, 2023, from https://goop.com/whats-goop/

Hayden, B. (n.d.). *Case study:* How content marketing saved this brick-and-mortar business – Copyblogger. 2013. Retrieved April 20, 2023, from https://copyblogger.com/brick- and-mortar-content-marketing/

Hetler, A. (2022). 8 reasons why blogs are important for businesses. www.techtarget.com/ whatis/feature/Reasons-why-blogs-are-important-for-businesses

Kujur, F., & Singh, S. (2020). Visual communication and consumer-brand relationship on social networking sites – uses & gratifications theory perspective. *Journal of Theoretical and Applied Electronic Commerce Research*, *15*(1), 30–47. 10.4067/S0718- 18762020000100104

Lin, K.-Y., & Lu, H.-P. (2011). Why people use social networking sites: An empirical study integrating network externalities and motivation theory. In *Computers in Human Behavior* (Vol. 27, pp. 1152–1161). 10.1016/j.chb.2010.12.009

Locker, M. (2018). Branded podcasts are the ads people actually want to listen to. FastCompany. www.fastcompany.com/40533210/branded-podcasts-are-the-ads-people- actually-want-to-listen-to

Lou, C., Xie, Q., Feng, Y., & Kim, W. (2019). Does non-hard-sell content really work? Leveraging the value of branded content marketing in brand building. *Journal of Product and Brand Management*, *28*(7), 773–786. 10.1108/JPBM-07-2018-1948

Merriam Webster Dictionary (n.d.). Infographic definition & meaning – Merriam-Webster. 2023. Retrieved April 20, 2023, from www.merriam-webster.com/dictionary/infographic

Muntinga, D. G. M. (2011). Introducing COBRAs. *International Journal of Advertising, 30,* 13–46.

Naseri, Z., & Noruzi, A. (2018). Content marketing process model: A meta-synthesis of the literature. *Webology, 15,* 8–18.

Oberlo (2023). 10 video marketing statistics you should know in 2023 [Infographic]. www.oberlo.com/blog/video-marketing-statistics

Ridings, C. M., & Gefen, D. (2004). Virtual community attraction: Why people hang out online. *Journal of Computer-Mediated Communication, 10*(1). 10.1111/j.1083-6101.2004.tb00229.x

Shahbaznezhad, H., Dolan, R., & Rashidirad, M. (2021). The role of social media content format and platform in users' engagement behavior. *Journal of Interactive Marketing, 53,* 47–65. 10.1016/J.INTMAR.2020.05.001

Statista. (n.d.). Number of sent and received e-mails per day worldwide from 2017 to 2025. 2021.

Sutter, B. (2016). Want to be successful with content marketing? Teach, don't sell. Forbes. www.forbes.com/sites/briansutter/2016/02/19/want-to-be-successful-with-content-marketing-teach-dont-sell/?sh=5e13f1487847

Whiting, A., & Williams, D. (2013). Why people use social media: A uses and gratifications approach. *Qualitative Market Research: An International Journal, 16,* 362–369. 10.1108/QMR-06-2013-0041

Yang, Q., Li, H., Lin, Y., Jiang, Y., & Huo, J. (2022). Fostering consumer engagement with marketer-generated content: The role of content-generating devices and content features. *Internet Research, 32*(7), 307–329. 10.1108/INTR-10-2021-0787

5 Value Creation Through Digital Content: Entertainment Value

By Dr Agata Krowinska and Dr Clidna Soraghan

Learning Outcomes

- To explore the importance of entertainment value in content marketing and to gain insights into different types of branded entertainment.
- To develop a clear understanding of the differences between product placement and branded entertainment.
- To discuss the role that humour and aesthetics play in driving positive brand-related engagement.

Entertainment Value

The digital revolution has significantly changed the entertainment industry and media consumption patterns by enabling new ways of media creation and distribution (Ahuja, 2021). In turn, this has given rise to what is now known as the creators' economy, where not only traditional media outlets, but also users and brands can become entertainment providers who compete for audience attention. Early research on social media have shown that entertainment benefits are one of the most important drivers of social media usage (Groups et al., 2009; Raacke & Bonds-Raacke, 2008; Urista et al., 2009). Previous studies have demonstrated that entertaining branded content on social media is an important factor stimulating users' engagement. For example, Sabate et al. (2014) found that the richness of entertainment is positively correlated with the number of likes received, while Zhang et al. (2012) proposed that branded entertainment can foster user participation. Furthermore, Mafe et al. (2013) identified entertainment as one of the key drivers of customer loyalty on brand pages and Rohm et al. (2013) proposed that young digital natives interact with brands on social media primarily with the intention of seeking entertainment. Overall, these findings highlight the importance of providing entertaining content to stimulate positive brand engagement behaviours. In the following sections, we discuss the most effective tactics which brands can utilise to provide users with entertainment value.

DOI: 10.4324/9781003346500-5

Branded Entertainment

The concept of branded entertainment is not new. Promoting products using content that entertains the audience has been used in marketing for decades (Hudson & Hudson, 2006). However, until early 2000s, the term 'branded entertainment' was not commonly used by marketers, and it was often confused with conventional product placement. The pivotal moment for the branded entertainment industry happened in 2001, when BMW created the 'The Hire' – their own branded series of eight short films starring a famous Hollywood actor Clive Owen (Kim et al., 2019). The series had cinematic quality with the focus on delivering entertainment value, which at that time was unique. In contrast to product placement, the BMW brand wasn't just inserted into an existing piece of entertainment; instead, the content was co-created by the brand. This marketing tactic was something new that marketers had not seen before. Shortly after the series was released the term branded entertainment gained some traction (Kim et al., 2019) and later, in 2003, the Branded Content Marketing Association was developed to offer space for advertising and entertainment professionals who specialise in producing branded entertainment (Hudson & Hudson, 2006).

While there are many different conceptualisations of branded entertainment (Hudson & Hudson, 2006; Kunz et al., 2016a, 2016b; Zhang et al., 2010), the one provided by London International Awards encompasses all the important elements of the notion; it defines branded entertainment as:

> … any piece of content (scripted or unscripted, comedy or drama, series or a single) that is made with a brand's personality, positioning, and marketing objectives in mind. Its primary intention is delivering an entertaining and engaging experience to consumers.
>
> (London International Awards, 2019 cited in
> Loggerenberg et al., 2021, p. 325)

Given the prevalence of entertaining content available across digital platforms, branded entertainment must compete with other entertainment forms. Therefore, it is essential that brands develop content that is professionally produced, has high quality and is designed in a way that encourages voluntary consumption and at the same time has a potential to go viral (Kunz et al., 2016).

As pointed out by Loggerenberg et al. (2021), branded content that has an authentic narrative can achieve brand resonance. Therefore, when developing branded entertainment, it is important to remember that a branded message should only be embedded unobtrusively (Kunz et al., 2016) and that the primary focus should be on the entertainment benefits that a specific piece of content offers its audience. There are different forms of branded entertainment available for marketers to use and below we outline some of the most popular formats.

Branded TV Series on Streaming Platforms

Digital branded series as a form of branded entertainment content have only recently entered the marketing game. This type of content is delivered in the long video format – just a usual TV mini-series on the popular streaming platforms. Brands such as Goop, Studio McGee, as well as Formula 1, have recently published their branded TV shows on Netflix. This type of content requires a lot of time and production cost but is one of the most sophisticated forms of content-marketing practice. At this point in time, branded series are not widespread, but it can be anticipated that more and more brands are going to utilise this content format in near future.

As branded entertainment aims to develop long term engagement with the consumer (Kunz et al., 2016b) providing users with regular programming can be a great way to attract a regular viewership, encourage some external third-party publications, and help brands to achieve greater reach. It is also worth adding that, as many companies are now content creators with their own production teams, there are also opportunities for content co-creation between brands (Bang et al., 2020). A good example here would be Red Bull's collaboration with GoPro on the video series focused on high flying video (Bang et al., 2020). Such partnerships can help brand more followers and reach a wider audience.

Music Playlists

Another way to provide entertaining benefits is through branded playlists published on music-sharing platforms such as Spotify or Apple Music. By creative their own playlists, brands can reach new consumers and establish a stronger connection with popular culture, resulting in increased relevance. Furthermore, music playlists allow brands to connect with users and offer them additional benefits that can be seen as extensions of their products or services. For instance, Peloton has developed over 90 playlists on Spotify for users to enjoy during their exercise. Similarly, Nike and Adidas have curated their own exercise playlists. Moreover, to further entertain and connect with users, brands can create playlists catered around specific events and trends such as Christmas or Mother's Day. Creating a playlist on Spotify is an inexpensive and effective way to engage the audience and it can easily be utilised by small organisations with limited marketing budgets.

It is also worth noting that this form of branded entertainment can be particularly effective for brands for which music is an important part of their product or service category. For example, iconic music venues like Ibiza Rocks, Pacha, or Café Mambo have all created shareable playlists on Spotify. This type of playlist can evoke nostalgia among their customers and further strengthen brand loyalty.

Branded Competitions

Companies can also provide entertainment benefits to users by organising branded competitions on social media. This type of practice can also be seen as a type of remunerative content (Dolan et al., 2015) as users are often offered some reward in exchange for their participation. Many studies have suggested offering rewards and monetary incentives to be one of the key drivers contributing to positive user engagement on social media and on branded communities (Dessart et al., 2015; Gummerus et al., 2012; Kang et al., 2014; Romero, 2015). Consumers who participate in 'games-like' incentives can derive both hedonic as well as utilitarian benefits from such engagement. This type of branded entertainment can be a very effective tactic for stimulating user engagement.

Also, branded competition can be a fantastic opportunity for an organisation to encourage development of user-generated content. However, this type of content should be used sporadically so that maximum engagement can be achieved. Otherwise, users may lose interest in this type of content. To learn more about different forms of UGC please see Chapter 7.

Humorous Branded Content

Another prominent way in which entertainment value could be delivered is via humour. The use of humour in social media marketing has been extensively researched and many studies have found that humorous content can drive positive consumer engagement behaviours (Barry & Graça, 2018; Hosanagar & Nair, 2018; Yang, 2022). Furthermore, use of humour can also help brands to express their personality and in turn help them to become more relatable to online users. A great example of this type of practice can be seen in Rare Beauty's recent branded content posted on April Fool's Day. The brand shared a video via its official TikTok channel, announcing the launch of a new version of its best-selling liquid blush. The brand mentioned increased demand and consumer feedback as the main reason behind the new product development. However, the product demonstrated in the branded video was of an unrealistically large size, quickly revealing that it was an April Fool's joke. The audience response to this piece of branded entertainment was overwhelmingly positive, with the video receiving over 3.2 million views and over 9000 positive impressions. In the comments section under the video, many users expressed how funny and engaging they found the content and their also expressed their brand love for Rare Beauty.

To watch the video, access with the link: www.tiktok.com/@rarebeauty/video/7217077579512073515?lang=en

Use of memes is another effective and inexpensive way that companies can use to entertain their audience. With their potential to increase brand exposure, memes have recently become a popular content tactic among marketing practitioners (Yang, 2022). Leveraging memes online can also help a brand reach a wider audience due to its ability to go viral (Guadagno et al., 2013). Memes can be categorised into two types: existing memes that can be adapted by brands to convey their own branded message, and original memes that are created by brands (Yang, 2022). Use of memes can not only entertain the users, but it can also display the brand's sense of humour, which yet again can enhance the brand's identity and relatability.

An effective use of memes by brands can be demonstrated by IKEA's branded content titled 'Get the look'. The brand has used the iconic image of US Senator Bernie Sanders wearing mittens and sitting with folded arms at President Joe Biden's inauguration. The meme has gained widespread popularity across the internet and has become a viral sensation. IKEA seamlessly incorporated this meme into its branded content to entertain their audience and promote products. The content has become a global marketing success spreading across all countries.

To learn more about this campaign, access with the link: www.youtube.com/watch?v=YYxwE4vYuKc

The example of IKEA successfully demonstrates that creative use of memes can lead to viral success for brands, which can be achieved at a relatively low cost. As such, even creators with little experience in content development can easily use this format to entertain online users and capitalise on the existing viral phenomenon.

Branded Games

In recent years, there has been a growing trend of brands creating their own signature branded games tailored specifically for their audience (Kinard & Hartman, 2013). Branded games can be played free of charge on social media or on the brand's dedicated mobile apps (Kinard & Hartman, 2013) and are sometimes referred to as gamified content (Pepper Content, 2022). Branded games can come in different forms, such as slot games, augmented reality (AR) games, and simulations (Pepper Content, 2022). Many brands such as Audi, Perfume Shop, and Benefit have developed successful branded games which have generated impressive levels of engagement.

Branded games can be an effective way to engage the target audience and further enhance the brand's personality. However, the development of a branded game can be expensive, so it is essential for brands to ensure that the game is suitable for their target market to guarantee user engagement. For example, users who do not typically download branded apps or have little interest in gaming may not be interested in such content. Therefore, prior research and game testing should always be conducted before developing gamified content to ensure its relevance and appeal to the target audience.

An alternative way of using gamified content is by placing the brand into an existing popular social or app game. For example, McDonald's has effectively been embedded on Facebook social games, Farmville and CityVille (Zhu & Chang, 2015). This type of strategy can help a brand to raise brand awareness and improve brand recall. The main advantage of this strategy is that brands can monetise on the game without the need to spend money on game development. We further explore digital product placement in the section below.

Digital Product Placements

Product placements are well-known marketing practice that can be viewed as 'the insertion of a product into mass media content with the intention of influencing consumer attitude or behavior' (Roehm & Roehm, 2019, p. 283). Product placement has been used in different entertainment settings, including radio, featured films, TV shows or reality TV. Product placements have been proven to be an effective way of promoting the product in a way that does not feel commercial to the audience and therefore might be viewed more favourably (Um, 2014). This marketing practice can generate positive associations with the brand (Cowley & Barron, 2008) and lead to increased profits (Jan & Martina, 2013). Product placements can take the form of visual appearance, be mentioned as part of a dialogue between the main characters of the story or be an integral part of the plot (Russell, 1998). It is important to underline that product placements are viewed positively by the audience if they are used in moderation (Meyer et al., 2016). Therefore, organisations should exercise caution in order to avoid excessive and overwhelming integration of product images or mentions within the entertainment context. Furthermore, for the product placement to work, it is essential that the brand is presented in a positive manner (Um, 2014). Otherwise, the product placement can creative negative associations and lead to a crisis management situation. A good example of product placement failure was the recent placement of a stationary Peloton bike in the reboot of a Sex in the City TV series called 'And just like that'. In the series one of the main characters dies of heart attack after exercising on a Peloton bike. Shortly after the episode aired the stocks on Peloton fell significantly (NBC, 2021).

With the advancements in digital technology, product placements are no longer just limited to movies or TV shows (Um, 2014). Product placements can now be integrated in various formats of digital entertainment such as videos, games, and social media posts. Digital product placement offers marketers many benefits over the traditional product placement. Product placements can now be digitally inserted providing brands and entertainment creators with a lot of flexibility. For example, digital product placement can now be adapted to different graphical locations, languages, and audience behaviours. Product placements have the potential to personalise the entertainment product by incorporating product placements that are specifically selected for each consumer based on their online behaviours, interests, and preferences. Trifts and Aghakhani (2018, p. 607) offered the following example that successfully illustrates the practice of personalised product placement:

> Imagine a scenario in which a consumer surfs the web to buy a new watch. She searches multiple sites and finds a Fossil watch that catches her eye on Amazon.com. She clicks on the model and spends several minutes looking at it before placing it on her wish list for later. Later that day, this same customer decides to buy an eBook from Amazon and uses the 'look inside' feature to preview a book. As she reads through the text, the heroine of the story is described as wearing the exact Fossil watch the customer placed on her wish list during a previous shopping trip.

The marketing technique described above shows that personalised product placements have a potential to be integrated into the customer online journey, creating a seamless experience that fits perfectly with the unique interests and preferences of the specific user. As such, modern content marketers might need to focus more on the specific behaviour of the user and provide digital product placement that corresponds with the interests of that user. As suggested by Hsu (2019) 'in the near future, according to marketing executives who have had discussions with streaming companies, the products that appear onscreen may depend on who is watching'. A similar approach might be taken by content creators on social media who will be able to display different product placements based on their viewer's preferences. In future this may also apply to content posted by social media influencers.

The Role of Aesthetics in Content Marketing

Visual content dominates the content marketing environment and can be found to be more effective in grabbing users' attention and stimulating positive engagement (Sabate et al. 2014). Internet users are exposed to a lot of visual content on daily basis. Therefore, brands and content creators need to make sure that the images that they share have high aesthetics value and highlight a product or a service in the best possible way. A great example of how to effectively use images can be found on the Instagram profile called Nathy's Kitchen (see Figures 5.1 and 5.2). The page is run by Dr Nathalia Tjandra, a content creator who uses visual content marketing to share her delicious food recipes and promote her cookbook. The profile is full of captivating and visually stunning images that effectively stimulate users' engagement.

Figure 5.1 Instagram profile of Nathy's Kitchen

Figure 5.2 Visual content examples from Nathy's Kitchen

End of Chapter Questions

- What is branded entertainment and how different is it from the well-known concept of product placement?
- What are the main benefits of digital product placements and how can modern marketers adapt them on Netflix?
- What types of branded entertainment can be used to make a brand more relatable to its target market?

- What are the two types of memes that marketers can use to entertain their audience?
- What role does aesthetics play in content marketing?

Task I

Fictional case study/scenario: Gats is a new UK-based fitness company specialising in providing online fitness classes to consumers of all ages who want to stay fit without leaving the house. As part of their monthly membership (£22.99 per month), users can enjoy 22 fitness programs and 150+ motivating workouts adapted to individual fitness levels and goals, and they also get help from a personal trainer. The company was launched in April 2023 and since then it has achieved over 15,000 sign ups, which were generated mostly from the local radio ads and WOM.

Currently, Gats has a very limited social media presence and they have decided to employ you to help them to develop some branded entertainment which can help them to engage potential customers.

You task here is to develop a plan for three pieces of branded entertainment that will engage potential users.

References

Ahuja, V. (2021). Transforming the media and entertainment industry: Cases from the social media marketing world. *Journal of Cases on Information Technology (JCIT)*, *23*(4), 1–17. 10.4018/JCIT.296255

Bang, H., Choi, D., Baek, T. H., Oh, S. Do, & Kim, Y. (2020). Leveraged brand evaluations in branded entertainment: Effects of alliance exclusivity and presentation style. *International Journal of Advertising*, *39*(4), 466–485. 10.1080/02650487.2019.1672328

Barry, J. M., & Graça, S. S. (2018). Humor effectiveness in social video engagement. *Journal of Marketing Theory and Practice*, *26*(1–2), 158–180. 10.1080/10696679.2017.1389247

Cowley, E., & Barron, C. (2008). When product placement goes wrong: the effects of program liking and placement prominence. *Journal of Advertising*, *37*(1), 89–98. https://login.napier.idm.oclc.org/login?qurl=https%3A%2F%2Fwww.proquest.com%2Fscholarly-journals%2Fwhen-product-placement-goes-wrong-effects-program%2Fdocview%2F236506162%2Fse-2%3Faccountid%3D16607

Dessart, L., Veloutsou, C., & Morgan-Thomas, A. (2015). Consumer engagement in online brand communities: A social media perspective. *Journal of Product & Brand Management*, *24*(1), 28–42. 10.1108/JPBM-06-2014-0635

Dolan, R., Conduit, J., Fahy, J., & Goodman, S. (2015). Social media engagement behaviour: A uses and gratifications perspective. *Journal of Strategic Marketing*, online (May), 1–17. 10.1080/0965254X.2015.1095222

Guadagno, R. E., Rempala, D. M., Murphy, S., and Okdie, B. M. (2013). What makes a video go viral? An analysis of emotional contagion and Internet memes. *Computers in Human Behavior*, *29*(6), 2312–2319.

Gummerus, J., Liljander, V., Weman, E., & Pihlström, M. (2012). Customer engagement in a Facebook brand community. *Management Research Review*, *35*(9), 857–877. 10.1108/01409171211256578

Hosanagar, D., & Nair, K. (2018). Advertising content and consumer engagement on social media: evidence from Facebook. *Management Science.* 10.1287/mnsc.2017.2902

Hsu, T. (2019) Future product placement in films and television 'will be tailored to individual viewers', *The Independent.* www.independent.co.uk/news/business/product-placement-future-film-tv-individual-viewers-direct-marketing-a9257046.html (Accessed: 04 August 2023).

Hudson, S., & Hudson, D. (2006). Branded entertainment: A new advertising technique or product placement in disguise? *Journal of Marketing Management, 44*(116), 489–504. 10.1362/026725706777978703

Jan, K., & Martina, K. (n.d.). Product placement: A smart marketing tool shifting a company to the next competitive level. 10.7441/joc.2013.04.06

Kang, J., Tang, L., & Fiore, A. M. (2014). Enhancing consumer-brand relationships on restaurant Facebook fan pages: Maximizing consumer benefits and increasing active participation. *International Journal of Hospitality Management, 36*, 145–155. 10.1016/j.ijhm.2013.08.015

Kim, K., Park, C., Yoon, S., Choi, Y. K., Oh, S., & Lee, J. (2019). Branded entertainment: Gender differences in reactions to star ratings. *Journal of Consumer Behaviour, 18*(2), 166–176. 10.1002/cb.1755

Kinard, B. R., & Hartman, K. B. (2013). Are you entertained? The impact of brand integration and brand experience in television-related advergames. *Journal of Advertising, 42*(2–3), 196– 20.

Kunz, R., Elsässer, F., & Santomier, J. (2016). Sport-related branded entertainment: The Red Bull phenomenon. *Sport, Business and Management: An International Journal, 6*(5), 520–541. Elected as Outstanding Paper in the 2017 Emerald Literati Network Awards for Excellence. 10.1108/SBM-06-2016-0023

Loggerenberg, M. J. C. van, Enslin, C., & Terblanche-Smit, M. (2021). Towards a definition for branded entertainment: An exploratory study. *Journal of Marketing Communications, 27*(3), 322–342. 10.1080/13527266.2019.1643395

Meyer, J., Song, R., & Ha, K. (2016). The effect of product placements on the evaluation of movies. *European Journal of Marketing, 50*(3–4), 530–549. 10.1108/EJM-12-2014-0758

NBC News By Variety (2021). Peloton stock drops after 'and just like that' character's shocking post-workout death, NBCNews.com. www.nbcnews.com/pop-culture/pop-culture-news/peloton-stock-drops-just-characters-shocking-post-workout-death-rcna8420 (Accessed 04 August 2023).

Park, N., Kee, K. F., & Valenzuela, S., (2009). Being immersed in social networking environment: Facebook groups, uses and gratifications, and social outcomes. *Cyberpsychology & Behavior: The Impact of the Internet, Multimedia and Virtual Reality on Behavior and Society, 12*(6), 729–733.

Pepper Content (2022). What are branded games, and how can they help content marketing? www.peppercontent.io/blog/using-branded-games-for-content-marketing/ (Accessed 04 August 2023).

Raacke, J., & Bonds-Raacke, J. (2008). MySpace and Facebook: Applying the uses and gratifications theory to exploring friend-networking sites. *Cyberpsychology & Behavior, 11*(2), 169–174. 10.1089/cpb.2007.0056

Roehm, H. A., & Roehm, M. L. (2019). Using advertising alignment to improve product placement effects on product choice: The power of facilitating analogies. *Journal of Consumer Behaviour, 18*(4), 283–290. 10.1002/CB.1763

Romero, J. (2015). Exploring customer engagement behavior: Construct proposal and its antecedents. 2nd International Symposium on Partial Least Squares Path Modeling, 31517, 1–12.

Ruiz-Mafe, C., Marti-Parreno, J., & Sanz-Blas, S., (2014). Key drivers of consumer loyalty to Facebook fan pages. *Online Information Review, 38*(3), 362–380.

Russell, C. A. (1998). Toward a framework of product placement: theoretical propositions. ACR North American Advances, NA-25. www.acrwebsite.org/volumes/8178/volumes/v25/NA-25/full

Sabate, F., Berbegal-Mirabent, J., Cañabate, A., & Lebherz, P. R. (2014). Factors influencing popularity of branded content in Facebook fan pages. *European Management Journal*, 1–11. 10.1016/j.emj.2014.05.001

Trifts, V., & Aghakhani, H. (2018). Enhancing digital entertainment through personalization: The evolving role of product placements. https://doi-Org.Napier.Idm.Oclc.Org/10.1080/13527266.2018.1452046, 25(6), 607–625. 10.1080/13527266.2018.1452046

Um, N.-H. (2014). Practitioners' perspectives on branded entertainment in the United States. *Journal of Promotion Management, 20*(2), 164. https://doi.org/info:doi/

Urista, M. A., Dong, Q., & Day, K. D. (2009). Explaining Why Young Adults Use MySpace and Facebook Through Uses and Gratification Theory. *Human Communication, 12*, 215–229.

Yang, G. (2022). Using funny memes for social media marketing: The moderating role of bandwagon cues. *Journal of Promotion Management, 28*(7), 944–960. 10.1080/10496491.2022.2054904

Zhang, J., Sung, Y., & Lee, W.-N. (2010). To play or not to play: An exploratory content analysis of branded entertainment in Facebook. *American Journal of Business* (Vol. 25, pp. 53–64). 10.1108/19355181201000005

Zhu, D. H., & Chang, Y. P. (2015). Effects of interactions and product information on initial purchase intention in product placement in social games: The moderating role of product familiarity. *Journal of Electronic Commerce Research, 16*(1), 22–33. https://login.napier.idm.oclc.org/login?qurl=https%3A%2F%2Fwww.proquest.com%2Fscholarly-journals%2Feffects-interactions-product-information-on%2Fdocview%2F1661993789%2Fse-2%3Faccountid%3D16607

6 Value Creation Through Digital Content: Social Value

By Jasmiina Milne

Learning Outcomes

- To define the concept of social value in the context of marketing practice.
- To develop an in-depth understanding of the benefits associated with the use of social value in content marketing practice.
- To understand different formats of social value content and their benefits and discuss the practicalities of social value content.

Social Value

As discussed in Chapter 1, content marketing has become the core element of digital marketing practice. Traditional marketing methods are no longer sufficient to attract and retain consumers with increasingly diversified needs and broader social interactions (Zhu, 2019). Digital channels, and social media particularly, have changed marketing communications. Organisations interact with consumers in the digital space creating interrelationships which deliver value. This value has become a critical digital currency for organisations (Cheng et al., 2021).

Social – also referred to as interaction – value plays a crucial role in content marketing practice. It has several benefits, including increasing consumer trust, enhancing the reputation of the brand, and consumers' loyalty to the brand (W. Zhu et al., 2022; X. Zhu, 2019).

According to Sheth et al. (1991), social value is 'the perceived utility acquired from an alternative's association with one or more specific social groups'. (p. 161). Sweeney and Soutar (2001) defined it as 'the utility derived from the product's ability to enhance social self-concept' (p. 211). Social value can reflect the association with stereotyped demographic and socio-economic and ethnocultural attributes (Sheth et al., 1991) and refers to the value of feelings or emotional characteristics of the consumer (W. Zhu et al., 2022). Social value captures the brand perceptions of the consumer in relation to their socio-cultural upbringing, reference groups, and identities. Therefore, family, peers, and celebrities influence consumers' perceptions of brand value (Park & Rabolt, 2009).

Consumers make decisions based on the perceived social value of products and services, aiding them in creating the desired identity (Laverie & Arnett, 2000).

DOI: 10.4324/9781003346500-6

These social identities are built based on how consumers see themselves, and consumption choices are made accordingly. This is particularly true for highly salient identities, where consumption is based on social expectations of a specific identity (Reed, 2004).

The social value of branded content can be viewed as valuable content that helps to achieve social benefits, such as popularity or likeability, from others (Lou & Xie, 2021). Social value centres around themes, such as trends, and embodies the perceived utility related to symbolic or conspicuous consumption and often includes interpersonal communication (Robertson, 1967). It is particularly relevant for choices involving highly visible products, such as fashion items, including clothing and jewellery, as well as goods and services, which are shared with others, such as gifts, entertainment, and experiences. Consumers might, for example, buy a certain car brand based on the social image it evokes rather than its basic functionalities. However, products that are traditionally associated more with functional or utilitarian rather than social value, such as kitchen appliances, are also regularly purchased based on their social value (Sheth et al., 1991).

Togetherness and Belongingness

Fundamentally, people are social beings looking for belongingness, the need to belong to a group and to be accepted (Baumeister & Leary, 1995). Consumers can achieve social value by forming social connections with others (Kietzmann et al., 2011), fulfilling their need for belongingness and satisfying their need for cognition with others who share the same norms, values, and interests (Gangadharbatla, 2008). Belongingness or need to belong refers to people's need to be loved and socially accepted (Baumeister & Leary, 1995), while the need for cognition refers to 'an individual's tendency to engage in and enjoy effortful cognitive endeavours' (Cacioppo et al., 1984, p.1).

Belongingness, together with social and cultural affiliation (Laroche et al., 2012), leads consumers to join brand communities to be identified or linked with groups or symbols they find desirable and want to be associated with (Schembri et al., 2010). The shift to the online environment has opened a variety of virtual communities that consumers can choose from to find the most suitable option for them to connect with and derive social value (Jiao et al., 2018). Understanding the consumer and their behaviour is essential for marketers to optimise the use of online communities, which are discussed in more detail later in this chapter.

Individuals are driven by different motivations, and although all people demonstrate a need to belong (Baumeister & Leary, 1995), some are more motivated by the sense of community and belonging in a group than others. In particular, the behaviour of people from collectivist cultures tends to be driven by derived values and benefits (M. K. O. Lee et al., 2005). They experience social value by connecting to others, such as family, peers, groups, or society as a whole (Ryan & Deci, 2000).

How consumers perceive themselves in relation to other users is also an essential part of social value. Self-construal plays an important role in bringing distinction to how individuals think, feel, behave, and act in a social context. It consists of two aspects, independent and interdependent self-construal, which coexist among individuals (Markus & Kitayama, 1991). People with interdependent self-construal tend to value connectedness, and harmony in the group is essential for them. These individuals see themselves as part of the group and pursue goals of social cohesion in particular social contexts (D. Lee et al., 2012; Trafimow et al., 1991). They appreciate relationships and connections and tend to alter their behaviour to fit with others. The interdependent self-construal incorporates the social value aspect of social media (Jiao et al., 2015).

Social Media

The universal adoption and popularity of social media enable consumers to experience value in novel ways in this new media. Social value is encountered across content marketing; however, it plays a particularly large role in social media marketing. Social value is at the core of social media and embodies user participation and interaction there (W. Zhu et al., 2022). This is due to social media possessing characteristics such as openness, participation, interaction, sharing, connectedness, creativity, autonomy, collaboration, and reciprocity (Constantinides & Fountain, 2008; Kaplan & Haenlein, 2010; O'Reilly, 2007), which enable consumers to fulfil their social value (Jiao et al., 2015).

Consumers' perceived value on social media is mainly social value (Kaplan & Haenlein, 2010; O'Reilly, 2007), which can be enhanced by being connected to others. Social media incorporates social value through interaction and offering users social aspects by providing relevant content from other like-minded social media users, such as family, peers and influencers (Jiao et al., 2015, 2017). These connections enhance the consumer's perception of the brand's equity (Jiao et al., 2018). The social value represents the social consequences of what the product communicates to others (Sweeney & Soutar, 2001). Therefore, it is essential for those working in social media to actively take measures to improve the consumers' perceptions of social value (W. Zhu et al., 2022).

Social value can be obtained in social media by building interpersonal relationships, communicating information, and exchanging feelings in virtual situations. Shared values and social connections around specific topics strengthen interactions among social media users (W. Zhu et al., 2022). Social value helps to create emotional connections between consumers and brands, as well as strengthen the relationships between them and brand communities as a whole (Kaur et al., 2016). These features also increase users' loyalty to social media platforms (Chatterjee & Nguyen, 2021).

Self-presentation theory (Goffman, 1959) is an important social dimension to consider in social media. People wish to present themselves in certain ways to others and have control over how they present themselves in social interactions and what kind of views others form of them. What an individual wishes to show to others varies from situation to situation. Some motivations driving self-presentation include objective influencing to gain rewards, such as making a positive impression on future in-laws or creating an image corresponding to personal identities, such as fashionable clothes to be deemed trendy. Self-presentation extends beyond social media; for example, the key motivator to create a personal webpage is to present oneself online (Jensen Schau & Gilly, 2003).

Benefits of Social Value to the Content Marketing Strategy

Brands should actively take steps to enhance the consumer's perceived social value, as it presents multiple benefits for the content marketing strategy. For example, it has been found to positively impact consumer satisfaction rates (Hu et al., 2015), increase consumer trust, and enhance the reputation of the brand and loyalty to the brand (Zhu et al., 2022; X. Zhu, 2019). Perceived social value can also indirectly affect CRM performance via customer satisfaction (Wang et al., 2004).

Social value can be enhanced by being connected to others. These connections enhance the consumer's perception of the brand's equity (Jiao et al., 2018). Social value is known to positively impact consumers' experiential evaluation of low-product involvement brands particularly (Xie & Lou, 2020). Social value embodies the perceived utility related to symbolic or conspicuous consumption and often includes interpersonal communication (Robertson, 1967).

The social value of branded content also brings benefits to the consumer and can be viewed as valuable content that helps to achieve social benefits, such as popularity or likeability, from the consumers' social network (Lou & Xie, 2021) and contributes to the enhancement of their self-image (Sheth et al., 1991). For example, mobile technology adoption and use are both motivated by consumers' desire to express their image, status, and personality publicly (Leung & Wei, 2000).

Below are some concrete examples of specific areas where research has proven the positive role of social value in consumer behaviour and brand loyalty. These include entertainment streaming applications (Oyedele & Simpson, 2018), online retailing platforms (J. M. Cheng et al., 2009), and travel destinations (Luo et al., 2020).

Entertainment streaming applications provide social value as consumers can share these experiences with others by discussing trending films, TV series or songs. Entertainment can play an essential role in consumers' self-identity and socialisation; therefore, consuming the content creates social value. Popular culture, films and music included are common topics in social conversations and are a source of social connections. By watching the latest films or listening to new songs, entertainment streaming application users can strengthen their self-identity by being digitally connected and seen as fans of certain genres (Oyedele & Simpson, 2018). According to Oyedele and Simpson (2018), perceived social value is likely to impact the use of entertainment streaming applications as long as the use reinforces salient self-identities since consumer choice behaviour is positively influenced by social value through identity salience.

In a study researching online retailing platforms, J. M. Cheng et al. (2009) concluded that social value has a particular impact on information collection, whereas emotional value was the key factor in order placement. Even though face-to-face communication is reduced in the online environment (Vijayasarathy, 2002), e-commerce platforms, such as eBay and TripAdvisor, offer an efficient and effective way to communicate and features to share information and experiences with like-minded individuals who share similar interests (Breitenbach & van Doren, 1998). In addition, many social media platforms, such as Facebook and Instagram, offer e-commerce – known as s-commerce – which can enhance social value. Efficiency and effectiveness lead to increased consumer trust (J. M. Cheng et al., 2009), which is known to impact future purchase intentions positively (Garbarino & Johnson, 1999), customer acquisition, sales, and loyalty offline and online (Gefen & Straub, 2003).

Social value captures consumers' perceptions of the brand, endorsement, and attachment in relation to their social upbringing and identities (Park & Rabolt, 2009). Social value is associated with demographic, socio-economic, and ethnocultural attributes (Sheth et al., 1991). Making good impressions and social interactions are important. Hence, social value has a significant role in destination loyalty (Luo et al., 2020). Tourists want to learn from culture, history and lifestyle by interacting with locals (Ashton, 2015), as well as collect evidence from their travels, such as images and souvenirs, to express identity and signal this to those around them (Feldwick, 1996).

Social Value Content

Organisations can create social value through digital content in multiple ways. Social value content includes any content used in content marketing that promises social value to consumers (Xie & Lou, 2020). Consumers can experience this content in multiple ways; for instance, video-sharing platforms, such as YouTube and TikTok, provide an abundance of multisensory and emotional content (Lou & Xie, 2021), while Facebook offers tools for creating online communities and Instagram and Twitter offer social value, for instance, via trending hashtags.

Brands create content that provides social value to their followers. They can, for example, build online communities and share behind-the-scenes stories, intriguing legacy narratives, and content that highlights the unique features of the brand, such as the content of craftsmanship and aesthetic close-ups (Xie & Lou, 2020).

Low-involvement brands in particular can benefit from social value content (Xie & Lou, 2020), as this can positively shape consumers' brand experiences and, therefore, brand loyalty. Branded content that entertains helps consumers to relax or works as a conversation starter and contributes to building relationships between consumers. Besides low-involvement brands, also luxury brands, such as fashion, jewellery, cosmetics, wine, automobile, hotel, tourism or private banking, benefit from social, symbolic, and hedonic value (H. Kim, 2005; J. E. Lee & Watkins, 2016). Luxury brands have features, such as prestige price, craftmanship, exclusivity, and in certain cases, heritage, which can be used to induce psychological and emotional values in consumers (Vinerean & Opreana, 2019).

The following presents practical examples of content on how social value can enhance and be incorporated into the marketing strategy.

Online Communities

Socialisation, such as sharing experiences, is essential for social value (J. M. Cheng et al., 2009). Traditional characteristics of human interactions are still present in the online environment, although face-to-face socialisation is reduced (Vijayasarathy, 2002). Hence, online communities that allow communication between users and members an opportunity to have their opinions heard are useful for brands when it comes to creating social value (J. M. Cheng et al., 2009).

Online communities are a form of socialisation that combines sharing experiences with information needs and games (Seraj, 2012). They are particularly prominent on social networks, which allow consumers to engage with brands in various ways (Carvalho & Fernandes, 2018).

The internet provides an evolutional way to communicate and interact socially (Weiser, 2001) through efficient and effective communication, such as information and experience sharing with like-minded members of online communities and interest-based websites (Breitenbach & van Doren, 1998). Efficiency and effectiveness are known to increase communication and interaction frequency and lead to a higher degree of consumer trust (J. M. Cheng et al., 2009). Increased trust leads to a constructive relationship that positively impacts future purchase intentions (Garbarino & Johnson, 1999), and can lead to increased customer acquisition, sales, and loyalty offline and online (Gefen & Straub, 2003).

Content quality and playful interactivity are crucial for building social bonds and fostering community culture. Online communities facilitate the formation of social, intellectual, and cultural values, therefore increasing the members' loyalty to the brand and encouraging them to purchase (Seraj, 2012). Other benefits include, for example, an increase in business profits, consumer knowledge of the brand and improved consumers' social experience and enjoyment (Chou & Sawang, 2015).

Online social interactions can capture the differences between consumers' willingness to interact with each other in an online environment and the impact of these on consumer behaviour, including, for instance, online engagement and participation (Blazevic et al., 2014). Social interactions help to develop positive consumer-brand relationships as the feeling of being connected carries beyond the interaction and helps to drive loyalty as well as sharing of more information. However, if the consumer realises that these interactions become automated, these effects may not be sustained (Labrecque, 2014). Therefore, the high quality of the online community is essential to gain positive impacts, such as an increase in sales and consumers' emotional well-being (Chou & Sawang, 2015).

Quality content and keeping interactions engaging and playful are key to creating social bonds and self-governing community culture, which facilitate the formation of social value in online communities (Seraj, 2012). Engagement, interactivity, and flow experience attract consumers to brand communities and foster trust, referrals, and long-term commitment (Carvalho & Fernandes, 2018). Vivid, frequent interactions are more likely to convert in online space (Cork & Eddy, 2017), and passion impacts participation in social commerce and user engagement. Feelings and cognitive experiences are found to increase participation and engagement, while passion helps to spread positive word-of-mouth (Herrando et al., 2017).

However, there are also factors outside of the brand's scope which impact how successful the online community will be, such as personal traits. For instance, a collectivist mentality influences consumer behaviour in online communities (Chou & Sawang, 2015). The more consumers spend time in online communities absorbing information, the more their participation increases. Moreover, the more participation increases, the greater the consumers perceive the social value of an online community (Zhou et al., 2013).

Moment Marketing

Moment or real-time marketing campaigns, where content is inspired by a current topic, trend, or event (Kerns, 2014), are one of the most attractive ways to target consumers on social media (Pathirage & DK, 2021). Trending topics and current events are a great way for brands to stimulate engagement, drive reach, and create social value.

Since timing is essential in moment marketing, it requires marketers to be agile and adapt the content in real time. The marketing team should keep up to date with current events and trends based on the interests of the target audience while keeping true to the brand – not every trend is suitable for every brand. Moment marketing is an excellent way to start conversations and allows brands to connect with consumers while keeping the cost often relatively low. However, marketers must remember to keep the conversation flowing and engaging with consumers continuously. Reaching the right person at the right time (Pathirage & DK, 2021) on the right platform is also essential for moment marketing to be successful and drive sales.

There are different ways to create moment marketing content, and depending on the social media platform used, hashtags can be an effective way to mobilise the right audiences, for example on Instagram (Vinerean & Opreana, 2019), Twitter or TikTok. Consumers often use hashtags for inspiration and research, and marketers can leverage the use of them to reach new audiences and participate in viral discussions on social media platforms. Furthermore, the use of hashtags can result in a sense of community and belongingness as social media users might not know each other, but using the same hashtag means that they share something in common and therefore form networks (Kozinets, 2015).

Behind-the-Scenes Content

With the abundance of content shared on social media platforms, such as Instagram and TikTok, brands must find intriguing ways to grab consumers' attention and create content that engages consumers. The use of features available on social media platforms, such as Instagram's Boomerangs, Highlights, Stories, Filters, Reels, and Shopping, has been demonstrated to improve brand image and awareness and drive engagement (Vinerean & Opreana, 2019). Furthermore, the content can enhance the legacy of the brand, highlight its uniqueness and lead to desired behaviour (Herrando et al., 2018). Storytelling is a powerful form of content, which includes, for instance, behind-the-scenes videos of brands, which advocate the brand voice and bring consumers closer to an authentic experience, for example, by showing people behind the brand. This humanises the brand and creates a sense of inclusion and togetherness. Backstage cues, which include images and text, are found to be particularly effective in reducing consumers' perceived pre-purchase risk (Liu et al., 2017).

The backstage stories allow brands to tell their story in intriguing new ways and add social value to the brand. Whether the behind-the-scenes content focuses on staff members, celebrities, or influencers through relevant partnerships, people should be at the heart of the content. Partnerships with celebrities and influencers can help to raise brand awareness and increase reach on social media platforms. Behind-the-scenes content can, for instance, show employees choosing materials (Wongkitrungrueng & Assarut, 2020) or designing the products or influencers or celebrities preparing for an event or advertising campaign. For example, Burberry led 38 per cent of the discussion on Instagram when it used an engaging behind-the-scenes content during London Fashion Week (Vinerean & Opreana, 2019).

Depending on the outlet, the content should be tailored to suit the platform. For instance, Instagram posts should obtain a timeless, editorial look and feel, whereas momentary and ephemeral content has more value on Instagram Stories (Vinerean & Opreana, 2019).

eWOM

The internet has created an excellent source for electronic word-of-mouth (eWOM) as a way for brands to communicate with consumers (Hennig-Thurau et al., 2004). eWOM is a great way to highlight the product or service quality using a variety of forms that result in value for consumers. eWOM may result in economic, utilitarian, or social value (Balasubramanian & Mahajan, 2001;

Hennig-Thurau et al., 2004), and consumers can have different motivations for engaging with eWOM whether it is using or generating it (Hennig-Thurau et al., 2004). Similar to traditional word-of-mouth (WOM), eWOM can have even higher credibility and relevance to consumers than other forms of marketing (Bickart & Schindler, 2001).

Testimonials are a form of eWOM, which reassure consumers of the product quality by using, for instance, attractiveness, professionalism, and reliability (Arens, 1996). Often, endorsers can be well-known people, such as celebrities or influencers, professionals, experts, or relatable consumers.

Another form of eWOM is customer-to-customer (C2C) know-how exchange, and meanwhile, it often is primarily connected to utilitarian value due to providing expertise to understand better, use, operate, modify, or repair products; some consumers also derive social and hedonic value, such as self-enhancement from participation as they can feel good about solving problems, answering questions, and helping others (Hennig-Thurau et al., 2004).

Consumers can indeed have different reasons for taking part in eWOM activities and achieving social benefits. These are primarily similar reasons to motivations of participants taking part in traditional WOM and vary among consumers. For instance, self-interested helpers are mainly motivated by economic incentives, while consumer advocates are mainly motivated by the concern of other consumers, and true altruists are driven by a motivation to help other consumers as well as businesses (Hennig-Thurau et al., 2004).

Brands can improve the social benefits, for example, by creating a discussion forum, which is separate from the product-review section, for frequent users or allowing the creation of social profiles in the eWOM space, which can increase attractiveness. These would help foster a sense of community and togetherness with other users (Hennig-Thurau et al., 2004). However, marketers should be aware that consumers quickly learn to differentiate between the social value derived from interaction with other consumers and economic transactions with a business (Balasubramanian & Mahajan, 2001). The concept of co-creation and user-generated content is discussed in Chapter 7.

Live Streaming

Several social media platforms offer live streaming features, which offer a great source of social value. New features on online platforms allow consumers to position themselves as they desire in the marketplace (Crawford, 1992; Sandikci & Holt, 1998) and feel innovative. Consumers do not only form perceptions of themselves but also about the brands and other customers of the brand (el Hedhli et al., 2013; Sandikci & Holt, 1998). They like to be associated with brands whom they can identify with and whose clientele is similar to their desired identity. Live streaming allows sellers and consumers to coexist in the same space and, thus, aids social identification, which depicts belongingness with specific groups (Ashforth & Mael, 1989). Identifying with the brands and other consumers enhances consumers' participation and social interaction on social media (Badrinarayanan et al., 2015) as well as leads to a long-term relationship with the brand (M. Hu et al., 2017; Tuškej et al., 2013).

Online consumers rely mainly on information created and shared by other consumers, eWOM, such as reviews, feedback and even the number of likes (S. Kim & Park, 2013). Live streaming allows consumers to observe the brand representative's personality and appearance, which can lead to admiration (M. Hu et al., 2017). If their taste matches and they identify with the seller, they are more likely to trust recommendations. In addition, the consumers observe and evaluate other consumers' identities (M. Hu et al., 2017). Live streaming provides real-time information, which helps consumers to interpret other consumers' characteristics, the popularity of products and whether the product is accepted by their social networks (Wongkitrungrueng & Assarut, 2020).

Games

Digital games offer an excellent way for brands to enhance social value, which is prominent in many online gamer groups (Gilbert & Han, 2005). Social value can be achieved in different ways, either by creating a game or in-game advertising, such as product placement.

Some games generate social value through the recruitment of friends. This game model is a so-called 'freemium model'. Players can either choose to spend money to sustain their gaming addiction or generate social value by recruiting friends (Ramirez, 2015). While the free players might not bring direct revenue, they make a crucial contribution to the success of the game by helping to spread awareness, boosting the ranking and visibility of the game, and producing social value through social networking sites (SNS) and other advertising avenues (Ramirez, 2015). One popular example of a game using the freemium model is Candy Crush Saga, which encourages players to produce social value by turning to friends for help, for instance, when running out of lives. Players can either wait, pay, or ask for help from their Facebook friends. Sharing the game on SNS helps to recruit new players. In addition, players can compare their scores and process in the game, creating a sense of community and competition.

In addition to games themselves, advertising in games can be used to create value. For instance, games with high product quality and interactivity generate favourable brand attitudes for in-game advertising, creating attention, and engagement (Vashisht & Chauhan, 2017). This is often due to highly interactive and challenging games increasing emotional and cognitive engagement resulting in stronger brand connection (Berger et al., 2018). For example, Redecor, an interior design game, uses product placements. Players can purchase or win branded items from genuine brands to use in the game. Players take part in challenges, and other players can vote for the best designs. Winners are encouraged to share their results on social media to attract new players to join the game.

Personalised Communications

Personalised communications, such as tailored apps and newsletters, can also add social value. Social value can be derived from shopping, and personalising the experience can assist consumers in achieving social value. Social codes, symbolic meanings, relationships and consumers' identities can all be enhanced by social acts (Firat & Venkatesh, 1993), such as shopping. Personal values of self-actualisation, such as self-fulfilment and social affiliation, such as friendly relationships, have a positive impact on how consumers perceive the online store (Koo et al., 2008). Experiences that reflect and enhance a consumer's personal identity (Erdem et al., 1999; Sirgy et al., 2000) and achieve social integration (Hewer & Campbell, 1997) are valued.

Personalising the marketing messages can increase the feeling of togetherness. For instance, offering expert team members to assist online and to answer any questions can improve the sense of togetherness.

Interactive Content

Interactive content, such as interactive posts, allows two-way communication (Ko et al., 2005), which can increase social value. Novel interactive features of social media advertisement allow consumers to communicate with brands effortlessly (Sreejesh et al., 2020; Wang & Chen, 2021). For example, Instagram, Facebook and Twitter allow consumers to send direct messages to the brand, answer polls, and check real-time results.

Interactivity promotes interpersonal communication, which helps consumers feel socially connected and thus enhances the overall social value of the brand experience. Connecting with the brand and other consumers through interactivity can increase interest in the brand, online information search, brand engagement, such as sharing the ads with others, and purchase intention (Kim et al., 2023). The social value derived from interactive content depends upon product category, content and design of the ad and perceived brand characteristics. However, Stories can be an affordable tool for brands with relatively low brand awareness to reach more users (Kim et al., 2023).

Mapping Social Value Content

Social value content has several benefits, among which it increases consumer trust, and enhances the reputation of the brand as well as consumers' loyalty to the brand. Social value is encountered across content marketing; however, it plays a particularly large role in social media marketing. Consumers can achieve social value by forming social connections with others, fulfilling their need for belongingness, and satisfying their need for cognition with others who share the same norms, values, and interests. In Table 6.1 you can find an overview of the key types of social value content.

Table 6.1 Table content types

	Benefits	Downsides	Best uses	Most suitable channels
Online community	Online communities allow members to engage with brands in various ways. Members can share experiences and information freely. They are a great way for brands to get constant feedback on their products and services.	Requires resources to monitor the community and ensure that the community stays active. When listening to the feedback from online communities, marketers should bear in mind that not all intentions necessarily translate to purchases.	Online communities are great for keeping the brand in customers' minds. They boost brand exposure, heighten engagement and customer retention, offer a channel to present products and services, as well as get feedback from them, and can lower customer support cost, as consumers can share information with each other.	Facebook Groups.
Moment marketing	Trending topics and current events are a great way for brands to stimulate engagement, drive reach, and create social value.	Since timing is essential in moment marketing, it requires marketers to be agile and adapt the content in real-time. Marketers should also consider carefully, which topics suit the brand as whole.	Hashtags are a great way to participate in trending conversations.	Newsletters and social media channels.
Behind-the-scenes content	Humanises the brand and creates a sense of inclusion and togetherness. It can also reduce pre-purchase risk.	The content should suit the overall look of the brand and be of high quality.	Showcase people behind the brand or share backstage content from an event or partnership.	Social media channels. Tailor content to suit the platform. For instance, Instagram posts should obtain a timeless, editorial look and feel,

(Continued)

Table 6.1 (Continued)

	Benefits	Downsides	Best uses	Most suitable channels
				whereas momentary and ephemeral content has more value on Instagram Stories.
eWOM	eWOM can have even higher credibility and relevance to consumers than other forms of marketing. Allows marketers to start and analyse buzz.	Little control over what is said about the brand.	Marketers can listen to what is said about the brand, engage with the customers, and share positive content directly through their own channels.	Can be created across platforms that allow users to generate content.
Live streaming	Live streaming allows social identification, which depicts belongingness with specific groups.	Live streaming requires resources and time. It can be challenging to reach audiences across different time zones and consumers with different lifestyles.	Live Q&A sessions, competitions, such as quizzes, event coverage, and influencer partnerships.	Social media channels, such as YouTube, Facebook, Instagram, TikTok or Twitch.
Games	Highly interactive and challenging games increase emotional and cognitive engagement resulting in stronger brand connection. They also increase engagement.	Games can take resources to design and be costly, hence, it is essential to ensure ROI.	Product placements in already existing games or a game on the company website or app.	Game platforms or branded app.

Personalised communications	Personalising the marketing message increases the feeling of togetherness.	Personalising marketing communications requires handling personal data and strictly adhering to data protection regulations.	Newsletters and auto-responses on social media channels.	Emails and private messages on social media platforms. Can also be used to a certain extent in social media advertising.
Interactive content	Helps consumers feel socially connected.	Time-consuming as requires continuous interaction.	Polls, quizzes, and opinions, and invite followers to ask questions about the brand. Instagram Stories offers great options for all of these.	Social media platforms, particularly Instagram, TikTok, and Twitter.

Case Study – MAN Truck & Bus

Background and Challenge

MAN Truck & Bus, a TRATON SE company, is one of Europe's leading commercial vehicle manufacturers; it provides transport solutions and has an annual turnover of over 10.9 billion € (2021). Its product portfolio includes vans, trucks, buses, diesel and gas engines, and a range of services relating to the transport of passengers and goods.

In Germany, the proportion of women in the logistics sector is shockingly low. In fact, only two per cent of truck drivers are women. Hardly any other industry has such a low proportion of female employees. According to market research, one key barrier relates to work-life balance, with the sector requiring drivers to work very flexibly and for long hours, often away from home. In recent times, transport and logistics companies have struggled to find and attract new staff. Thereby, a very large part of the pool of potential candidates – women – have not yet explicitly been encouraged to pursue careers in this sector.

For the transport industry to further develop and thrive, traditional thinking patterns needed to be overcome, making the industry more attractive to women.

Passionate about solving this challenge, MAN embraced their values PRIDE and CARE across the industry.

- With PRIDE, MAN underlines how much they value their drivers and how proud the company is of every one of them.
- With CARE, MAN wants to take on the responsibility of being a reliable partner for all drivers, making sure their interests are being taken care of.

Campaign Objectives

The objective of the campaign was to honour female drivers by raising awareness of their daily lives. As such, the main KPIs of the campaign focused on increasing reach and generating greater awareness.

In line with its values, PRIDE and CARE, MAN aimed to celebrate women working in logistics and driving their trucks. Doing so, they intended to inspire more women to pursue a career in logistics. In line with the campaign objectives, the targeted segments for the campaign were female truck drivers; women who have an interest in driving.

Campaign Outline

To utilise the budget available for maximum impact, MAN and all partners needed to think creatively. Specifically, it was crucial to design a cutting-edge content marketing strategy, delivered at the right time.

In terms of timing, an obvious day stood out: International Women's Day (IWD) – when the world commemorates the cultural, political, and socio-economic achievements of women. it would be the perfectly appropriate time to launch the campaign. But how could we turn MAN's message into a WOMAN's message?

The idea was right in front of us: we would change the company name to WOMAN for the duration of the campaign. By adding the 'WO' prefix to the MAN logo, we would turn the brand upside down, prompting curiosity and inspiration.

To ensure the message would be delivered effectively, we would rebadge the TGX, MAN's latest vehicle, as the WOMAN-TGX with a WOMAN logo on the radiator grille. Without a specific budget dedicated to paid media, the strategy aimed at leveraging earned coverage and content to stimulate campaign-related conversation across the country.

To achieve this, two further tactics were employed:

- First, to generate buzz amongst our female target group, we partnered with Julia Beitler, Germany's most famous female truck driver, influencer, and star of the reality TV series, Trucker Babes.
- Second, to drive broader awareness, we integrated Germany's most famous MAN vehicle into the campaign: the Bayern Munich team bus. Given the team's large fan base and massive social-media presence, it was a sure-fire way to get the redesigned logo noticed amongst a huge number of people. To support the campaign launch, professional female truck drivers were invited to apply via the MAN website to unveil the new TGX and win a test drive.

Just in time for IWD, we staged the new WOMAN-TGX as the HERO, or rather the SHE-RO of our campaign, and used the truck as a vehicle for all media implementations.

Göran Nyberg, a former MAN board member, dropped the cape of our SHE-RO and handed over the keys to professional driver Steffi S., the winner of the first raffle round and now test driver for a week.

The video footage was shared on Facebook and Instagram, highlighting the WOMAN lettering on the radiator grille.

We also shared the video on YouTube in a form of TrueView placement. In addition, we used Twitter, Facebook, and Instagram to attract females to join our MAN competition to win a test drive with the new WOMAN-TGX.

Supporting this activity, we hosted a video interview with Julia Beitler, our female trucker, on YouTube. In the video, Julia explained what life was really like for female drivers, allaying the concerns women might have about the realities of the job. To generate further reach, Julia also shared the video with her followers on Facebook and Instagram.

Finally, we branded the FC Bayern team bus as the WOMAN bus and posted humorous video content across socials. Shared with the club's 31 million Instagram followers, the video featured the team bus on its way to training. As part of a humorous conversation, the new WOMAN logo was revealed. Subsequently, the bus driver turned towards the camera to thank all the female truck drivers on this special day.

Campaign Results

Through the campaign, we got Germany talking:

- The campaign's videos generated over five million views across all social channels. The FC Bayern Munich video promoting 'WOMAN' generated over 1.7 million views making it the best performing video of the campaign.
- The reveal video, which was implemented as a TrueView video on YouTube, achieved a strong rate of 41 per cent versus the TrueView benchmark on YouTube of approx. 30 per cent.
- One million positive expressions of user engagement were generated, including comments, shares, and likes on social channels (Facebook, YouTube and Instagram), which showed how our message spread and, despite the small budget, we were able to generate a lot of attention on Google Trends. The index (IX) value of the search term 'Truck Driver' jumped from 53 on 7 March, the day before the kick-off, to 87 IX on 8 March, on IWD (maximum rating is 100 – meaning they are the most popular search terms of the day).
- During the entire campaign period, index values between 90 and 100 IX were recorded.
- The search term 'Bayern Bus' increased from the zero line (on 7 March) to 37 IX (on 8 March, at IWD) and in the further days to the maximum of 100 IX at the end of the campaign.

And one year later, on International Women's Day 2022, the proportion of women among truck drivers had doubled to 4.3 per cent.

Takeaways From This Campaign

The campaign has demonstrated that – and also given a comparatively small budget – topics with a high social impact in connection with current trends and events can achieve high reach, attention, and engagement. The video showcasing campaign can be accessed at www.youtube.com/watch?v=Pqd3hmaQwz0

Suggested Tutorial Exercises

After learning about social value and practical examples of how to add social value content in the marketing practice, now try putting your newly learned skills into practice.

In small groups, imagine that you oversee the social media marketing of a brand of your choice. Look at their social media channels and create a content plan focusing on social value.

When making the plan, consider the brand overall, its audience, which social media platforms they use, or perhaps could use, and what kind of content would work for them.

If you would like some inspiration to get started, look at the social media presence of some brands you are familiar with. You can use, for example, Canva or PowerPoint to create three examples of social-value content. Once the exercise is completed, each group should share their content ideas with the rest of the class. Please remember to provide justification of your content choices.

References

Arens, W. F. (1996). *Contemporary Advertising.* (J. J. Whidden, Ed.; 6th edn). Irwin.

Ashforth, B. E., & Mael, F. (1989). Social identity theory and the organization. *The Academy of Management Review, 14*(1), 20. 10.2307/258189

Ashton, A. S. (2015). Developing a tourist destination brand value: The stakeholders' perspective. *Tourism Planning & Development, 12*(4), 398–411. 10.1080/21568316.2015.1013565

Badrinarayanan, V. A., Sierra, J. J., & Martin, K. M. (2015). A dual identification framework of online multiplayer video games: The case of massively multiplayer online role playing games (MMORPGs). *Journal of Business Research, 68*(5), 1045–1052. 10.1016/J.JBUSRES.2014.10.006

Balasubramanian, S., & Mahajan, V. (2001). The economic leverage of the virtual community. *International Journal of Electronic Commerce, 5*(3), 103–138. https://www.jstor.org/stable/27750984

Baumeister, R. F., & Leary, M. R. (1995). The need to belong. *Psychological Bulletin, 117*(3), 497–529. 10.1037/0033-2909.117.3.497

Berger, A., Schlager, T., Sprott, D. E., & Herrmann, A. (2018). Gamified interactions: Whether, when, and how games facilitate self–brand connections. *Journal of the Academy of Marketing Science, 46*(4), 652–673. 10.1007/s11747-017-0530-0

Bickart, B., & Schindler, R. M. (2001). Internet forums as influential sources of consumer information. *Journal of Interactive Marketing, 15*(3), 31–40. 10.1002/DIR.1014

Blazevic, V., Wiertz, C., Cotte, J., de Ruyter, K., & Keeling, D. I. (2014). GOSIP in cyberspace: Conceptualization and scale development for general online social interaction propensity. *Journal of Interactive Marketing, 28*(2), 87–100. 10.1016/J.INTMAR.2013.09.003

Breitenbach, C. S., & van Doren, D. C. (1998). Value-added marketing in the digital domain: Enhancing the utility of the Internet. *Journal of Consumer Marketing, 15*(6), 558–575. 10.1108/07363769810241436

Cacioppo, J. T., Petty, R. E., & Feng Kao, C. (1984). The efficient assessment of need for cognition. *Journal of Personality Assessment, 48*(3), 306–307. 10.1207/s15327752jpa4803_13

Carvalho, A., & Fernandes, T. (2018). Understanding customer brand engagement with virtual social communities: A comprehensive model of drivers, outcomes and moderators. *Journal of Marketing Theory and Practice, 26*(1–2), 23–37. 10.1080/10696679.2017.1389241

Chatterjee, S., & Nguyen, B. (2021). Value co-creation and social media at bottom of pyramid (BOP). *The Bottom Line, 34*(2), 101–123. 10.1108/BL-11-2020-0070

Cheng, J. M., Wang, E. S., Lin, J. Y., & Vivek, S. D. (2009). Why do customers utilize the internet as a retailing platform? *Asia Pacific Journal of Marketing and Logistics, 21*(1), 144–160. 10.1108/13555850910926290

Cheng, M., Liu, J., Qi, J., & Wan, F. (2021). Differential effects of firm generated content on consumer digital engagement and firm performance: An outside-in perspective. *Industrial Marketing Management, 98*, 41–58. 10.1016/J.INDMARMAN.2021.07.001

Chou, C. Y., & Sawang, S. (2015). Virtual community, purchasing behaviour, and emotional well-being. *Australasian Marketing Journal, 23*(3), 207–217. 10.1016/j.ausmj.2015. 06.001

Constantinides, E., & Fountain, S. J. (2008). Web 2.0: Conceptual foundations and marketing issues. *Journal of Direct, Data and Digital Marketing Practice, 9*(3), 231–244. 10.1 057/palgrave.dddmp.4350098

Cork, B. C., & Eddy, T. (2017). The retweet as a function of electronic word-of-mouth marketing: A study of athlete endorsement activity on Twitter. *International Journal of Sport Communication, 10*(1), 1–16. 10.1123/ijsc.2016-0107

Crawford, M. (1992). The world in a shopping mall. In M. Sorkin (Ed.), *Variations on a Theme Park: The New American Theme Park and the End of Public Space* (pp. 3–30). Hill and Wang.

el Hedhli, K., Chebat, J.-C., & Sirgy, M. J. (2013). Shopping well-being at the mall: Construct, antecedents, and consequences. *Journal of Business Research, 66*(7), 856–863. 10.1016/J.JBUSRES.2011.06.011

Erdem, O., ben Oumlil, A., & Tuncalp, S. (1999). Consumer values and the importance of store attributes. *International Journal of Retail & Distribution Management, 27*(4), 137–144. 10.1108/09590559910268435

Feldwick, P. (1996). Defining a brand. In D. Conley (Ed.), *Understanding a Brand* (pp. 17–30). Kogan Page.

Firat, A. F., & Venkatesh, A. (1993). Postmodernity: The age of marketing. *International Journal of Research in Marketing, 10*(3), 227–249. 10.1016/0167-8116(93)90009-N

Gangadharbatla, H. (2008). Facebook me: Collective self-esteem, need to belong, and internet self-efficacy as predictors of the Igeneration's attitudes toward social networking sites. *Journal of Interactive Advertising, 8*(2), 5–15. 10.1080/15252019.2008.10722138

Garbarino, E., & Johnson, M. S. (1999). The different roles of satisfaction, trust, and commitment in customer relationships. *Journal of Marketing, 63*(2), 70. 10.2307/1251946

Gefen, & Straub. (2003). Managing user trust in B2C e-Services. *E-Service Journal, 2*(2), 7. 10.2979/esj.2003.2.2.7

Gilbert, A. L., & Han, H. (2005). Understanding mobile data services adoption: Demography, attitudes or needs? *Technological Forecasting and Social Change, 72*(3), 327–337. 10.1016/J.TECHFORE.2004.08.007

Goffman, E. (1959). *The Presentation of Self in Everyday Life*. University of Edinburgh, Social Sciences Research Centre.

Hennig-Thurau, T., Gwinner, K. P., Walsh, G., & Gremler, D. D. (2004). Electronic word-of-mouth via consumer-opinion platforms: What motivates consumers to articulate themselves on the Internet? *Journal of Interactive Marketing, 18*(1), 38–52. 10.1002/DIR.10073

Herrando, C., Jimenez-Martinez, J., & Martin de Hoyos, M. J. (2018). Surfing or flowing? How to retain e-customers on the internet. *Spanish Journal of Marketing – ESIC, 22*(1), 2–21. 10.1108/SJME-03-2018-006

Herrando, C., Jiménez-Martínez, J., & Martín-De Hoyos, M. J. (2017). Passion at first sight: How to engage users in social commerce contexts. *Electronic Commerce Research, 17*(4), 701–720. 10.1007/s10660-016-9251-6

Hewer, P., & Campbell, C. (1997). Research on shopping: A brief history and selected literature. In Pasi. Falk & C. Campbell (Eds.), *The Shopping Experience* (pp. 186–206). Sage Publications.

Hu, M., Zhang, M., & Wang, Y. (2017). Why do audiences choose to keep watching on live video streaming platforms? An explanation of dual identification framework. *Computers in Human Behavior*, *75*, 594–606. 10.1016/J.CHB.2017.06.006

Hu, T., Kettinger, W. J., & Poston, R. S. (2015). The effect of online social value on satisfaction and continued use of social media. *European Journal of Information Systems*, *24*(4), 391–410. 10.1057/ejis.2014.22

Jensen Schau, H., & Gilly, M. C. (2003). We are what we post? Self-presentation in personal web space. *Journal of Consumer Research*, *30*(3), 385–404. 10.1086/378616

Jiao, Y., Ertz, M., Jo, M.-S., & Sarigöllü, E. (2018). Social value, content value, and brand equity in social media brand communities. *International Marketing Review*, *35*(1), 18–41. 10.1108/IMR-07-2016-0132

Jiao, Y., Gao, J., & Yang, J. (2015). Social value and content value in social media: Two ways to flow. *Journal of Advanced Management Science*, *3*(4), 299–306. 10.12720/joams.3.4.299-306

Jiao, Y., Jo, M.-S., & Sarigöllü, E. (2017). Social value and content value in social media: Two paths to psychological well-being. *Journal of Organizational Computing and Electronic Commerce*, *27*(1), 3–24. 10.1080/10919392.2016.1264762

Kaplan, A. M., & Haenlein, M. (2010). Users of the world, unite! The challenges and opportunities of social media. *Business Horizons*, *53*(1), 59–68. 10.1016/J.BUSHOR.2009.09.003

Kaur, P., Dhir, A., & Rajala, R. (2016). Assessing flow experience in social networking site based brand communities. *Computers in Human Behavior*, *64*, 217–225. 10.1016/J.CHB.2016.06.045

Kerns, C. (2014). *Trendology: Building an advantage through data-driven real-time marketing*. Palgrave MacMillan.

Kietzmann, J. H., Hermkens, K., McCarthy, I. P., & Silvestre, B. S. (2011). Social media? Get serious! Understanding the functional building blocks of social media. *Business Horizons*, *54*(3), 241–251. 10.1016/J.BUSHOR.2011.01.005

Kim, H. (2005). Consumer profiles of apparel product involvement and values. *Journal of Fashion Marketing and Management*, *9*(2), 207–220. 10.1108/13612020510599358

Kim, K., Chung, T.-L. (Doreen), & Fiore, A. M. (2023). The role of interactivity from Instagram advertisements in shaping young female fashion consumers' perceived value and behavioral intentions. *Journal of Retailing and Consumer Services*, *70*, 103159. 10.1016/J.JRETCONSER.2022.103159

Kim, S., & Park, H. (2013). Effects of various characteristics of social commerce (s-commerce) on consumers' trust and trust performance. *International Journal of Information Management*, *33*(2), 318–332. 10.1016/J.IJINFOMGT.2012.11.006

Ko, H., Cho, C.-H., & Roberts, M. S. (2005). Internet uses and gratifications: A structural equation model of interactive advertising. *Journal of Advertising*, *34*(2), 57–70. 10.1080/00913367.2005.10639191

Koo, D., Kim, J., & Lee, S. (2008). Personal values as underlying motives of shopping online. *Asia Pacific Journal of Marketing and Logistics*, *20*(2), 156–173. 10.1108/13555850810864533

Kozinets, R. v. (2015). *Netnography: Redefined* (2nd edn) Sage.

Labrecque, L. I. (2014). Fostering consumer–brand relationships in social media environments: The role of parasocial interaction. *Journal of Interactive Marketing*, *28*(2), 134–148. 10.1016/J.INTMAR.2013.12.003

Laroche, M., Habibi, M. R., Richard, M.-O., & Sankaranarayanan, R. (2012). The effects of social media based brand communities on brand community markers, value creation practices, brand trust and brand loyalty. *Computers in Human Behavior*, *28*(5), 1755–1767. 10.1016/J.CHB.2012.04.016

Laverie, D. A., & Arnett, D. B. (2000). Factors affecting fan attendance: The influence of identity salience and satisfaction. In *Journal of Leisure Research*, *32*(2).

Lee, D., Kim, H. S., & Kim, J. K. (2012). The role of self-construal in consumers' electronic word of mouth (eWOM) in social networking sites: A social cognitive approach. *Computers in Human Behavior*, *28*(3), 1054–1062. 10.1016/J.CHB.2012.01.009

Lee, J. E., & Watkins, B. (2016). YouTube vloggers' influence on consumer luxury brand perceptions and intentions. *Journal of Business Research*, *69*(12), 5753–5760. 10.1016/J.JBUSRES.2016.04.171

Lee, M. K. O., Cheung, C. M. K., & Chen, Z. (2005). Acceptance of Internet-based learning medium: The role of extrinsic and intrinsic motivation. *Information & Management*, *42*(8), 1095–1104. 10.1016/J.IM.2003.10.007

Leung, L., & Wei, R. (2000). More than just talk on the move: Uses and gratifications of the cellular phone. *Journalism & Mass Communication Quarterly*, *77*(2), 308–320. 10.1177/107769900007700206

Liu, Y.-F., Xu, Y., & Ling, I.-L. (2017). The impact of backstage cues on service evaluation. *International Journal of Quality and Service Sciences*, *9*(2), 165–183. 10.1108/IJQSS-04-2016-0024

Lou, C., & Xie, Q. (2021). Something social, something entertaining? How digital content marketing augments consumer experience and brand loyalty. *International Journal of Advertising*, *40*(3), 376–402. 10.1080/02650487.2020.1788311

Luo, J., Dey, B. L., Yalkin, C., Sivarajah, U., Punjaisri, K., Huang, Y., & Yen, D. A. (2020). Millennial Chinese consumers' perceived destination brand value. *Journal of Business Research*, *116*, 655–665. 10.1016/J.JBUSRES.2018.06.015

Markus, H. R., & Kitayama, S. (1991). Culture and the self: Implications for cognition, emotion, and motivation. *Psychological Review*, *98*(2), 224–253. 10.1037/0033-295X.98.2.224

O'Reilly, T. (2007). What is Web 2.0: Design patterns and business models for the next generation of software. *Communications & Strategies*, *65*(1), 17.

Oyedele, A., & Simpson, P. M. (2018). Streaming apps: What consumers value. *Journal of Retailing and Consumer Services*, *41*, 296–304. 10.1016/J.JRETCONSER.2017.04.006

Park, H.-J., & Rabolt, N. J. (2009). Cultural value, consumption value, and global brand image: A cross-national study. *Psychology & Marketing*, *26*(8), 714–735. 10.1002/mar.20296

Pathirage, D., & DK, T. (2021). Impact of real-time social media content marketing on emotional brand attachment with special reference of Sri Lanka food and beverage industry. *Business Law, and Management (BLM2): International Conference on Advanced Marketing (ICAM4) An International Joint e-Conference-2021*, 312.

Ramirez, F. (2015). Affect and social value in freemium games. In Tama Leaver and Michele Willson (Ed.), *Social, Casual and Mobile Games: The Changing Gaming Landscape* (pp. 117–132). Bloomsbury Collections. http://dx.doi.org/10.5040/9781501310591.ch-009

Reed, A. (2004). Activating the self-importance of consumer selves: Exploring identity salience effects on judgments. *Journal of Consumer Research*, *31*(2), 286–295. 10.1086/422108

Robertson, T. S. (1967). The process of innovation and the diffusion of innovation. *Journal of Marketing*, *31*(1), 14. 10.2307/1249295

Ryan, R. M., & Deci, E. L. (2000). Intrinsic and Extrinsic Motivations: Classic Definitions and New Directions. *Contemporary Educational Psychology*, *25*(1), 54–67. 10.1006/CEPS.1999.1020

Sandikci, O., & Holt, D. B. (1998). Malling society. Mall consumption practices and the future of public space. In J. F. Sherry (Ed.), *Servicescapes: The Concept of Place in Contemporary Markets* (pp. 305–336). NTC Business Books.

Schembri, S., Merrilees, B., & Kristiansen, S. (2010). Brand consumption and narrative of the self. *Psychology & Marketing, 27*(6), 623–637. 10.1002/mar.20348

Seraj, M. (2012). We create, we connect, we respect, therefore we are: Intellectual, social, and cultural value in online communities. *Journal of Interactive Marketing, 26*(4), 209–222. 10.1016/J.INTMAR.2012.03.002

Sheth, J. N., Newman, B. I., & Gross, B. L. (1991). Why we buy what we buy: A theory of consumption values. *Journal of Business Research, 22*(2), 159–170. 10.1016/0148-2963(91) 90050-8

Sirgy, M. J., Grewal, D., & Mangleburg, T. (2000). Retail environment, self-congruity, and retail patronage: An integrative model and a research agenda. *Journal of Business Research, 49*(2), 127–138. 10.1016/S0148-2963(99)00009-0

Sreejesh, S., Paul, J., Strong, C., & Pius, J. (2020). Consumer response towards social media advertising: Effect of media interactivity, its conditions and the underlying mechanism. *International Journal of Information Management, 54*, 102155. 10.1016/J.IJINFOMGT. 2020.102155

Sweeney, J. C., & Soutar, G. N. (2001). Consumer perceived value: The development of a multiple item scale. *Journal of Retailing, 77*(2), 203–220. 10.1016/S0022-4359(01)00041-0

Trafimow, D., Triandis, H. C., & Goto, S. G. (1991). Some tests of the distinction between the private self and the collective self. *Journal of Personality and Social Psychology, 60*(5), 649–655. 10.1037/0022-3514.60.5.649

Tuškej, U., Golob, U., & Podnar, K. (2013). The role of consumer–brand identification in building brand relationships. *Journal of Business Research, 66*(1), 53–59. 10.1016/ J.JBUSRES.2011.07.022

Vashisht, D., & Chauhan, A. (2017). Effect of game-interactivity and congruence on presence and brand attitude. *Marketing Intelligence & Planning, 35*(6), 789–804. 10.1108/ MIP-01-2017-0018

Vijayasarathy, L. R. (2002). Product characteristics and Internet shopping intentions. *Internet Research, 12*(5), 411–426. 10.1108/10662240210447164

Vinerean, S., & Opreana, A. (2019). social media marketing efforts of luxury brands on Instagram. *Expert Journal of Marketing, 7*(2), 144–152.

Wang, Y., & Chen, H. (2021). Self-presentation and interactivity: Luxury branding on social media. *Journal of Product & Brand Management, 30*(5), 656–670. 10.1108/JPBM-05-2019-2368

Wang, Y., Po Lo, H., Chi, R., & Yang, Y. (2004). An integrated framework for customer value and customer-relationship-management performance: A customer-based perspective from China. *Managing Service Quality: An International Journal, 14*(2/3), 169–182. 10.1108/09604520410528590

Weiser, E. B. (2001). The functions of internet use and their social and psychological consequences. *Cyberpsychology & Behavior: The Impact of the Internet, Multimedia and Virtual Reality on Behavior and Society, 4*(6), 723–743. 10.1089/109493101753376678

Wongkitrungrueng, A., & Assarut, N. (2020). The role of live streaming in building consumer trust and engagement with social commerce sellers. *Journal of Business Research, 117*, 543–556. 10.1016/J.JBUSRES.2018.08.032

Xie, Q., & Lou, C. (2020). Curating luxe experiences online? Explicating the mechanisms of luxury content marketing in cultivating brand loyalty. *Journal of Interactive Advertising, 20*(3), 209–224. 10.1080/15252019.2020.1811177

Zhu, W., Huangfu, Z., Xu, D., Wang, X., & Yang, Z. (2022). Evaluating the impact of experience value promotes user voice toward social media: Value co-creation perspective. *Frontiers in Psychology*, *13*, 4911. 10.3389/fpsyg.2022.969511

Zhou, Z., Wu, J. P., Zhang, Q., & Xu, S. (2013). Transforming visitors into members in online brand communities: Evidence from China. *Journal of Business Research*, *66*(12), 2438–2443. 10.1016/J.JBUSRES.2013.05.032

Zhu, X. (2019). Research on the impact of content marketing on brand equity. Proceedings of the International Academic Conference on Frontiers in Social Sciences and Management Innovation (IAFSM 2018), 230–235. 10.2991/iafsm-18.2019.35

7 Value Creation Through Digital Content: User Co-creation Value

By Dr Denitsa Dineva

Learning Outcomes

- Defines user-generated content (UGC) and explains the role of customer co-creation value in content marketing.
- Discusses the key benefits and challenges of customer co-created content.
- Outlines the main forms of UGC and considers their pros and cons.
- Introduces the key steps that organisations must take to stimulate the highest quality of UGC.

User-Generated Content and Co-creation

User-generated content (UGC) or consumer-generated content is original, brand-specific digital content created and published by customers, rather than brands (Hootsuite, 2022) that adds value to brands. In recent years, the use of UGC has grown rapidly due to its inexpensive and influential nature, with more than half of consumers seeking advice before making a purchase (Google Consumer Insights, 2018) and trusting the opinions of others (Forbes, 2022a). UGC allows content suppliers to be rewarded and recognised for their contributions, while providing receiving consumers with entertaining, real data, and unsanitised-by-brands content. A fundamental premise of UGC is the process of co-creation, whereby customers actively participate in firms' value creation processes by being empowered to co-develop product and service solutions that meet their needs. Co-creation is a paradigm shift that has been taking place over the last couple of decades, and moves content marketing from value creation *for* to value creation *with* customers (Vargo & Lusch, 2004).

There are **three key components to customer value co-creation** that improve the firm's competitive advantage by contributing to its innovativeness (Mahr et al., 2014). First, customer co-creation allows brands to use new and external knowledge to develop innovations and consequently achieve competitiveness. This is because the co-creation process enables brands to access resources external to the firm (e.g., customer feedback) and as such add value to their products and services by offering a new or improved solution to a

DOI: 10.4324/9781003346500-7

customer problem. Second, customers are not only active participants in the co-creation, but also the beneficiaries through, for example, achieving stronger feelings of accomplishment, an increased sense of belonging to a community, or a better fit of the firm's value to their own needs. Third, customer co-creation outcomes can vary significantly across customer segments, which necessitates brands to deliberately select participating customers on the basis of their individual qualities such as their expertise or the qualities of their relationship with the brand, such as trust and loyalty. This interactive nature of UGC differs from traditional static marketing research and allows for the emergence of unexpected needs or ideas that are suited to dynamic and unpredictable digital environments.

Value co-creation through UGC is at the core of modern content marketing and a direct consequence of Web 2.0 ('The Social Web') and the emerging Web 3.0 ('The Semantic Web') that are characterised by highly interactive, democratised, and decentralised conditions. In other words, consumers are no longer the recipients of firm value, but also invariably its active and participating co-creators. It is important to note that while brands aim to encourage desirable collaborative practices with their consumers, the outcomes of UGC can often be outside of the firm's control. In turn, this chapter explores not only the benefits and different forms of user value co-creation content, and how brands can plan for UGC, but also important considerations for minimising its unintended consequences.

Benefits of User Co-creation in Content Marketing

User value co-creation benefits firms in several ways, which can be categorised into three distinctive groups: customer empowerment, peer-to-peer feedback, and external resource optimisation.

First, including target consumers in the content creation process empowers them, which in turn engenders **collaborative spirit**. Value co-creation promotes consumer participation in the brand's growth, which reinforces a sense of belongingness, community, and affinity with the brand and like-minded consumers (Muniz & O'Guinn, 2001). As a consequence, brands can build engaged online and offline communities of supporters. Furthermore, co-created content that takes place in the form of consumer-to-consumer (C2C) interactions within virtual communities enables brands to establish sources of innovation that involve varied customer roles in new product and service development. For instance, research found that an innovative product development strategy that encompasses customer co-creation experiences fosters a sense of community among users, facilitates communication within that community, allows the brand to act on customer feedback, and to continuously develop and maintain the community relationships (Rowley et al., 2007). At the minimum, co-producing content with customers helps develop and deepen relationships, thus generating brand loyalty.

The second benefit of user co-creation lies in the **peer-to-peer effect of marketing**, which is stronger than a brand's own advertising or marketing communications since it produces perceptions of *authenticity* and *trust* (Busser & Shulga, 2019). Nowadays, firms have to compete for their customers' attention in a highly saturated digital content environment whereby buyers are selective about the brands they interact with and purchase from. Typically, content that is perceived as authentic constitutes successful content and UGC is among the best practices to showcase the legitimacy of product or service performance. A related outcome of the peer-to-peer marketing effect is the generation of *trust*. Trust is an important consideration for brands with the increase of misinformation in recent years (World Health Organisation, 2022), making it challenging for brands to establish their trustworthiness. This is where UGC plays a crucial role. Individuals trust other individuals more than brand-generated commercial content (Forbes, 2022b), and so user co-creation can be viewed as the modern-day word-of-mouth (WOM). Indeed, market research shows that consumers are twice as likely to perceive user content as authentic compared to content created by brands (Business Wire, 2019).

Third, user co-creation allows brands to access **a cost-effective resource** that is adaptable and drives conversion rates (Timoshenko & Hauser, 2019). Brands can harness user content as a form of inexpensive resource of knowledge, ideation, and improvement. Thus, UGC can help brands scale in a way that is far less expensive compared with celebrity endorsers or influencers and can be particularly suited to smaller brands and enterprises. Moreover, customer value co-creation is an adaptable and flexible resource, which can be incorporated in other marketing campaigns and channels and represent a key theme in an omnichannel marketing strategy. For example, UGC is particularly influential in the final stages of the consumer decision-making journey whereby brands seek to convert prospects into customers.

Prominent Forms of Digital Content Co-creation

UGC comes in many forms, from simpler, low user involvement such as product and service reviews, testimonials, social Q&A sessions, to more complex and higher user involvement content such as blogs, crowdsourcing, thought leadership and podcasts. These are summarised in Table 7.1 – Forms of UGC.

Table 7.1 Forms of UGC

UGC form	*Advantages*	*Limitations*
Online customer reviews	Enhanced trust perceptions Free advertising Improved awareness Improved conversion rates	Little control over sentiment or content Possible reputational or credibility loss

(*Continued*)

Table 7.1 (Continued)

UGC form	Advantages	Limitations
Testimonials	Humanise the brand Provide authentic social proof of the brand's competence Quality assurance Improved conversion rates	Challenging to obtain Time-consuming compared with electronic WOM
Social Q&A sessions	Easy and inexpensive to implement Help brands to reach and engage with their online followers Two-way interaction	Careful planning is required ROI may be difficult to measure
Blogs	Improve search optimisation Help build brand authority	Time- and resource-consuming
Crowdsourcing	Improve consumers' sense of belonging to and relationship with the brand Product innovation Authentic co-creation with users	Little control over the content produced Possible reputational or credibility loss Can backfire easily
Thought-leadership articles	Establish credibility and improve reputation by reinforcing the brand story from an impartial perspective Generate backlinks, mentions and shares that improve SEO Attract new clients	Divisive, irrelevant, unhelpful, or generic content Negative user sentiment or feedback
Podcasts	Engagement with a captive on-the-go audience Improved brand awareness through regular content dissemination Improved social sharing and community-building	Costly and difficult to measure ROI Time-consuming Require compelling content on a regular basis

Online customer reviews are a form of electronic WOM (eWOM) that entails consumers posting content about a product or service on a brand's website, social media, or a third-party website (e.g., Trustpilot). Customer reviews are one of the most recognised forms of UGC and these have become a key source of product information for brands and prospect customers alike. For brands, customer reviews represent a rich source of product improvement and innovation through real-time customer feedback. For consumers, it assists them in making the purchase decision after reading impartial product performance information generated by existing brand customers. From a marketing mix perspective, customer reviews can be considered as an emerging promotion element, because brands are extensively using customer reviews to understand their attitudes, perceptions, and behavioural intentions towards their products and services (Babić Rosario et al., 2020). Brands thus largely benefit from customer reviews in terms of enhanced trust perceptions, free advertising and improved awareness, and better conversion rates. Nonetheless, like with other forms of UGC, brands have little control over the sentiment or content of the reviews they will receive, and that may lead to reputational loss and damaged credibility, leading to further increased costs and lower profitability. According to Trustpilot reviews data, the hotel and airline industries are rated worst for customer care with approximately 77 per cent and 73 per cent of reviews respectively being negative reviews.

Testimonials are a form of reference marketing (Jalkala & Salminen, 2010), and represent written or spoken statements that praise or endorse a brand, its product, or service. The key difference between customer reviews and testimonials is that the focus in testimonials is on encouraging delighted consumers to share positive experiences with the brand. To generate testimonials, brands often refer to their satisfied clients to share their opinions and encouraging experiences, and subsequently these are included in the brand's marketing materials. Testimonials are challenging to obtain since they are only limited to highly satisfied customers and necessitate the brand's time investment and commitment from customers. They are, however, highly valuable for brands since they humanise the brand (e.g., generate warmth perceptions), provide authentic social proof of the brand's competence (e.g., functionality, superiority), which in turn generate trust and build credibility, and ultimately lead to conversions. Aside from more conventional text-based testimonials featured on brands' websites, a good example is RokuTV's customer testimonial video, which showcases opinions from several customers on the usability of the product. The video features simple, informative storytelling, and emphasises the ease of use through on-screen text highlighting the specific benefits of the product.

Social Q&A sessions with target audiences are used by brands to answer any customer questions in real time and in this way helps to solidify the brand's proposition or address any issues. These are valuable to brands because they not only allow prospective and existing customers to learn more about the brand, its products, or services, but also contribute to knowledge-gathering, which can then be utilised in marketing promotions or value proposition improvements. This method of co-creation is relatively easy and inexpensive to implement, while it helps brands to reach and engage with their online followers. Social Q&A sessions generate a two-way conversation between the brand/brand representatives and the target audience, which improves authenticity perceptions as well as enhancing customers' sense of belonging to and connection with the brand. This format of UGC requires careful planning, timing, and call-to-action (e.g., hashtags, clickable links). Webinars and social media are particularly suited to this method of UGC with polls, open-ended questions, multiple-choice questions representing some examples of it.

Among the most common forms of co-creation that require high customer involvement are **blogs**. Blogs represent personal Web logs or journals in which a brand user shares information or their opinion on a variety of topics related to that brand. A blog post, in contrast, is an individual Web page on a website that discusses a particular sub-topic of the main blog. There are three categories of blog posts: 1) brand-owned – those developed by the brand and hosted on its official website, 2) blogs sponsored by brands, and co-designed by influencers or opinion leaders, and 3) blogs solely created by brand users or fans. Consumer-generated blog posts allow brands to improve their ranking on search engines through keywords and earning backlinks (i.e., third-party links that promote the brand's website or social media channels), because these are organic, perceived as more trustworthy (compared with paid-for content) and of higher quality. Thus, user-generated blogs are valuable to brands because they drive traffic to the brand's website and help generate leads and conversions (e.g., sales) that in turn meet business objectives. Moreover, brand reach is greatly improved through customer-generated blogging, and brands can utilise this in various ways (e.g., by guest posts on their website), which can help earn traffic both ways. For instance, Karen's Makeup&Beauty website is a consumer-generated blog where multiple brands are featured on different blog posts with the content creator clearly distinguishing organic and paid-for posts. Seeking to implement organic customer-generated blogging, however, is time- and resource-consuming and often adopted by brand loyalists or fans. Controlling the content or sentiment of the message on these blogs may also be challenging, particularly in instances where the blog posts are created by anti-brand communities and users.

Another common form of co-creation is **crowdsourcing**. Crowdsourcing is the deliberate use of 'crowds' (i.e., groups of consumers) to solve problems, create new products, or improve consumer experiences. Crowdsourcing involves consumers by asking them to participate in a deliberate and predefined call-to-action (CTA), and as such provides brands with novel and dynamic marketing opportunities (Bal et al., 2017). There are four main modes of crowdsourcing that companies use: *contests, collaboration, complements*, and *labour* (Bal et al., 2017).

Contests are a widely applied practice of crowdsourcing whereby a company designs a contest and consumers are encouraged to enrol by the promise of gaining cash rewards if they win. Customer ideation contests are a form of co-creation that is not geographically constrained and provides an opportunity for brands to access a worldwide pool of talented users. Typically, contestants can submit their own designs and comment on those of other contributors. These options offer contributors the space to publish content such as ideas, comments, opinions. Participation in customer ideation contests is predominantly extrinsically motivated but it can also be motivated by users' intrinsic goals. A good example of a contest where the brand used both types of motivation to encourage participants is Lay's 'Do Us a Flavor' campaign. In the campaign the participants had the opportunity to win $1 million (extrinsic motivator) as well as be recognised for inventing a new flavour (intrinsic motivator). Beyond constructive and useful content, however, contests may generate destructive deviant content that comprises visible and malicious protests or results in mocking and ridiculing the brand on the contest platform and other social media, thereby exposing the contest host to reputational risks (Gatzweiler et al., 2017). This was the case of McDonald's New Zealand 'Make Burger History' campaign where users were encouraged to build their own unique burger, but instead this resulted in racist, homophobic, and otherwise offensive suggestions.

To improve product or service usage and functionality, brands invite consumers to work on *collaborations* – a second form of crowdsourcing. These consumers are predominantly intrinsically motivated to engage in value co-creation since they are not compensated financially for their work. As such, the risks of failed campaigns, poor ideas or contributions are lower since consumers have a genuine interest to participate and are not financially motivated. Wikipedia is the best example of a large-scale collaboration crowdsourcing. On social media platforms, user polls are a cost-effective and quick way to collaborate in order to gather feedback from consumers and followers on topics related to the brand. A third form of crowdsourcing are complements, which represent the co-creation customer segments that work with technology (e.g., open source) in order to facilitate a complementary function. For instance, applications that are not created by the smart device manufacturer but can be downloaded to smart devices to complement the functionality or usability of the smart device and, as such, increase the value of that device are an example of a complement. Another example is Nexar, which works as a crowdsourced dashcam and while using their Nexar application or Wi-Fi-enabled dashcam, drivers are connected to their Nexar vehicle-to-vehicle network. The final form of crowdsourcing for value co-creation is labour. In a labour crowdsource scenario, individuals seeking employment are matched with companies or individuals who need labour. For instance, through its MTurk, Amazon has created crowdsourcing opportunities for individuals or corporations looking for labour. As such, MTurk enables researchers to gain access to individuals who take surveys for a fee.

Co-authoring **thought-leadership pieces** is another way to deliver authentic and genuine content that uses the expertise, insight, and experience of the contributor with the goal of reaching others by organically and indirectly promoting the brand. Generally, thought leadership represents creating value, building knowledge, or taking a stand. According to market research, thought leadership can consist of inspirational content that drives change, educational content, content exploring industry trends, industry research, and opinion commentary (Semrush, 2022) with the latter particularly suited to user co-creation. Co-authored thought-leadership content enables the brand to: 1) establish credibility and improve its reputation by reinforcing the brand story from an impartial perspective, 2) generate backlinks, mentions and shares that improve the brand's overall search engine optimisation (SEO) ranking, and 3) act as a mechanism to attract new clients since thought-leadership content is not intended for direct conversion of prospects. Thought-leadership articles are particularly influential in the B2B industry since they solidify a firm's authority in the market and generate customer engagement. IBM, for example, has dedicated an entire section on their website to the topic of growth through knowledge. On the downside, good thought-leadership pieces are by nature never about the brand, its products or services and therefore not linked to a specific industry and may be deemed generic. Moreover, thought-leadership articles may be viewed by some users as divisive, irrelevant, or unhelpful, generating negative sentiment and feedback.

Similarly to thought-leadership articles, **podcasts** are not intended to attract the brand's audience immediately, but instead spark interest, which other content marketing tools can then convert into sales. Podcasting represents a digitally evolved form of radio broadcasting that involves the creation of a series of audio or video files that are released episodically and often downloaded through internet syndication. Podcasting offers niche brand audiences a clear and concise way to understand its value proposition or learn more about topics related to it. Podcast listenership has increased dramatically in recent years (Statista, 2022) due to the on-demand digital culture created by emerging Web 2.0 and Web 3.0 technologies. It allows businesses and brands to tell their stories or co-create them with consumers anywhere and anytime, reinforcing their authority among competitors and creating brand advocates. There are certain benefits that podcasts generate including: engagement with a captive audience that consumes the content on-the-go, improved brand awareness through regular content dissemination, improved social sharing and community-building, and improved SEO. On the flipside, podcasts can be costly with tracking return-on-investment (ROI) challenging. Podcasts are time-consuming and require compelling content on a regular basis to retain the audience captivity, and the podcast creator-brand fit can be a source of risk (e.g., creator personality or background does not fit those of the brand). An example of a successful podcast is Annie Zhang's user-generated audio series 'Hello Metaverse' that discuss emerging topics pertinent to the metaverse.

How to Plan for User-Generated Content Campaigns

When designing for content campaigns that are co-created with customers, the firm must follow five key stages starting with setting out the objectives, choosing the target audience, deciding on the storyline and how to promote it, and ending with measuring the success of the campaign. These key stages are outlined in Table 7.2.

Table 7.2 UGC marketing campaign step-by-step process

Campaign stage	What it involves
1 Purpose and goals	Why are you encouraging UGC and what value will it provide?
2 Audience	For whom are you encouraging UGC and how will they benefit?
3 Story	What specific, unique, and valuable ideas will you build your UGC around?
4 Process	How will you structure, manage, and promote the campaign?
5 Measurement	How will you assess the performance and continually optimise your efforts?

The first stage is to define the *purpose* of the UGC and what *goals* it sets out to achieve. It is important for brands to first understand whether and where the value of UGC lies for their products and services and how best to capture and promote it. Additionally, brands must have clear objectives that UGC specifically helps them to achieve that other content marketing methods cannot. These objectives should be SMART (specific, measurable, achievable, relevant, and time-bound) since UGC can be a time-consuming venture that requires ongoing commitment from the brand. The next important consideration is for brands to select their *target audience*. Typically, brands have several target audiences based on which target personas can be created. A target persona is part of user-centred marketing and represents a fictional character that reflects a customer type that might use a brand's product or services. It is challenging for brands to attract different personas with the same piece of co-created content. Personalising UGC for different audiences or utilising it in a way that targets certain audiences helps brands achieve a better return on the co-created content. In establishing the persona demographics and their demand for content, brands must primarily consider what and who influences their day-to-day life as well as how they consume content and how these factors may in turn make UGC attractive to them.

In the next stage, the brand must choose what story to tell its target audiences; a marketing practice often referred to as storytelling. Storytelling in co-created content entails using real characters, ideally brand users or customers, and a plot to convey a message that indirectly markets the brand's products or services. Storytelling helps solidify a brand message and simplify complex product or service features. High quality UGC is characterised by its narrative being imaginative, interactive, and attention-grabbing storytelling. Broadly speaking, co-created content can be grouped into three distinct categories: functional, emotional, and essential. Functional content is predominantly fact-based and is less emotive since it focuses on the hard sell. As such, this type of content is typical for B2B content where the emphasis is on the industrial selling of products and services. The emotional content humanises the brand and allows customers to better relate to the business. This content often draws from the human experience and showcases the brand's personality. Finally, essential content provides minimum information that a consumer requires to know to be convinced to interact with the brand and buy its products or services. Storytelling represents a healthy mixture of elements from each of these three content categories. Table 7.3 showcases broad ideas for a storytelling narrative based on whether this originates from the brand, its products or services, or knowledge and expertise – with the latter most suited to UGC.

Table 7.3 Content marketing storybox

The brand	Brand's products and services	Knowledge and expertise
• Brand values and mission • The heritage of the brand • Corporate responsibility • Company achievements • Milestones and highlights • Quality assurance • The team • Team and employee achievements	• The products, services • Original ideas or designs • How the product or service evolved • Behind the scenes • The market covered • Customer stories • Customer success • Educational stories	• Research and opinions • Surveys • Conference feedback • Forecasting the future • Resources • Reading list • Templates • Point of view • FAQs

Once the content has been co-created, the brand must decide how to promote it to its target audiences and typically there are two ways to do that with brands typically opting for a combination of the two. On the one hand, **organic content promotion** entails SEO, bots and messaging applications, email marketing, social media, live events and webinars, influencer marketing, content syndication and content repurposing. Value co-creation is typically done to improve *SEO* and optimising such content to make it easy to be discoverable on search engines is a common method to promote UGC. Creators incorporate specific topics and keywords that help build brand authority and organically acquire inbound links to generate traffic to the brand's website or social media. *Conversational marketing*, that is the use of bots and messaging apps to promote relevant content (e.g., customer forum for questions) is another organic way to promote content and convert visitors to the brand's website. *Email marketing* is a good technique to target different audiences and personas through segmentation and personalised content that adds different value to different target audiences. *Social media* is a seamless way to promote content organically via hashtags and posting real-time, visual, and engaging content from consumers (e.g., comments from 'Top fans', re-sharing consumer posts). Another good organic way to increase exposure to prospects is through live events and webinars with opinion leaders or industry experts that are external to the brand and enhance the brand's credibility and authenticity. Establishing partnerships with existing *influencers* that are relevant to the brand or co-creating content with them is another popular method of promoting content. *Content syndication* is when a brand republishes existing content on additional websites to get more value of it, because this way it is exposed to different audiences and redirects them back to the brand's website (e.g., a user writing a blog). Lastly, *content repurposing*, for example, through turning a blog post into an infographic, is a good way to visually engage with prospect consumers and attract them to the brand.

On the other hand, **paid content promotion** is typically done via Google and social media ads, paid influencer marketing and native display advertising. Paid content promotion is used to supplement organic efforts and reach audiences more difficult to reach than just with organic promotion. *Google ads* are particularly influential in this respect as the first page of Google results receives the majority of page traffic clicks and remarketing (i.e., online advertising aimed at consumers based on their previous digital behaviour and footprint). *Social media* ads further increase awareness of and exposure to the brand and each platform has its own take on what advertising entails with brands able to choose between more visual picture- and video-based sites (e.g., Instagram, TikTok) to more informative, text-based ones (e.g., Twitter). In a similar vein to organic influencer marketing, *paid influencer marketing* is a suitable way to promote content in a way that reaches new and different audiences. Lastly, *native display advertising* represents content created and paid for by advertiser that allows the advertiser to sponsor content on websites relevant to the brand's industry. This form of paid content promotion fits in with the rest of the content on the brand's website and is suited to capturing the audience's attention without being intrusive or interruptive.

The final fifth stage of planning for content co-creation is the **measurement** of the campaign. This is done based on the brand's choice of promotion techniques and ranges from *Web metrics* (e.g., unique page visitors, bounce rate), *social media metrics* (e.g., impressions, engagement), email metrics (e.g., open rate, click-through rate) and *social listening*. Social listening is the process of identifying overall conversation or sentiment about the brand on social media platforms. A good content strategy benefits significantly from succinct social listening activity that identifies the sentiment towards the brand and its competitors. It also helps monitor how audiences use and engage with the content that is being promoted and whether any improvements are required. Importantly, social listening is crucial for brands to be able to identify, strategise, and monitor for any potential crisis moments. This helps brands to pre-empt for the impact of any possible negativity and manage brand equity.

Considerations for User Co-created Content

Customer co-created content is valuable for brands, but it also has a dark side due to the little control brands have over it. There are certain measures brands can take to ensure that content co-creation process and outcomes are appropriate and advantageous.

Obtain Permission for Reusing UGC Content

When using UGC for their promotions, brands must ensure that they obtain permission to reuse such content. The best way to do this is by directly asking users for permission to repost their content.

Credit Content Creator

Acknowledging the source of the UGC by mentioning their name, publication, or providing a direct link to the original content is a responsibility of the brand; this ensures transparency and improves authenticity.

Soliciting UGC = Little Control Over the Message

Brands should accept that when they solicit UGC, it can be challenging to control the content or sentiment of the message. Creative freedom is often at the core of UGC, but ensuring the content meets the brand's expectations is difficult, so brands must make sure that their audience knows what is expected from them. Since co-created content is an external resource, it cannot be controlled like internal resources (e.g., employees) and brands require distinct mechanisms for knowledge transfer, data protection, and incentivising.

Observe Safety Regulations and Legal Boundaries

Using common sense with UGC and adhering to safety regulations and legal boundaries is an important requirement for brands when co-creating content. Ways to do this include: creating clear Terms and Conditions that users are aware of; considering a licence agreement; or covering UGC in the brand's Privacy Policy.

Transparency With Paid UGC

Brands must ensure that any payments or incentives made towards the generation of UGC should be declared with #ad or #spons for transparency with consumers. This is now a legal requirement and brands as well as content creators can be fined if they do not comply.

Content Can Be Positive and Negative

In addition to accepting that controlling the message is constrained when co-designing for UGC, brands must develop strategies to deal with both positive and negative content. This constitutes real-time, consistent, and professional webcare, which praises complimentary consumer content and competently addresses transgressive or undesirable content.

Clear Expectations of Creators and Content

Brands must make sure their intention with UGC is clear and not misleading for the content creators. Moreover, brands should not attempt to fake user-generated posts or campaigns, because when consumers uncover false sentiment, this will result in damaging the brand's reputation in the long-term. Instead, brand must ensure that UGC comes from one of three cohorts: customers, brand loyalists, or opinion leaders.

Case Study – McDonalds Big Mac Art Project

Figure 7.1 Big Mac.

Background and Challenge

Fewer and fewer teens & tweens were getting excited about McDonald's. Brand love in these important target groups has declined significantly, and constant promotional campaigns were not bringing them back either. To turn this around, credible communication was key. But credibility in this young target group was a tricky issue: It can only come from the target group itself. Meaning, the target audience must become brand ambassadors.

Campaign Objectives

The primary goal of this campaign was to increase the levels of brand love among McDonald's teenagers and young adults. This group was found to become increasingly unreceptive to traditional methods of marketing communications, and McDonald's needed to come up with a novel approach that would enable the brand to connect with this audience in a meaningful way. The main objective of the brief was to develop a User Generated Content campaign that teens and tweens will engage in by producing creative content related to McDonald's.

Overview of the Campaign

To achieve these objectives, McDonald's developed a four-phase campaign centred around its iconic Big Mac product. The campaign was designed to encourage the target group to design and submit their own 'Big Mac' artwork.

The first phase of the campaign was the initiation phase, during which three artists – Hombre, Pepiart, and Dxtr – created their own 'Big Mac' artwork. This content was then shared on owned channels, such as the campaign hub and social media, and served as a call-to-action for the target group.

In the second phase, four macro-influencers from different pop cultural areas joined the campaign and created their own 'Big Mac' art, along with a call for participation. These macro-influencers helped to spread the word about the campaign and inspire the target group to get involved.

In the third phase, around 30 micro-influencers were enlisted to spread the word about the campaign and create their own 'Big Mac' art. These micro-influencers had smaller, more specific followings and helped to further promote the campaign and encourage participation from the target group.

Finally, in the participation phase, the target group was invited to submit their own 'Big Mac' art to the campaign hub. The result was a unique collection of highly diverse works, including paintings, photo retouching, and fashion items such as shoes, sweaters, and shirts.

The Results

The campaign was extremely successful, with the results significantly exceeding McDonald's expectations. The campaign hub was accessed over 1 million times, and more than 500 artworks were submitted. Positive sentiment towards the campaign was a high 94%. In addition, the buzz volume around McDonald's increased by 60% during the campaign period, and the positive rating of the McDonald's brand increased by an impressive 135%.

Takeaways From This Campaign

This campaign demonstrates the power of user-generated content in driving brand engagement and love, particularly among younger audiences. By giving the target group the opportunity to express themselves creatively and become part of the brand's marketing efforts, McDonald's was able to connect with them in a meaningful way and drive positive sentiment towards the brand. This approach could be used by other brands looking to engage younger audiences in a more authentic and relevant way. Additionally, the campaign's success shows the potential impact that a well-executed, targeted campaign can have.

References

Babić Rosario, A., De Valck, K., and Sotgiu, F. (2020). Conceptualizing the electronic word-of-mouth process: What we know and need to know about eWOM creation, exposure, and evaluation. *Journal of the Academy of Marketing Science*, 48(3), 422–448.

Bal, A., Weidner, K., Hannah, R., and Mills, A. J. (2017). Crowdsourcing and brand control. *Business Horizons*, 60(2), 219–228.

Business Wire (2019). Stackla Survey Reveals Disconnect Between the Content Consumers Want & What Marketers Deliver. Available at: www.businesswire.com/news/home/20190220005302/en/Stackla-Survey-Reveals-Disconnect-Content-Consumers-Marketers

Busser, J. A. and Shulga, L. V. (2019). Involvement in consumer-generated advertising: Effects of organizational transparency and brand authenticity on loyalty and trust, *International Journal of Contemporary Hospitality Management*, 31(4), 1763–1784.

Forbes (2022a). The Rise Of User-Generated Content And Its Impact On Brand Loyalty And Affinity. Available at: www.forbes.com/sites/forbesagencycouncil/2022/09/12/the-rise-of-user-generated-content-and-its-impact-on-brand-loyalty-and-affinity/?sh=365adccd29ac

Forbes (2022b). Customers Don't Trust Businesses As Much As Executives Think They Should, PwC Study Finds. Available at: www.forbes.com/sites/edwardsegal/2022/06/21/new-survey-shows-a-big-gap-in-trust-between-companies-and-consumers/?sh=4da03f836811

Gatzweiler, A., Blazevic, V., and Piller, F. T. (2017). Dark side or bright light: Destructive and constructive deviant content in consumer ideation contests. *Journal of Product Innovation Management*, 34(6), 772–789.

Google Consumer Insights (2018). Consumer Insights. Available at: www.thinkwithgoogle.com/consumer-insights/consumer-trends/shopping-research-before-purchase-statistics/

Hootsuite (2022). What is user-generated content? And why is it important? Available at: https://blog.hootsuite.com/user-generated-content-ugc/#What_is_user_generated_content

Jalkala, A., and Salminen, R. T. (2010). Practices and functions of customer reference marketing—Leveraging customer references as marketing assets. *Industrial Marketing Management, 39*(6), 975–985.

Mahr, D., Lievens, A., and Blazevic, V. (2014). The value of customer co-created knowledge during the innovation process. *Journal of Product Innovation Management,* 31(3), 599–615.

Muniz, A. M., and O'Guinn, T. C. (2001). Brand community. *Journal of Consumer Research,* 27(4), 412–432.

Rowley, J., Kupiec-Teahan, B., and Leeming, E. (2007). Customer community and co-creation: A case study. *Marketing Intelligence & Planning, 25*(2), 136–146.

Semrush (2022). Thought leadership: What it is and how to master it in 2023. Available at: www.semrush.com/blog/complete-guide-to-thought-leadership-for-business/#the-benefits-of-thought-leadership-marketing

Statista (2022). Podcasts in the UK – statistics & facts. Available at: www.statista.com/topics/6908/podcasts-in-the-uk/#editorsPicks

Timoshenko, A., and Hauser, J. R. (2019). Identifying customer needs from user-generated content. *Marketing Science, 38*(1), 1–20.

Vargo, S. L., and Lusch, R. F. (2004). The four service marketing myths: Remnants of a goods-based, manufacturing model. *Journal of Service Research,* 6(4), 324–335.

World Health Organisation. (2022). Infodemics and misinformation negatively affect people's health behaviours, new WHO review finds. Available at: www.who.int/europe/news/item/01–09-2022-infodemics-and-misinformation-negatively-affect-people-s-health-behaviours--new-who-review-finds

8 Digital Content and Social Media Influencers

By Dr Ashleigh Logan-McFarlane

Learning Outcomes

*   To develop an in-depth understanding of social media influencers and their main domains.
*   To be able to identity the main differences between different levels of social media influencers.
*   To learn about the key criteria for selecting social media influencers for social media campaigns.

Social Media Influencers (SMIs)

According to Statistica (2023), the global marketing influencer, advertising market size has practically doubled since 2019 and is now worth $16.4 billion. This is not surprising given that in 2020, 75 per cent of advertisers used influencers and a further 43 per cent were actively pursuing ways to increase their overall advertising budget spend on influencers (Campbell & Farrell, 2020). Social media influencers (SMIs) are everyday people who use social media to create and share written and visual narrated content to connect with their followers in digital spaces in authentic ways and, in doing so, generate income from the incorporation of sponsored content into blogs and/or social media posts (Abidin 2015, 2016a, 2016b; Khamis, Ang & Welling, 2017). This means that using social media platforms such as TikTok, Instagram, Facebook, Twitter etc. anyone can produce interesting and entertaining images with engaging explanations with the aim of capturing the attention of followers who share that same interest and/or point of view on a particular topic. The key difference between you or me sharing content, and an SMI, is that the SMI normally receives some form of compensation from organisations for embedding paid and/or sponsored content into these written and visual narrations, most of which feature products, services, and experiences. Today, the SMI concept encompasses all types of influential users on digital platforms including: influencer, blogger, vlogger, YouTuber, Instafamous personalities etc. and has become the most commonly used term for advertisers, commercial sponsors and academic researchers (Ye et al., 2021).

DOI: 10.4324/9781003346500-8

Cornwell and Katz (2020, p. 6) redefine an SMI as 'a persona (related to a person, group of people, or organisation) that possesses greater than average potential to sway others in terms of thoughts, attitudes and behaviours due to attributes of their communication frequency, persuasiveness, social network or other characteristics'. This definition foregrounds the importance of the 'persona' and just how SMIs enact roles or characters which can be genuine to their own sense of self, to that of an entity, and/or entirely fictional.

Social Media Influencers (SMIs) and the 'Demotic Turn'

The origin of the SMI can be traced back to the early noughties with the rise of Web 2.0 and what Turner (2009 refers to as the 'demotic turn'. That is, the emergence of democratic communication platforms that facilitated two-way interaction between individuals and large audiences. This change in technology enabled ordinary individuals to achieve fame in new ways. For example, through 'blogging' and/or sharing intimate details of private thoughts, images, and videos of personal physical spaces. Senft's (2008) ethnographic study of 'cam girls' captures the beginnings of what we know about the character of SMIs today. The study focused on young women who displayed themselves over the Web using video and social media platforms including LiveJournal, YouTube, Myspace and Facebook in pursuit of some measure of celebrity. These women revealed the inside of their bedrooms to offer an intimate glimpse into their private lives and Senft (2008, p. 25) coined the term micro-celebrity to depict this 'new style of online performance that involves people "amping up" their popularity over the Web using technologies like video, blogs and social networking sites'. Emerging interactive online platforms and social media channels such as Live Journal, Myspace, Facebook, YouTube, Twitter and Instagram, meant that technology facilitated autonomy and permitted ordinary people access to audiences that were once difficult to reach and controlled by media institutions such as the British Broadcasting Corporation (BBC) in the UK.

SMI Domains

In 2023, many influencers are well-known within a particular domain. Some of the most widespread spheres of influence include lifestyle, fashion, beauty, music, food, travel, technology, and sports. It is of utmost importance to identify SMIs who are active within the domain that your organisation seeks to work within. This is because these SMIs already have experience creating and posting content while engaging with the type(s) of audience that you wish to reach. We will focus on the types of content posted in lifestyle, fashion, beauty, and sports domains before introducing emerging influencer domains.

The *lifestyle domain* captures behind-the-scenes day-to-day activities shared by SMIs including daily habits such as the commute to work and other travel, snippets from getting dressed in the morning, physical workouts, food consumed throughout the day, and much more. This was the largest domain among UK Instagram influencers in 2020 with 8.22 per cent of SMIs positioning their content to cover these topics (Statistica, 2023).

The *fashion domain* captures SMIs who set and establish trends on which brands, items of apparel, and styles are in vogue. This domain is always evolving. Academic research on fashion influencers has identified that the fashion ideal is depicted in images and has stable qualities which include the body as the subject of the fashion that is worn. Disguising certain limitations to the body, such as imperfections/ageing, the body is open to change and can be interpreted in a number of different ways (de Perthuis & Findlay, 2019). This means that digital technologies are facilitating the constant evolution of fashionable style, and content creators are involved in the process of negotiating the staples of this fashion look. For example, a particular style gaining momentum among SMIs is the 'advanced age style movement'. This depicts influencers aged 50+, who are renegotiating and challenging body ideals and fashion designs available in traditional Western beauty and fashion markets to accommodate on-trend options and embrace their ageing bodies (McFarlane & Samsioe, 2020; Veresiu & Parmentier, 2021).

The *beauty domain* is comprised of make-up tutorials and tips that offer anyone anywhere in the world access to the latest professional techniques. Beauty vlogs on YouTube are a popular method of communicating these tips and techniques (Mardon, Molesworth, & Grigore, 2018) and attract millions of active subscribers. Increasingly, beauty vloggers are connecting across platforms to link TikTok videos with bright visuals, engaging music, and relevant hashtags, e.g., @babsbeauty with 56.6+ thousand followers.

The *sports domain* captures the activities of sports figures including footballers, basketball players, cricketers etc. and offers a glimpse into their professional opinions on sports techniques. A worldwide football report (2022) revealed that 72 per cent of supporters now view apps to watch games. The Nielsen Influence Scope measured the social media branded posts of influential footballers on Instagram, where players such as Lionel Messi and Neymar have an audience engagement rate of 2 per cent and 1.8 per cent respectively and a social media value of $2,631,388 and £1,152,495 (Nielsen, 2022). Sports accounts such as @leomessi's Instagram, not only share relevant sports and football content, but also give a more personal account of private life and share images which convey family values.

The heightened increase in social media consumption during the COVID-19 pandemic has led to the emergence of new categories such as petinfluencers, genuineinfluencers, finfluencers (finance influencers) and virtual influencers (Influencer Marketing Hub, 2022). Brands such as Dyson are beginning to realise the significance of (for example) pet accounts as nano-influencers (e.g., promoting the product through the demonstration of 'drying kitty @mochi_fluffpom's hair' to 3,165 followers (MNFST, 2019)). 'Genuineinfluencers' might expose their weaknesses and imperfections. They amass followers by being more relatable and sharing simple and comprehensive explanations of a product/ brand, such as a toothbrush or chocolate bar, its composition, production and how its usage affects us, the environment and wider society (Avallone, 2021). 'Finfluencers' attempt to fill the 'advice gap' concerning how best to manage decisions about financial matters, including savings, mortgages and other high-risk investments (Barrett, 2022). The danger lies in the fact that many of these 'finfluencers' are unregulated by the Financial Conduct Authority (FCA) and generate an income from selling online courses, and other add-ons (ibid.).

The Influencer Marketing Hub have a search tool that enables you to identify the top influencers deemed most authentic by followers, engagement rate, and authentic engagement. It measures how strong an influencer is outside of the base country that they work within. In January 2023, the top-rated lifestyle and music SMI was Korean @agustd with 42.1+ million Instagram followers, a 20.96 per cent engagement rate and 8.8 million authentic engagement. @agustd offers an artsy aesthetic, which often features verandas, sports, consuming food in restaurants, art, and various music-related posts. This is a useful tool for searching for SMIs as it also enables you to identify SMIs whose content reaches beyond a single domain, e.g., lifestyle *and* music. This reinforces the importance of being informed on how the content created by SMIs can reach several domains and different audience interests simultaneously. Marketers must be aware of these different interest groups to ensure that the brand and/or product with which they are seeking to collaborate does not offend and/or isolate the values of other SMI-interested audiences across domains.

SMI Levels – Mega, Macro, Micro, and Nano

If we are to understand the SMI phenomenon, we must consider the different levels of SMI and how these are often used by advertisers to select the most apt SMI for a particular brand and/or product to reach the intended audience. Boerman (2020) aptly outlined micro, meso and macro-influencers but the Influencer Marketing Hub (2023) has since updated these to incorporate mega- and nano-influencers. In what follows we review each in turn and focus on Instagram influencers. This is because 90 per cent of all influencer campaigns use this platform (ibid.).

- **Mega-influencers** are social celebrities with more than a million followers. This group is considered elite due to the amount of following and engagement that they typically attract. The top six social media mega-influencers (according to total number of followers on Instagram) at the time of writing this chapter, include: professional football athletes Cristiano Ronaldo (787 million) and Leo Messi (530 million followers), musician and actress Selena Gomez (499 million), Canadian musician

Justin Bieber (477 million), and US influencers and reality TV personalities Kylie Jenner (530 million) and Kim Kardashian (530 million) (Frederick, 2023). It is interesting to note here that most of these individuals are worldwide celebrities in the traditional sense (Logan, 2016), achieving fame through athleticism, academy awards, and multiplatinum albums. Also of note, is the premium fee that these individuals can command for engaging in sponsorships with organisations. In 2016, Selena Gomez was rumoured to have collaborated with the luxury fashion brand Coach for an estimated fee of $10 million (Schneier, 2016).

- **Macro-influencers** are full-time professional influencers with national recognisability who have between 100,000 and one million followers (McFarlane and Samsioe, 2020). Macro-influencers often provide audiences with content surrounding a specialised or niche focus and have an impressive number of followers. For example Jean Lee @jeaniuseats (111 thousand followers as of January 2023) is a New York City based food and travel influencer. Her Instagram feed features mouth-watering images of food consumed at trendy restaurants, most often in NYC, but she also features the food she consumes when travelling. Lee contributes to the infamous Zagat guide, originally a NYC based organisation which now works with Google to collect and compare ratings from 250,000 individuals to produce guides' ratings on travel and tourism from restaurants to hotels to museums, movies, and leisure (Burton, 2019).

- **Micro-influencers** are normal people turned Instafamous with up to 100,000 followers. This is the largest group of influencers and according to the Influencer Marketing Hub (2023). While their following is not considered to be large, they have a high level of authenticity because followers believe their content and find it relatable. Indeed, a study by Kay, Mulcahy and Parkinson (2020) revealed that micro-influencers have greater influence than macro-influencers. This is because followers resist macro-influencers' advertising content and perceived their increased levels of popularity and content creation as a forced effort to become more persuasive. For example, Erika Fong @ericawfong founded luxury skincare brand Dewystone. With a following of 51.3+ thousand, Erika effortlessly portrays a luxury lifestyle aesthetic that her followers appear to perceive as genuine. Moreover, Luke Preece @iamdooom is a freelance illustrator who has amassed 48+ thousand followers. Luke has designed for several prominent organisations including popular band Panic at the Disco. Both Erika and Luke are listed in affiable.ai's Top 1000 Micro-Influencer Instagram Influencers in United Kingdom list as available for collaboration.

- **Nano-influencers** are individuals who have an enormous influence, and who possess niche characteristics that have a high appeal to a distinctive community of consumers, e.g., parents, property developers, gamers etc. They typically have fewer than 1,000 to no more than 10,000 followers.

Nano-influencers were found to have seven times the engagement rate than those of their macro-influencer counterparts (Geyser, 2022). Nano-influencers can be a lower-cost option for organisations and can often be compensated through gifting products and experiences. With 7,116 followers John Adams @dadbloguk is a UK-based dad blogger, who has won awards for his commentary on parenting and family lifestyle. He revealed that he is taking a break from blogging to pursue further study and a career change focused on young teenagers. This is an account to watch and potentially collaborate with, as his followers eagerly anticipate a return.

Each level of SMI has its own unique advantages and drawbacks. The selection of an SMI for a particular campaign will depend on the advertising budget available and the sought-after return on investment (ROI). This is often determined through identifying the desired level of awareness and engagement from followers.

In Figure 8.1, the vertical axis represents the budget spent from high to low/ no budget and the horizontal axis represents the desired level of campaign awareness sought from high to low. We can now review each scenario.

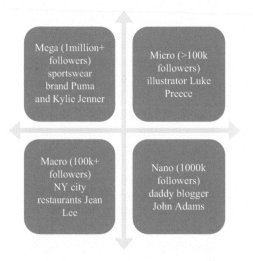

Figure 8.1 How to select SMI level based on desired campaign awareness and advertising budget.

Scenario I

You are looking to raise awareness of a product/brand on a global scale and have a large advertising budget. In this case you might consider a mega-influencer, e.g., sportswear brand Puma selected Kylie Jenner.

Scenario 2

You have a medium budget, are looking to raise awareness on a national scale, and are looking to target a niche group of consumers with your product/brand. Here, you might consider using a macro-influencer, e.g., New York City restaurants inviting food influencer Jean Lee to dine in restaurants and feature this in Instagram posts and the Zagat guide.

Scenario 3

You have a medium to small budget and would like to engage followers who believe your product/brand to be authentic, you might consider using a micro-influencer, e.g., normal people turned Instafamous such as illustrator Luke Preece.

Scenario 4

You have a very limited budget and are seeking to engage a community or niche following with your product/brand. Here, you might consider a nano-influencer, e.g., daddy blogger John Adams.

We have considered the different levels of SMI and the characteristics of each and how they might be beneficial depending on the desired level of awareness and engagement from followers. Now we will consider the significance of sponsorships and how to select effective SMIs to maintain consumer trust and authenticity.

SMI Partnerships, Trust, and Authenticity

SMIs have overtaken traditional celebrities and are now first choice for organisations seeking to engage in paid partnerships to promote brands, services, and experiences (Schouten, Janssen & Verspaget, 2020). This is because individuals identify more with SMIs than traditional celebrities, feel more akin to them, and this results in a higher level of trust. For this reason, perceived similarity, identification, and trust are all significant for organisations seeking to partner with SMIs. Influencers prompt consumer engagement and participation in the form of likes, comments, and share posts to their networks, and this increases the reach and visibility of the original post (Boerman, 2020). However, research has established that when consumers recognise the use of hashtags on Instagram such as #sponsored and #paidad, which reveal influencers' commercial partnerships, this lessens the likelihood that they will share this via eWOM (Evans et al., 2017) and this can also have an unintended negative impact on the influencers' perceived credibility among consumers (De Veirman & Hudders, 2020).

In order to avoid this, research has suggested that SMIs maintain a balance when posting content (Hudders, De Jans, & De Veirman, 2021). This is because too much commercial content can lead to the dilution of authenticity and the influential power of the SMI (ibid.). When this occurs, audiences start to question whether the SMI is legitimately narrating their own personal experience as opposed to bigging up the brand, product, service, experience etc. because they are being paid to do so. In this case, partnering with the SMI can become a risky advertising spend for the organisation because the audience's perceived trust of what is being promoted is also reduced.

Let us consider a situation where an SMI has engaged in posting commercial content when the legitimacy of the sponsorship is questioned, leading to reduced audience trust. In June 2022, mega-influencer football star Cristiano Ronaldo engaged in a partnership deal with Binance, a digital organisation specialising in crypto exchange, to create exclusive, non-fungible tokens (NFTs) worth over $2 million (Oliver et al., 2022). The partnership raised some questions. Although Ronaldo sought to engage his audiences on the advantages, the value of crypto and NFTs were in decline at that time and, the UK's Financial Conduct Authority (FCA) cautioned that there was a lack of consumer laws protecting such investments (ibid.).

Therefore, to achieve the correct balance between authentic and commercial content, and to obtain consumer trust, organisations seeking to partner with an SMI should first focus their efforts on identifying the intended audience for their brand, product, service, and/or experience. This is not an easy task, and it is one that requires knowledge of, not only the different social media platforms and how they operate, but also active SMIs and the types of audiences that they engage. For example, TikTok is a visual video platform with a unique algorithm which curates content and recommendations based on the videos that an individual watches, and the content the platform displays is dependent on one's mindset at a particular point in time (Newberry, 2022). If you are unfamiliar with a platform such as TikTok and the advantages of working with an active SMI within the desired audience and community, e.g., fitness fanatics interested in challenges, tutorials, and finding inspiration for their fitness goals #FitTok, it is probably wise to consider working with a specialised influencer agency. Fortunately, influencer agencies are on the rise and a quick Google search can reveal several organisations that specialise in connecting sponsors with SMIs. Influencer agencies can help with identifying SMIs that are a good fit – see Table 8.1.

Table 8.1 Criteria checklist for selecting SMIs for SM campaigns

Criteria	*Focus*
Number of followers	Mega, macro, micro, nano etc.
Engagement rate with followers	Replying to followers' comments and interacting via likes etc. – high, medium, low.
Relevance to the particular campaign	Creating content that actually reflects the values of the product/brand being promoted and is of use to audiences potentially considering engaging in its usage.

(Continued)

Table 8.1 (Continued)

Criteria	Focus
Authenticity	Genuineness of the person. To what extent the character that they project on social media is in line with the product/brand they are promoting. A body builder promoting protein shakes who has credibility and high likelihood of authentically using the product being promoted versus beautician promoting a mortgage deal. The latter is unlikely to be a good fit if all posts across social media platforms relate to beauty.
Trustworthiness	To what extent an honest review about the product/brand is offered based on real qualities, rather than an SMI bigging up the product because they will receive compensation for doing so.
Values	Does the product/brand align with SMI beliefs and ethical stance.
Content quality	Good aesthetics, use of visuals, engaging language, use of relevant hashtags etc.
Frequency of posts	Finding a good balance is key. This because posting irregularly can lead to follower drop off and losing followers but, equally, posting too often can also lead to this.
Audience quality	The importance of interactions, comments that convey positive reactions to and reinforcement of the item being promoted in the posts.

Aspire is an example of one such agency where you can search, compare, and contact creators across platforms such as TikTok, Meta, YouTube etc. who are active within the required audiences and communities. You can also receive requests for collaboration from active content creators (Aspire, 2023). Aspire enables sponsors to build campaigns around anyone with influence, approve content before it goes live, license content as it is created, and measure which content is most successful. Aspire highlight some of their brand collaborations on their website and social media. @Drinkevolve is a brand which develops sustainably sourced plant-based protein shakes, powders, and bars and is part of the Aspire portfolio. A recent post on the @drinkevolve Instagram features a collaboration with micro-influencer @relauren whose profile features a US beach lifestyle where sustainability is the core focus in posts to her 38.6+ thousand followers in collaboration with @drinkevolve: www.instagram.com/reel/CnAe8neK9u7/?utm_source=ig_web_copy_link.

Fohr is another influencer platform that concentrates on inspiring authentic advertisements of brands and products, and provides tools and analytics from a team of experts who suggest methods to improve SMI campaigns (Fohr, 2023). Fohr is committed to ensuring maximum campaign visibility to the desired audience and offers different pricing plans depending on organisation size and content campaign goals. Of interest, is how Fohr openly shares aspects of successful elements of SMI campaign collaborations. In one Instagram post, Fohr features a breakdown of a successful fragrance collaboration between luxury brand @Aerin and macro lifestyle influencer @taniasarin with 416+ thousand followers: www.instagram.com/p/CmzEuDNOWTg/. Fohr highlights important features of the post, including the image which features the fragrance bottle, brand, and text on the bottle, the well-narrated explanation of the fragrance, the use of #Ad and paid partnership in line with Federal Trade Commission online influencer (FTC) guidelines, and the ability to evoke positive opinions of the audience which are visible in the comments on the post.

Influencer agencies actively create and follow the latest developments in influencer marketing and can assist with identifying invisible and emerging trends. They are a quick and comprehensive option to maximise reach (e.g., SocialPubli offers access to 200+ thousand influencers across 35 countries (Forbes, 2022) and you can search by filtering social network,, and/or domain fashion/gaming) whilst maintaining trust and authenticity. This approach is perhaps more suited to those working with an advertising budget, although many agencies do offer free access to certain features on the platform, e.g., AiInfluencer, where you can select category, hashtags, keywords, number of followers, etc. Even with limited to zero advertising budget, you can take time to research these platforms and identify different types and levels of influencer that will best address your audience needs. In this case, the focus should be on ensuring that the SMI selected for your campaign is able to establish and nurture a strong relationship with their audience through building an appealing and enticing profile. As we have seen with @relauren and @taniasarin, to achieve this you need to increase the relevance of sponsored content and integrate commercial content into genuine non-sponsored content in a carefully balanced way (Hudders, De Jans, & De Veirman, 2021).

Parasocial Interaction and SMI

Parasocial interaction theory was coined to capture communication between a media personality and an ordinary individual which is perceived as being 'real' (Horton & Wohl, 1956). This was understood as a one-directional interaction through an individual's perceived and often imagined relationship with a famous person (Logan, 2016) where the media personality did not engage in reciprocal communication and the individual receiver was unable to obtain a direct, personal reply. With the rise of Web 2.0 and social media, the term 'parasocial relationship' emerged to capture the shift towards the often two-directional, reciprocal relations that SMIs develop with their audiences (Aw & Chuah, 2021). These relationships can resemble close personal ones such as friendships, family members, and significant others. This is because SMIs communicate intimate details of their everyday lives through their social media interactions, granting audiences access to behind-the-scenes, which establishes a familiar and perceived closeness (Abidin, 2015). The format of these exchanges often centres around self-presentation, as aspects of SMIs real, authentic lives are displayed in real time largely through the commodification of characteristics of their private lives (Duffy, 2015). @StaceySolomon is a UK music star, TV personality, and mega lifestyle influencer with 5.5+ million followers, who reveals intimate details surrounding her family life at home with her TV personality husband mega-influencer @realjoeswashy and soon to be five children. Follower comments on aspects of her Instagram posts discuss intimate aspects of her family life in detail and Stacey often rewards her followers with positive, emotional affirmations for their support and interactions in her live stories. Stacey achieves the perfect balance of interactions with commercial content and paid partnerships which, to use Kozinets et al.'s (2010) term, are effortlessly woven into a 'character narrative'. Therefore, establishing parasocial relationships is a well-practised SMI strategy to maintain the balance between, what appears to be genuine, and non-sponsored content. Parasocial relationships help maintain SMI credibility and authenticity.

Lueck's (2012) exploratory analysis of celebrity-fan interactions on Kim Kardashian's Facebook page was one of the first studies to demonstrate the power of embedding personal stories (emotional and transformational) into social media posts. It revealed how an emotional connection is used to engage audience members in effective parasocial interaction as the audience is 'constantly rewarded' with information about the celebrity's private life, her/his everyday activities, and lifestyle. The audience also follows closely as they seek to emulate the celebrity's way of life by purchasing the same brands and products. Recent studies, such as Aw and Chuah (2021, p. 154) highlight just how important it is for SMIs to engage with audiences more interactively. For example, directly responding to followers' comments, and taking advantage of content analysis methods to 'identify and learn' from posts which depict desirable parasocial relationship characteristics, including SMI 'attractiveness, prestige and expertise'. They explain that consumers are more likely to participate in parasocial relationships with SMIs who they believe display visually appealing content, status, and knowledge in their domain. Attractive content could consist of certain types of social content such as vlogs, or physical features such as facial expressions and the way an individual looks directly at the camera, the positioning of the camera, and ability to zoom in on key features of the face and/or zoom out to capture full body shots, as well as the use of imaginative and engaging language. Ultimately, establishing parasocial relations with SMIs has been found to increase followers' likelihood of commenting, and this in turn boosts the credibility of the SMI for other online followers (Reinikainen et al., 2020).

Sometimes consumers engage in parasocial relationships for entertainment value, although they do not engage with the behaviours being promoted by the SMI. This was the case in Sokolova and Perez' (2021) study of the parasocial interaction of YouTube fitness SMIs. This calls into question audience motivations for engaging with SMIs. These motivations do not always relate to the intended strategic goals communicated in the content. This means that organisations seeking to work with SMIs who engage with their audiences in this way and have established emotional connections, and an audience who have a relationship with the SMI, need to be aware that the intended strategic goals of a campaign, and the desired results, may not always be achieved as they were originally envisioned.

SMI Gendered and Exploitative Labour

In our definition of SMI, we outlined that SMIs typically receive some form of compensation from organisations for embedding paid and/or sponsored content into their posts in the form of both written and visual narrations which feature products, services, and experiences. It is important to consider the labour involved in establishing oneself as an SMI, and how this might impact organisations seeking to establish collaborations with SMIs.

Digital labour is a term coined by Fuchs (2014, p. 4) to depict the 'collective work force that is required for the existence, usage and application of digital media'. The term captures all forms of paid and unpaid labour that have emerged from the internet and the rise of social media platforms (Scholz, 2013). Indeed, aspiring SMIs often engage in social media activities during their leisure time to create content for free, and this content is often used by organisations (Duffy, 2015; Duffy & Hund, 2015). The question of exploitation arises as this 'free content' is leveraged by organisations who can generate some form of profit from making use of this material.

This research questions the ways in which women's often low or unpaid digital labours require them to invest emotional energy and time as they produce content that generates profit for online platforms (Duffy & Schwartz, 2018). In their study of Kate Middleton fashion bloggers, McFarlane et al. (2022) revealed the discrepancy between content creators who were able to capitalise on their labour by generating the equivalent of a full-time income from click-through banner advertisements, affiliate sales, luxury brand collaborations, and developing online retail offerings, and other aspiring SMIs who were unable to successfully complete the journey from consumer to what Scaraboto and Fischer (2013) have elsewhere termed as 'institutional entrepreneurs'. This form of gender exploitation is also evident in Drenten, Gurrieri and Tyler's (2019) research on the sexualised labour performed by female influencers on Instagram, who create visually explicit and openly sexual body poses to capture followers' attention and increase their chances of earning more money per sponsored post.

Organisations seeking to collaborate with aspiring SMIs must therefore be cautious. When seeking to recruit SMIs, organisations should ensure that SMIs are compensated for the use of their content in a way that is agreed by both parties. Doing so will recognise the value of this labour, and help alleviate concerns surrounding exploitation of digital labour and the content it produces.

SMIs and Inequalities

Within the SMI literature, it is understood that SMIs often display levels of power and privilege in their social media content (Khamis, Ang, & Welling, 2017). This is often laden with comments and suggestions that draw attention to inequalities, including social class, and ethnicity (Abidin, 2016a, 2016b; Iqani, 2019; McFarlane & Samsioe, 2020). A study by Leban et al. (2021) revealed a tension that exists between high-net-worth (HNW) lifestyle SMIs such as Kylie Jenner and Paris Hilton (who become famous for sharing their luxurious lifestyle) and the need to remain true to morals in the consumption decisions and choices that they make by engaging in altruistic activities, e.g., hosting charitable celebrations, or establishing businesses in order to support a societal cause. Studies are bringing in wider voices such as that of the Korean 'ajumma', middle-aged married Korean women, whose digital self-presentation strategies based on external appearance help them to take responsibility for fostering media culture and communities across social media platforms (Moon & Abidin, 2021).

Certainly, as we have seen in earlier sections of this chapter, the global influencer industry incorporates SMIs from all nationalities. Yet, organisations seeking to collaborate with SMIs must be careful to be representative, and not exclude hard-to-reach groups such as low-income consumers and individuals experiencing poverty. These hard-to-reach groups are extremely important and many organisations within the third sector are increasingly looking to find new ways of engaging with these communities. Often, they seek to introduce campaigns that effect behavioural change. For example the Scottish government released a paper to reduce vaping rates among young people living in less wealthy areas (Todd, 2022). Hence, there is a lot of potential for organisations to collaborate with SMIs to address inequalities and engage hard-to-reach audiences.

Virtual Influencers (VI)

Virtual influencers (VIs) are artificial and computer-generated personas developed by programmers and media agencies who perform tasks like humans (Thomas & Fowler, 2021; Stein et al., 2022). VIs have no physical or virtual limitations and are able to nurture a large online audience in a short time frame, which enables content creators to maintain total control over content and campaigns from start to finish (Bringe, 2022). This is advantageous for organisations because it also means that posts and content can be created and released continually, regardless of the time zone. For these reasons, global brands such as

Samsung, Prada, Amazon, Puma, Nike, and even US music festival Coachella, are engaging in around-the-clock partnerships with VIs and the agencies that create and manage their content (Taslaud, 2022).

The possible forms and domains that VIs can depict and the various human tasks that can be performed through content creation are endless. Miquela Sousa or Lil Miquela debuted on Instagram in 2016 and quickly amassed millions of followers and paid partnerships with fashion brands, despite being open about being 'a robot'. In 2019 they featured on TIME magazine's '25 most influential People on the Internet' (Time, 2018). That same year, French luxury brand Balmain, famous for partnering with A-list celebrities Rhianna, Kendall Jenner, and Kim Kardashian, signed VIs Shudu, Margot, and Xhi, claiming that they better captured the inclusive and diverse values of the brand (Minton, 2018). In 2023, the top 10 VIs worldwide include a wide audience demographic. They feature fictional characters from Japan @imma.gram (macro-VIinfluencer 403+ thousand Instagram followers), Vietnam @e.m.oi (nano-VIinfluencer 1, 130+ thousand), South Africa and the first black virtual creator worldwide @shudu.gram (macro-VIinfluencer 239+ thousand), as well as domain specific VI sports and cycling ambassador @iongottlich (micro-VIinfluencer 70.6+ thousand) and a baby doll @re-alqaiqai (macro-VIinfluencer 335+ thousand) who is the family doll of Serena Williams and Alex Ohanian (Taslaud, 2022). Lastly, the World Health Organisation (WHO) used Knox Frost, a VI, for its COVID-19 campaign (Sands, Campbell, et al., 2022).

A VI study conducted in the US by the Influencer Marketing Factory found that 58 per cent of survey participants followed at least one VI, with 35 per cent admitting to purchasing a product endorsed by a VI (Influencer Marketing Factory, 2022). In terms of targeting specific audiences, the most lucrative seems to be the 18–44 age group who primarily use social media platforms YouTube (28.75 per cent), Instagram (28.4 per cent) and TikTok (20.5 per cent) to engage with VIs (Influencer Marketing Factory, 2022). Audiences are becoming increasingly comfortable with VIs and identify with their personalised content and recommendations in the same way as they do with human influencers (Sands, Campbell, et al., 2022). It has been suggested that consumers' experiences with artificial intelligence (AI) recommendation systems such as Netflix, has helped shaped this comfortableness, and it might be in the interests of VI developers to leverage this format (ibid.). However, organisations considering working with agencies specialising in VIs should exercise caution, and partner with those experienced with the brands and domains that they seek to work in. This is because VIs are also capable of transgressions, and these can have a negative impact on attitudes towards the brand and purchase intentions, even if this transgression is not related to the brand (Thomas & Fowler, 2021). For example, even Lil Miquela, who kissed model Bella Hadid in a Calvin Klein ad, was negatively received by audiences for 'queerbating' (Petrarca, 2019). That said, a crucial difference between SMIs and VIs is that when a VI transgression occurs, replacing a VI with a celebrity endorser was found to produce more favourable attitudes towards the brand and increase the likelihood of purchase (Thomas & Fowler, 2021). This means that VIs are still recognised as being not as unique as SMIs and it is consequently easier to replace them. This is perhaps because consumers find VI influencers to be more socially distant, and for that reason there is a greater need to develop parasocial interaction with followers (Sands, Campbell, et al., 2022).

Ethically, the use of VIs has raised some concerns, not only surrounding the question of who maintains control over content creation and audience in-teractions (e.g. the agency and/or the organisation commissioning a specific campaign for a desired target audience) but also over the unrealistic beauty standards and bodily depictions of many VIs (Sands, Ferraro, et al., 2022). Organisations seeking to engage in partnerships with VIs must therefore consider the potential negative societal effects of those involvements and take care to avoid setting unrealistic beauty and bodily standards. Collaborating with regulatory bodies and organisations such as Meta can help to set ethical standards and expectations in terms of how VI identities are created and communicated to audiences.

Conclusion

In this chapter we have defined what a social media influencer (SMI) consists of in the contemporary advertising sphere and charted the emergence of this phenomena alongside the 'demotic media' turn. We have captured the SMI's role as a content creator and discussed the various types of domains and shared common content ideals, beliefs, and values across each sphere of influence. Emerging new forms of SMI such as 'petinfluencers', 'genuineinfluencers', and 'fininfluencers' have been highlighted as, at present, emerging and growing domains. Organisations must be aware of these different interest groups to ensure that a brand and/or product does not offend and/or isolate the values of other SMI interested audiences across domains. Next, we considered the dif-ferent levels of SMI – mega, macro, micro, and nano – the advantages and disadvantages of these, and how advertisers can select the most apt SMI for a particular brand and/or product to reach the intended audience. This was followed by the role of sponsorships and the importance of selecting a credible and authentic SMI to establish trust among consumers. An SMI selection checklist was offered, and suggestions made as to how to achieve a careful balance of genuine versus sponsored content to maintain audience trust and achieve effective SMI sponsorships. Establishing parasocial relationships with followers that offer intimate details on the behind-the-scenes life of the influ-encer, and engaging in emotional two-way interactions (e.g. via comments functions etc.) is another strategy for maintaining the balance between genuine and commercial content. Organisations have a responsibility to ensure fair collaborations, safeguarding aspiring SMI content and ensuring that the labour involved in creating it is compensated. The role of inequalities within the SMI literature and domains was considered and suggestions made on how to better use SMIs to target hard-to-reach and under-represented consumer groups. Lastly, we explored the introduction of virtual influencers (VIs) and outlined some opportunities and challenges of partnering with the agencies that develop and manage their online presence.

References

Abidin, C. (2015). Communicative intimacies: Influencers and perceived interconnectedness. *Ada, 8,* 1–16.

Abidin, C. (2016a). Aren't these just young, rich women doing vain things online?: Influencer selfies as subversive frivolity. *Social Media + Society, 2*(2), 1–17.

Abidin, C. (2016b). Visibility labour: Engaging with influencers' fashion brands and #OOTD advertorial campaigns on Instagram. *Media International Australia, Incorporating Culture & Policy, 161*(1), 86–100.

Aspire (2023). About us. www.aspire.io/about-us. (Accessed: 16 August 2023).

Avallone, A. (2021). Farewell super influencer? The time has come for 'genuinfluencers', 19th November, Morning Future. Accessed online, 25/01/2023. www.morningfuture. com/en/2021/11/19/social-network-influencer-genuinfluencer/#:~:text=E2%80%9CThe %20term%20genuinfluencers%20was%20coined%20in%20January%202021,tips%20that %20are%20not%20bound%20by%20commercial%20agreements

Aw, E. C. X., and Chuah, S. H. W. (2021) "Stop the unattainable ideal for an ordinary me!" fostering parasocial relationships with social media influencers: The role of self-discrepancy, *Journal of Business Research*. Elsevier, *132*(April), pp. 146–157. doi: 10.1016/ j.jbusres.2021.04.025.

Barrett, C. (2022). Beware influencers plugging the financial advice gap. *Financial Times*. Accessed online, 20/01/2023. ft.com

Boerman, S. C. (2020). The effects of the standardized instagram disclosure for micro- and meso-influencers, *Computers in Human Behavior*. Elsevier, 103 (May 2019), pp. 199–207. doi: 10.1016/j.chb.2019.09.015.

Bringé, A. (2022). Council post: The rise of virtual influencers and what it means for brands, Forbes. www.forbes.com/sites/forbescommunicationscouncil/2022/10/18/the-rise-of-virtual-influencers-and-what-it-means-for-brands/

Burton, M. (2019). Zagat, Explained: The guidebook was once a go-to source for restaurant recommendations, updated 2nd April 2019, Eater online accessed 12/1/2023. www.eater. com/2018/3/5/17080772/zagat-guide-reviews-google-infatuation-sale

Campbell, C., and Farrell, J. R. (2020). More than meets the eye: The functional components underlying influencer marketing. *Business Horizons, 63*(4), 469–479.

Cornwell, T. B., and Katz, H. (2020). *Influencer*, Taylor & Francis. https://online.vitalsource. co.uk/books/9781000317862

Drenten, J., Gurrieri, L., and Tyler, M. (2019). Sexualised labour in digital culture: Instagram influencers, porn chic and the monetisation of attention, *Gender, Work & Organization*, (November 2018), pp. 1–26. doi: 10.1111/gwao.12354.

Duffy, B. E. (2015). Gendering the labor of social media production, *Feminist Media Studies, 15*(4), pp. 710–714. doi: 10.1080/14680777.2015.1053715.

Duffy, B. E., and Hund, E. (2015). "Having it all" on social media: Entrepreneurial femininity and self-branding among fashion bloggers, *Social Media+ Society, 1*(2), pp. 1–11. doi: 10.1016/j.chb.2015.08.026.

Duffy, B. E., and Schwartz, B. (2018). Digital "women's work?": Job recruitment ads and the feminization of social media employment, *New Media and Society*, *20*(8), pp. 2972–2989. doi: 10.1177/1461444817738237.

Evans, N. J., Phua, J., Lim, J., & Jun, H. (2017). Disclosing Instagram influencer advertising: The effects of disclosure language on advertising recognition, attitudes, and behavioral intent, *Journal of Interactive Advertising*, *17*(2), pp. 138–149.

Fohr (2023). Fohr Influencer Community. www.fohr.co/influencer

Forbes (2022). The state of influencer marketing: Top insights for 2022. 14th January 2022, Forbes. Accessed online 20/01/2023. www.forbes.com/sites/forbesagencycouncil/2022/01/14/the-state-of-influencer-marketing-top-insights-for-2022/?sh=1990bf8e5c78

Frederick, B. (2023). The top 100 social media influencers worldwide. *Search Engine Journal* (online) January 10th. Accessed online 12/1/2023. www.searchenginejournal.com/top-social-media-influencers/475776/#close

Fuchs, C. (2014). *Social Media: A Critical Introduction*. Sage, London.

Geyser, W. (2022). The State of Influencer Marketing 2020: Benchmark Report. Influencer Marketing Hub, 8th February 2022. Accessed online 18/01/2023. https://influencer marketinghub.com/influencer-marketing-benchmark-report-2020/

Horton, D., & Richard Wohl, R. (1956). Mass communication and para-social interaction: Observations on intimacy at a distance. *Psychiatry*, *19*(3), 215–229.

Hudders, L., De Jans, S., and De Veirman, M. (2021). The commercialization of social media stars: A literature review and conceptual framework on the strategic use of social media influencers, *International Journal of Advertising*. Routledge, *40*(3), pp. 327–375. doi: 10.1080/02650487.2020.1836925.

Influencer Marketing Factory (2022). Virtual influencers survey and infographic. 29th March. Accessed online 25/01/2023. https://theinfluencermarketingfactory.com/virtual-influencers-survey-infographic/

Iqani, M. (2019). Picturing luxury, producing value: The cultural labour of social media brand influencers in South Africa, *International Journal of Cultural Studies*, 22(2), pp. 229–247. doi: 10.1177/1367877918821237.

Kay, S., Mulcahy, R., and Parkinson, J. (2020). When less is more: The impact of macro and micro social media influencers' disclosure, *Journal of Marketing Management*. Routledge, *36*(3–4), pp. 248–278. doi:10.1080/0267257X.2020.1718740.

Khamis, S., Ang, L., and Welling, R. (2017). Self-branding, "micro-celebrity" and the rise of Social Media Influencers, *Celebrity Studies*, *8*(2), pp. 191–208. doi: 10.1080/193923 97.2016.1218292.

Kozinets, R. V. et al. (2010). Networked Narratives: Understanding Word-of-Mouth Marketing in Online Communities, *Journal of Marketing*, 74(2), pp. 71–89. doi: 10.1509/jmkg.74.2.71.

Leban, M. et al. (2021). Constructing personas: How high-net-worth social media influencers reconcile ethicality and living a luxury lifestyle, *Journal of Business Ethics*. Springer Netherlands, *169*(2), pp. 225–239. doi: 10.1007/s10551-020-04485-6.

Logan, A. (2016). Consuming Kate: Unpacking the Feminine Ideologies Surrounding the Celebrity Princess Brand. PhD diss., University of Strathclyde.

Lueck, J. A. (2015). Friend-zone with benefits: The parasocial advertising of Kim Kardashian. *Journal of Marketing Communications*, *21*(2), 91–109.

Mardon, R., Molesworth, M., and Grigore, G. (2018). YouTube beauty gurus and the emotional labour of tribal entrepreneurship, *Journal of Business Research*. Elsevier, *92* (January 2017), pp. 443–454. doi: 10.1016/j.jbusres.2018.04.017.

McFarlane, A., Hamilton, K., and Hewer, P. (2022). Putting passion to work: Passionate labour in the fashion blogosphere, *European Journal of Marketing*, *56*(4), pp. 1210–1231. doi: 10.1108/EJM-08-2019-0642.

McFarlane, A. and Samsioe, E. (2020). #50+ fashion Instagram influencers: Cognitive age and aesthetic digital labours, *Journal of Fashion Marketing and Management*, *24*(3), pp. 399–413. doi: 10.1108/JFMM-08-2019-0177.

Minton, M. (2018). Balmain drops the Kardashians in favor of CGI models, Page Six.: https://pagesix.com/2018/08/30/balmain-drops-the-kardashians-in-favor-of-cgi-models/

MNFST (2019). 8 brands already using the power of nano-influencers. *MNFST*, 24th July 2019. Accessed online 18/01/2023. https://mnfst.medium.com/8-brands-already-using-the-power-of-nano-influencers-fd4cdf8a6b8d

Moon, J. and Abidin, C. (2021). Online ajumma: Self-presentations of contemporary elderly women via digital media in Korea, *Mediated Interfaces*, pp. 177–189. doi: 10.5040/9781501356216.ch-008

Newberry, C. (2022). How the TikTok algorithm works (and how to work with it in 2023), 11th February, Hootsuite online. Accessed online 18/1/2023. https://blog.hootsuite.com/tiktok-algorithm/

Nielsen. (2022). Social currency: How much is a World Cup influencer worth? September. Accessed online 20/01/2023. www.nielsen.com/insights/2022/social-currency-how-much-is-a-world-cup-influencer-worth/#:~:text=According%20to%20the%202022%20Nielsen%20ROI%20Report%2071%25,who%20did%20not%20see%20the%20influencer%20ads%202.

Oliver et al. (2022). Cristiano Ronaldo signs NFT deal with crypto exchange Binance, *Financial Times*. Accessed online 18/01/2023. www.ft.com/content/607dfcce-3cea-43af-b94a-a311345a6ea3

de Perthuis, K. and Findlay, R. (2019). How fashion travels: The fashionable ideal in the age of Instagram, *Fashion Theory – Journal of Dress Body and Culture*. Routledge, *23*(2), pp. 219–242. doi: 10.1080/1362704X.2019.1567062.

Petrarca, E. (2019). Calvin Klein apologizes for Bella Hadid and Lil Miquela campaign. The Cut. Accessed online 18/1/2023. www.thecut.com/2019/05/bella-hadid-lil-miquela-calvin-klein-apol-ogy.html

Reinikainen, H. et al. (2020). "You really are a great big sister" – parasocial relationships, credibility, and the moderating role of audience comments in influencer marketing, *Journal of Marketing Management*. Routledge, *36*(3–4), pp. 279–298. doi: 10.1080/0267257X.2019.1708781.

Sands, S., Campbell, C. L., et al. (2022). Unreal influence: Leveraging AI in influencer marketing, *European Journal of Marketing*, *56*(6), pp. 1721–1747. doi: 10.1108/EJM-12-2019-0949.

Sands, S., Ferraro, C., et al. (2022). False idols: Unpacking the opportunities and challenges of falsity in the context of virtual influencers, *Business Horizons*. Elsevier, *65*(6), pp. 777–788. doi: 10.1016/j.bushor.2022.08.002.

Santora, J. (2023). Key Influencer marketing statistics to drive your strategy in 2023. Influencer Marketing Hub, 11th January. Accessed online 18/01/2023. https://influencermarketinghub.com/influencer-marketing-statistics/

Scaraboto, D. and Fischer, E. (2013). Frustrated fatshionistas: An institutional theory perspective on consumer quests for greater choice in mainstream markets, *Journal of Consumer Research*. doi: 10.1086/668298.

Schneier, M. (2016). Coach confirms its partnership with Selena Gomez, *New York Times* Accessed online 18/1/2023. www.nytimes.com/2016/12/16/fashion/selena-gomez-coach-partnership-confirmed.html

Scholz, T. (2013), *Digital Labor: The Internet as Playground and Factory*. Routledge, New York.

Schouten, A. P., Janssen, L., and Verspaget, M. (2020). Celebrity vs. Influencer endorsements in advertising: The role of identification, credibility, and Product-Endorser fit, *International Journal of Advertising*. Routledge, *39*(2), pp. 258–281. doi: 10.1080/026504 87.2019.1634898.

Senft, T. M. (2008). Camgirls: Celebrity and community in the age of social networks, 4, 189–193.

Sokolova, K. and Perez, C. (2021). You follow fitness influencers on YouTube. But do you actually exercise? How parasocial relationships, and watching fitness influencers, relate to intentions to exercise, *Journal of Retailing and Consumer Services*. Elsevier, 58(November 2019), p. 102276. doi: 10.1016/j.jretconser.2020.102276

Statistica (2023). Influencer marketing market size worldwide from 2016 to 2022. Accessed online 12/1/2023. www.statista.com/statistics/1092819/global-influencer-market-size/

Stein, J. P., Linda Breves, P., & Anders, N. (2022). Parasocial interactions with real and virtual influencers: The role of perceived similarity and human-likeness. New Media & Society, 14614448221102900.

Taslaud, G. (2022). Top 10 virtual influencers in 2023 – Most influential online creators to follow, INSG 28th December. Accessed online 25/01/2023. www.insg.co/en/virtual-influencers-world/

Thomas, V. L. and Fowler, K. (2021). Close encounters of the AI kind: Use of AI influencers as brand endorsers, *Journal of Advertising*. Routledge, *50*(1), pp. 11–25. doi: 10. 1080/00913367.2020.1810595.

Time (2018). The 25 most influential people on the internet. Accessed online 12/1/2023. https://time.com/5324130/most-influential-internet/

Todd, M. (2022). Vaping Products – tightening the rules on advertising and promotion: consultation 2022. 3rd February, Scottish Government. Accessed online. www.gov.scot/ publications/tightening-rules-advertising-promoting-vaping-products-consultation-paper-2022/

Turner, G. (2009). Ordinary people and the media: The demotic turn. *Ordinary People and the Media*, 1–200.

De Veirman, M., & Hudders, L. (2020). Disclosing sponsored Instagram posts: The role of material connection with the brand and message-sidedness when disclosing covert advertising. *International Journal of Advertising*, *39*(1), 94–130.

Veresiu, E. and Parmentier, M. (2021). Advanced style influencers: Confronting gendered ageism in fashion and beauty markets, *Journal of the Association for Consumer Research*, pp. 1–15.

Ye, G. et al. (2021). The value of influencer marketing for business: A bibliometric analysis and managerial implications, *Journal of Advertising*. Routledge, *50*(2), pp. 160–178. doi: 10.1080/00913367.2020.1857888.

9 Content Curation: Best Practices and Techniques

By Dr Jackie Cameron

Learning Outcomes

- To develop an understanding of the role that content curation plays in stimulating social media brand-related engagement.
- To identify key theories and concepts about consumer behaviour in the digital environment and apply these in marketing content curation.
- To appreciate the role of copyright and other laws that protect intellectual property in content curation.
- To develop practical skills in content curation, including best practice in the use of creative assets developed by other parties for marketing purposes.

Content Curation: Information Guide in a Digitally Networked Society

By 2023, according to data tracked by DataReportal, nearly two-thirds of the world's population were spending more than two hours a day, or 15 per cent of their waking hours, on social media sites (Kemp, 2023). Facebook, YouTube, WhatsApp and Instagram were the most frequently visited channels, though most social media users were accessing more than seven social platforms each month. While the main reason cited for this high usage has been to maintain contact with friends and family, the globe's nearly five billion social media users were also spending more time than ever actively looking for content such as videos and articles, finding things to do and buy, paying close attention to what their connections were talking about, and sharing and discussing ideas online. It is against this backdrop of the maturation of the network society (Castells, 2004), with cultural, political, economic, and social influences combining and evolving through digital technologies, that the professional content curator has emerged. Content curator is now an established specialist content marketing role in marketing communications and media businesses.

In this age of the digital economy, content is widely available on most topics to meet the insatiable demand for online information and entertainment. The purpose of curation is to sift through the deluge of social media

DOI: 10.4324/9781003346500-9

posts, articles, videos, podcasts, and other formats to find pieces that resonate with specific target markets and can be used in a way that responds to specific content marketing aims. It involves the use of content that already exists.

It is an alternative to conceptualising and developing creative assets, though it involves more than merely drawing on other people's work. In this marketing technique, content is typically produced by others with curators making or advising on adaptations or using the information in skilful ways that suit a brand or organisation's communications objectives. In another dimension to the re-framing, repurposing, and reposting of information, the marketing practitioner curator also draws on the content flows or curation activities of other information gatekeepers and guides in the social media environment. These moderators and mediators are also content curators and include customers, their contacts, and individuals regarded as influencers of consumers and social media users. In this chapter we look mainly at the processes and practices of marketers who are content curators. Tasked with selecting, packaging, and distributing information to achieve marketing objectives, the curator has an ever-expanding suite of technologies and tools to guide content cultivation activities.

Aggregation of content is a similar concept, with various applications and automation services put to work scouring the digital landscape and extracting sections or entire pieces for websites, social media feeds, email newsletters, and other platforms and formats.

Curation adds to this process the application of human judgement, as content is chosen, positioned, adapted, framed, embellished, and presented in a way that is valuable and relevant for pre-specified target audiences as well as the organisation paying for the curated content. Digital information, also known as artefacts in keeping with the theme of the editor working like a museum curator, is gathered and personalised, or tailored, for specific customers or content communities in a procedure known as mass customisation (see Lies, 2019). This information is also changed into new formats, for example complex technical articles aimed at specialists are distilled and demystified into interactive infographics for consumers.

Curators typically use technology for example Google Alerts and search engines to help them find content. However, they also apply nuanced understandings of specific content angles, topics, themes, and formats that are likely to resonate with people in their target markets and that will, ultimately, help to deliver on predetermined marketing objectives. Computers can sift and order content based on codes that reveal our appetites for certain types of information and serve up, or aggregate, posts. The human dimension of curation is often referred to as 'adding value' to the content, with curators finding ways to make aspects of the content borrowed from others more attractive or valuable.

For many content consumers, the 'added value' aspect of the curation is the discovery and sharing of content that is useful and timely. Others appreciate the extra insights that are included, through commentaries and visual and other interpretations of information.

The goal of curation is to reduce information overload by following a 'less is more' approach in selecting and distributing content (Cohen, 2012). The curator identifies what they believe are the most important, best quality pieces for target audiences that are also appropriate for the marketing agenda of the organisation paying for the work of sourcing and repurposing content. Sharing and discussing a selection of thoughtfully curated content can position you or the business you represent as an expert on a particular niche topic and can also help foster relations with specific people and brands (Sutherland, 2020, pp. 209–210). Content is used to create connections and build relationships among customers and between the brand and customers. As a growing body of studies (see Santos et al., 2022, p. 1) underscore: 'In the era of relational marketing, social media brand communities are vital and constitute strategic instruments to induce and nurture consumer-brand relations'.

As with all forms of content marketing, the content product of curation is not the end goal of activity. It is part of the tactical roll out of campaigns, is ideally underpinned by a content marketing strategy or plan, and is part of the overall digital marketing strategy. There is even more to the curation role than marrying content that is a suitable thematic and topic match with brands and target audiences. Instead, the curator must also understand how to combine digital marketing techniques and knowledge of how consumers behave in the digital environment so that they are stimulating conversations and interactions between individuals as well as the company and its clients. They should ideally be able to manipulate social media users to share content that Lies (2019, p. 138) describes as 'edutainment', which can be defined as 'appealing, playful and entertaining communication to trigger viral effects, especially in social media'. While content that gains traction and goes viral is highly sought-after, there are also many occasions where curating artefacts that may be seen or heard by fewer people is more effective for achieving marketing objectives. This is particularly the case for niche products and services and business-to-business information. Take, for example, insurance for ships: you may need less than a handful of people to receive your content – provided these are the right people with the ability to respond to the communications and ultimately influence a large purchase decision.

There is a belief that it is cheaper, faster, and often more efficient to curate rather than create content, but this is often not the case. Curation enables brands to piggyback off the intellectual property of other parties, and the time and resources that have been poured into the original production and distribution. However, it must be done with careful consideration of marketing objectives and principles, or it can backfire or simply not work at all. An example of how the expenses of curation can be just as high, or greater than the cost of original content creation, is where textual information is produced in a new format such as an animated video or interactive infographic. There are also many curation risks that must be mitigated, ranging from legal claims over copyright to reputational harm from using inappropriate content. This, in turn, suggests that the individuals who are tasked with curation require certain knowledge and skills to ensure that content complies with legislation while also delivering on marketing objectives. In the next section, we will focus on theories and concepts that help marketers to understand how to evoke decisions and consumer behaviour that meets direct and indirect business goals.

Stimulating Brand Engagement Through Content Curation

As social media continues to evolve, experts and practitioners have been grappling with how to work with content in this environment in a way that is good for a product or service. It is widely acknowledged among marketers that it is important to stimulate positive interactions between businesses and customers in the digital domain and content curation can fuel this activity. This interactivity between businesses and target audiences is understood as consumer brand engagement (CBE) and it is clearly a reflection of the state of the relationship between a brand and its customers and potential customers. Trunfio and Rossi (2021, p. 271) note that the concept of customer engagement emerged in 2006, with the Advertising Research Foundation, American Association of Advertising Agencies, and the Association of National Advertisers collectively characterising it as 'turning on a prospect to a brand idea enhanced by the surrounding context'. Knowledge is still being developed on how consumers influence and drive CBE, which is a multi-dimensional concept (see Santos et al., 2022). Nevertheless, CBE is understood to encompass cognitive, emotional, and behavioural elements and can be defined as 'a consumer's psychological state and behavioural manifestations that occur through the process of value co-creation involving resource integration and service changes in consumer-brand interactive service systems' (Ndhlovu & Maree, 2022, p. 229).

Content curators need to understand the key tenets of CBE so that they can source and shape content in a way that helps to generate the right type of engagement for the brands they represent. Among the examples of relevant marketing objectives are:

• Increasing brand awareness, which is the ability of a potential buyer to recognise a product.
• Brand loyalty, which reflects the attachment a consumer has to a brand (Aaker, 1991, in Schivinski, 2021, p. 595).
• Brand equity, which can be defined as the 'positive perception or emotional attachment that consumers have towards a brand, which can influence their purchasing decisions and overall loyalty to the brand' (Hayes, 2023).

An added challenge for the curator, compared to the original creator, is how to ensure that the awareness, loyalty and equity are focused on their own brands that they have been tasked with promoting rather than the brand that has provided the seed content. Furthermore, these underlying brands must be assessed carefully so that they are compatible with the curator's brand and also so that curation activities are viewed favourably by target audiences. There are cases where the curation is mutually beneficial for brands, and others where this approach has backfired because a brand is seen to be hijacked or organisational values between two brands that are tied together through content curation are incongruent.

Social media is seen as highly conducive to creating, nurturing, and monitoring relationships. Consumer engagement with brands in social media has become a considerable field of study because, as Schivinski (2021, p. 594) points out, it is an important feature of digital marketing strategy and performance. 'In order to effectively engage consumers in brand-related social media activities, practitioners must understand the drivers of engagement with brands online' (ibid). This includes:

- Identifying types of consumers and their motivations for engaging with brands.
- Intensity of brand engagement (low, medium, high) of subtypes of consumers.
- What drives specific ways for consumers to interact with a brand on social media, such as reading, watching, clicking, sharing, liking, and creating brand-related content (ibid. pp. 594–595).

Social media engagement as a concept, meanwhile, is still being clarified by experts, though they broadly agree that it is behaviour that goes beyond commercial transactions and is a state that includes cognitive and emotional dimensions (see Chahal et al., 2020, p. 193). Marketers work towards building positive associations as this in turn should have the effect of directly and indirectly driving profitable activity. Chahal, Wirtz and Verma (2020, p. 191) point out that customers' social media engagement with brands is viewed as an important performance indicator that needs to be factored into promotional strategies. They found, in a study involving more than 400 Generation Y social media users in India, that social media brand engagement is positively related to brand equity, or brand reputation. Gkikas et al. (2022, p. 1) highlight the close link between CBE in social media and increased conversion and purchase intention as well as brand trust and brand loyalty.

There are three main types of social media activities that play a role in CBE that curators should consider when making their editorial choices with a view to generating positive brand-related engagement (see Schivinski, 2021, p. 596):

- **Consumption**. Social media activities associated with a minimum, or passive, level of engagement. This includes looking at pictures and text on a brand's social media page without actively participating.

- **Contribution**. More engaged, or active, consumers share, comment, and discuss brand content, with the curator aiming to convert consumers into brand endorsers.
- **Creation**. Considered the highest level of engagement, this entails consumers producing, publishing and co-developing brand-related content. Examples include initiating posts, publishing reviews, and uploading user-generated media.

Curators can take into consideration the three main types of social media users – consumers, contributors, and creators – to develop ways the brand can connect with, and deepen links, with individuals from consumption through to contribution and creation. An example may be taking user-generated content and packaging it, with commentary, into a piece that is shared or reshared by the brand. This shows appreciation to the most active consumers and can encourage them to develop more content. Understanding the different levels of activity plays into ways that curation is measured. For example, metrics that indicate a post has been viewed may be acceptable to gauge consumption whereas you will be monitoring shares, likes, and comments to assess how successful you have been at motivating contributors. In addition, curators may want to focus on transforming contributors into creators as a way of widening the pool of social media users who are regarded as being the most brand loyal.

The three levels of activity broadly correspond to different stages of the customer buying funnel. You can combine curation with creation to develop content that aims to connect with and activate decisions at different stages of the

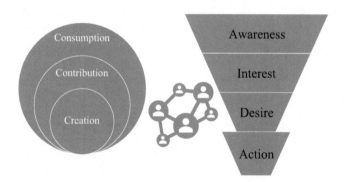

Figure 9.1 Stimulating brand engagement in social media environment.

Activating consumers on their buying journeys. Content curators must be highly skilled at finding, repurposing, and sharing digital artefacts that not only interest consumers but trigger actions that achieve marketing objectives. There are three main types of social media engagement, from passive consumption to active contribution and creation. Curators need to cater for buyers at different stages of the purchase funnel, starting with the awareness and interest phases to sparking the desire and encouraging people to become actively engaged with fellow consumers and build brand-related relationships (see Schivinski, 2021).

customer journey. Remember the seminal hierarchical model of the way consumers move from awareness to interest in a product to the desire to buy it and finally take action (AIDA, and variants). Think about how you can use curation as part of your content marketing plan to push consumers to different stages. It is worth noting, though, that levels of activity don't always correlate directly to intention to purchase. It is possible to have consumption-only social media engagement that leads to a profitable action. Conversely, creators don't always purchase.

Theories of Consumer Behaviour in the Digital Domain

It can be useful to understand the underlying reasons for consumers connecting with brands in social media to angle curated content so that it is effective and meets marketing objectives. In a systematic review of more than 130 studies on consumer engagement in social media brand communities, Santos et al. (2022, p. 9) found that two foundational theories underpin much of the research in this field:

- **Uses and Gratifications Theory (UGT)** (Blumler, 1979), which seeks to explain why people use media and what they get out of it or how it satisfies them. Reasons for individuals using social media include: social, such as making friends; entertainment, for example sharing jokes; and functional, for informational and educational purposes. Emotional motivations can range from escaping from reality to building a public persona that encapsulates self-identity. As a curator, it is important to understand which uses you are catering for with your choices of topics and formats.
- **Social Identity Theory (SIT)** (Tajfel & Turner, 1986), which relates to the way we define ourselves as a group member, in this instance as a part of the social group referred to as a brand community. Applying this theory to your curation activity: examine your communities' perceived characteristics and think carefully about how you position your community members and brand, your tone of voice, and how you refer to the audiences who are consuming, contributing, and co-creating your content. Explore how you can harness the desire for group belonging, for example, through campaigns and images in assets that help sharpen the links between individuals and the group.

Other theories to consider include:

- **Social exchange theory (SET)**, applied in some studies to explain the expectation that an effort to reach out or communicate will be reciprocated. Exchanging tangible and intangible benefits through social media can facilitate the creation and maintenance of valuable relationships between brands and consumers (see Santos et al., 2022, p. 9). In the curation context, this suggests that you should think of ways to reflect to those who reach out to your brand that you have heard them and are responding back. This can be directly, through a post, or you could incorporate, or embed, a comment into a digital artefact that is shared back to the community.

• **Social capital theory (SCT)**, which taps into the understanding that groups who share values and resources can benefit from personal connections. An example of where social capital is at work in the social media are intermediaries such as Airbnb where reviews can impact positively and negatively on bookings for accommodation providers (Kenton, 2022). Sharing a job opportunity with contacts on LinkedIn is another example of how social capital can be employed. Habibi et al. (2014) opine that the building blocks of a brand community are four relationships: customer-product, customer-brand, customer-company, and customer-other customers. Underlying this, meanwhile, is the concept of shared consciousness, which is a 'felt sense of connection among members within a brand community' and a feeling that 'an invisible hand connects them to each other and separates them from outsiders' (Habibi, 2014, p. 153). As a curator, you can investigate ways to build this connection, as the invisible hand, for example by paying close attention to community-specific jargon and topics and facilitating conversations. Community members also have a sense of commitment to the welfare of their fellow members (ibid), which you can foster as Airbnb has.

• **Trust transfer theory**. Trust is required for consumers to develop loyalty towards a brand and an exchange relationship. Trust among consumers and trust towards a company, which includes relying on that organisation

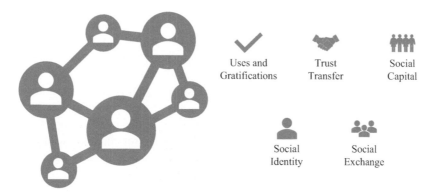

Figure 9.2 Understanding consumer motivations to connect with brands through content.

Curating content to target consumer engagement: theoretical considerations. Social media-related brand engagement is multi-faceted, with complex motivations at play. Curators with a deep understanding of theories of consumer behaviour in the digital world can use this knowledge to help them identify and position content with a view to achieving marketing objectives.

for information, can foster an intention to purchase. As Rajković et al (2021, p. 6) state: 'Trust in a company is influenced by the previous behaviour of the company and experiences of other members which, in the social media environment, have an opportunity to punish or reward the company through the power of eWOM'. This trust entails believing in the ability, competence, and integrity of the other party to do what was agreed, and is right, and in the online environment, trust is increased as the company is perceived as part of the group with more trustful subjects (ibid, pp. 3–4). For the curator, a key takeaway is to make sure that the content is borrowed and used with care and sources are properly attributed so that the curating organisation is not viewed as cannibalising or stealing content. Underlying messages in curated content should also help build trust, which is a major focus of the next section in this chapter.

Ethical and Legal Content Curation

Ethics relate to human conduct, morals, and the principle to minimise harm whenever making decisions; whereas legal issues are connected to specific pieces of legislation that govern activity. Laws are different in every country, and ethical considerations can vary too as they can be dependent on religious, cultural, and other factors. Both are vast fields of exploration. In this section we will summarise key practical considerations that are widely applicable and of relevance to content curators who seek to achieve best practice in the field and avoid negative brand perceptions. These issues are mostly connected to trust, which we discussed earlier in this chapter is an important factor in stimulating social media-related consumer brand engagement.

1   Check your facts

Factual accuracy is critical for building trust with your audiences. It strengthens credibility and integrity, which are both essential for strengthening connections with your target audiences and ultimately enhancing consumer brand engagement. Meanwhile reposting fake news or inaccurate information can damage your brand's value and deter social media users from consuming your content and interacting with your brand in a positive way.

Before you share content, assess every sentence for factual accuracy, including the meaning of your words so that your message projects what you intend to communicate. Also review your images. Go back to the original sources wherever possible and assess their credibility. Consider whether a certain view has been put forward based on a specific agenda, by evaluating the primary source of information. Make sure every point can be backed with evidence. If you are using statistics, check to make sure they are the right figures and add dates. Have the latest facts and figures because information can age and can become inaccurate as new details come to light or a situation changes.

2   Credit your sources clearly and prominently

Don't pass off other people's work as your own, as this is illegal, unethical and can damage perceptions of your brand. Acknowledge the original creators in a transparent way. Your audiences will appreciate your integrity and you will avoid the problem of being accused of plagiarising content. Where you are seen to be stealing intellectual property from others, you and your organisation can face a lawsuit – which can be costly to defend and can risk your brand's reputation.

You may need to ask for permission to use other people's work, though this depends on what content you use, where you found it, and how you display it. A tweet by a public figure that is embedded in an article along with other tweets will be subject to different considerations from a White Paper available only on a corporate website, with the former not necessarily needing permission for use and the latter requiring it. Often, creators stipulate usage rights. If in doubt, ask the primary source for permission to use their work – particularly if you want to use a piece of content in its entirety.

Where you take pieces of content, make sure you cite the source and add a hyperlink back to the original work so your audience is clear that you are being transparent and therefore trustworthy. Another advantage of linking to sources is that they may link back to you, particularly if they like your treatment of their content, and this can be beneficial for your search engine optimisation activities and promote your content to new, and preferably relevant, audiences.

3   Be aware that images, videos are easily manipulated

Software is so sophisticated that it can fool audiences into believing people have said and done things they have not. Undertaking multiple checks for factual accuracy is essential. Also be wary of manipulating your own images and photographs in a way that does not reflect reality, as you want to maintain your brand's integrity to maintain trust with your audiences.

4   Be wary of controversial topics

We heard in Chapter 3 (Content Ideation) that negative content is more likely to go viral than positive angles. However, negativity can damage perceptions about your brand and can interfere with your efforts to build a positive relationship with your online communities, so tread carefully on controversial topics. In extreme circumstances you, and your employer, can face legal action for sharing defamatory or libellous material where derogatory information about individuals or financially damaging content about businesses is disseminated. Remember, too, that ethical considerations can vary considerably on topics such as race, religion, gender, and politics, so sense-check whether a theme, comment or discussion is in the best interests of your particular community and brand before deciding on usage.

5   Tread carefully on jokes and satire as they are subjective

There is much emphasis put on entertainment in the social media. Before sharing, explore whether a meme or article is appropriate for your audience. Senses of humour vary considerably between groups, so also think about whether an angle will be well-received or could offend someone and backfire on your efforts to generate positive consumer engagement with your brand. Also examine whether humour fits your content marketing playbook, tone of voice, and other brand guidelines so that you remain compliant with efforts to build a cohesive image for the business you are representing.

6   Draw content from a variety of sources

If most curated content comes from a single source, this can be viewed by your audiences as, at best, laziness (Sutherland, 2020, p. 220). In addition, an over-reliance on a few sources detracts from the perception you are trying to create that, as a curator, you are a thought leader with expertise in selecting relevant content for niche audiences.

There is also an important legal reason to expand your search for relevant content. If you draw heavily from one source, you may fall foul of 'fair use' or 'fair dealing'. This is a woolly grey area that can make you and the organisation for whom you work vulnerable to costs. The UK government describes the challenge of getting the right balance when leaning on the work of others as follows:

> "Fair dealing" is a legal term used to establish whether a use of copyright material is lawful or whether it infringes copyright. There is no statutory definition of fair dealing – it will always be a matter of fact, degree and impression in each case. The question to be asked is: how would a fair-minded and honest person have dealt with the work? Factors that have been identified by the courts as relevant in determining whether a particular dealing with a work is fair include:
>
> • Does using the work affect the market for the original work? If a use of a work acts as a substitute for it, causing the owner to lose revenue, then it is not likely to be fair.
> • Is the amount of the work taken reasonable and appropriate? Was it necessary to use the amount that was taken? Usually only part of a work may be used.
>
> The relative importance of any one factor will vary according to the case in hand and the type of dealing in question.

Check the copyright status of content you want to use. For more, if you are working in the UK for UK audiences, see www.gov.uk/topic/intellectual-property/copyright.

Edit, Comment, Distil Content Into New Formats

Curating content entails more than sharing the work of others; you are exploring the content of others in a way that a new piece of content is created. As Sutherland (2021, p. 224) states:

> The audience is reading your work because they are generally interested in your perspective on a topic and your views on what other content creators think too. It ruins that expectation of reading a fresh perspective when your content is largely the work of someone else. Remember, copy and paste is not content curation.

Ways you can bring together this content in a new way include the following:

- **Add substantial commentary** at the beginning of a piece so that you contextualise a post you are sharing for your audience. This has the benefit of changing the copy (text) so that it is not identical to the article you have curated, which is good practice for search engine optimisation.
- **Refer to several pieces of content in one piece**. A common format is the listicle article, which includes summaries and links to a range of specific articles on a topic. You could also produce an infographic that includes text and hyperlinks produced by others but displayed on an image you have produced. Developing a timeline or narrative, with hyperlinks to specific pieces of content that relate to dates, can also help you distil information.
- **Always change headlines**. This is so that you do not simply copy the work of others. A fresh headline helps you create a fresh perspective that demonstrates you are adding value and presenting work from a specific point of view that is compatible with your brand and resonates with your target audiences. Another reason to rework your headlines is because the search engines are less likely to penalise your content if it is original.
- **Change the format**. White Papers can be distilled into infographics, animated videos, short articles or slide shows. You could also add a video or podcast to the slides. Other ways of changing format include précising, or summarising, articles into one piece or producing a podcast that summarises information across various sites.
- **Convert long pieces into a micro-blog series**. Carve out strong headlines and introductory paragraphs by picking out themes and topics for social media posts that in turn link to longer articles. Think of developing a series of posts that help you leverage off one substantial piece several times.

- **Develop a poll or ask questions about a topic**. You can make a piece of content the focus of a poll, and then use the results of your survey to build another article.
- **Bring out the voice of your community**. You can draw on comments, and quote commentators, on a specific topic, with hyperlinks to related articles on that issue. A 'Community Speaks' type of piece is a highly effective way to connect with your customers and let them know you are listening to them and facilitating conversations, while also rewarding them for taking the time to contribute to the community. Another way of using comments is to embed tweets, Facebook post comments and other social media discussions in articles that you repurpose.

Content Curation Tools

There is a large and ever-expanding suite of tools for curating marketing content. Here are a few popular options:

- **Feedly**: Feedly is a popular RSS reader that allows you to subscribe to multiple sources of content and view them in a single, organised location. This makes it easy to find and curate content on specific topics.
- **Pocket**: Pocket is a bookmarking tool that allows you to save articles, videos, and other content to view later. This can be useful for curating content for marketing purposes, as you can easily save content to review and share later.
- **Hootsuite Insights**: Hootsuite Insights is a social media monitoring tool that allows you to track keywords and hashtags, and see what's being said about your brand and industry on social media. This can be useful for curating content for thought leadership, as you can see what's trending and relevant in your industry.
- **Scoop.it**: Scoop.it is a content curation platform that allows you to curate and share content on specific topics with your audience. It offers a range of features, including content suggestion, topic analytics, and content scheduling, making it a useful tool for curating content for marketing purposes.
- **Curata**: Curata is a content curation platform that provides a range of tools for discovering, curating, and sharing content. It offers features such as content recommendations, content analytics, and a library of pre-curated content, making it a powerful tool for curating content.

Note that this list of curation tools was curated using a search on ChatGPT (the rest of this chapter was researched and written by a human with a wealth of experience as a content marketer and digital media content curator). You can do a search on ChatGPT and search engines for an updated list, though bear in mind that you should use your own creativity to add value to content as a curator. The use of tools such as ChatGPT is controversial. For more on the use of artificial intelligence (AI) chatbots in content marketing, see Chapter 12. In the meantime, this is what ChatGPT (February, 2023) produced instantaneously in response to the question: **Can ChatGPT curate content for marketing**?

- Yes, ChatGPT can assist in content curation for marketing purposes. As a language model trained by OpenAI, ChatGPT has been trained on a large corpus of text and can generate content based on various prompts, suggest relevant content to be curated, and provide insights and analysis to support content curation efforts.
- For example, ChatGPT can suggest topics or sources to curate content from, provide summaries of content for use in curation, and help you tailor your content to your target audience and specific marketing goals.
- However, it's important to note that the ultimate responsibility for curating content lies with the human user, who must use their judgement and expertise to ensure that the content being curated is relevant, high-quality, and aligns with their marketing goals and target audience.
- It's important to choose a tool that aligns with your specific needs and goals, and that offers the features and functionality you need to effectively curate content for your target audience.

Content Curation in the Content Marketing Plans

Content curation is an integral part of the development of your content calendar. The same principles apply to created and curated content. Your planning starts with identifying what you want to achieve with your content, usually contained in a brief that sets out the requirements. It is built on a foundation of research, with insights on the business and competitors fed into a strategy. For more on how to generate ideas and roll out content plans, see Chapter 3 (Content Marketing Ideation: How to Generate and Manage Creative Concepts).

Key Takeaways

In this chapter, you learnt:

- How content curation can play a vital role in stimulating social media brand-related engagement.
- About key theories and concepts that shed light on consumer behaviour in the digital environment, with insights on how to apply these in marketing content curation.
- Why ethical and legal considerations are at the heart of decision-making for marketing content curators.

- Practical skills in content curation, including best practice in the use of creative assets developed by other parties for marketing purposes.

Interview with Raphael Fix

Raphael Fix, Head of Innovation Management at Omnicom Media Group, Germany, is responsible for building new business models, products, and content. He has extensive experience in the field of innovation from previous positions at various companies, including Innovative Marketing at FinTech auxmoney and Brand Marketing at CHECK24. The focus of his work is the analysis of future scenarios, the scouting of new innovative startups and the steering of interdisciplinary innovation communities.

Raphael Fix

How would you define content curation?
Content curation is an innovative method that can help businesses efficiently gather and distribute a large volume of content across multiple channels. By carefully selecting and commenting on content, you can provide added value to target audiences and increase attention.

What are the differences between copying content and curating content?
Copying content is often seen as plagiarism and therefore not acceptable. In contrast, curating content refers to carefully selecting and sharing content from various sources while giving proper credit and recognition to the original creators. In a business context, content curation can be a creative way to share information and insights, promoting innovation.

What content do you curate?
In my role as a curator of business content, my focus is on gathering and curating trends, studies, and news related to new business and innovation. My aim is to provide my audience with a comprehensive overview that is easily digestible. Another crucial aspect of my role is selecting and curating trend reports and studies to understand emerging developments, new opportunities,

and insights supported by data. It's essential to curate not only obvious content but also to scrutinise the methods and sources to deliver to my audience with expert insights.

Do you have a set process for curating content?
Curating content from the areas of innovation, trends, and studies requires clear business processes and methods to curate the content objectively and with expertise. Tools such as trend radars or methods such as meta-analyses aid in selecting relevant content. On the other hand, curating innovation news is focused on clear business goals and a vision. It is essential to identify all news that is relevant to these goals, whether it is positive or negative, internal or external. Speed is a crucial factor here as innovation news from two months ago may no longer be relevant. Therefore, the curation process is focused on matching content to defined business goals and visions while ensuring its currency.

What are the benefits of content curation?
It saves time and costs, offers multiple perspectives and increases engagement. Innovation and creativity can be further enhanced through content curation by preparing unique perspectives and adding value to the audience.

What are the disadvantages of content curation? Please include some examples to illustrate your points.
Especially in the field of innovation and creation, there is a risk of inaccurate or outdated information. Content curation requires extensive clear research and fact-checking. Studies and methods must be checked for content just as much as the result from them.

How do you make your curated content stand out/how do you differentiate your content from other identical content? Are there unique ways to add value?
I have precise business goals, mission, and vision. Thus, my curation has a goal that is not identical to other curators in the same field. In addition, my goal is to incorporate professional expertise in a deeper way and also to challenge my own content again and again with external curated content.

What mistakes do you see in content curation that we should avoid – and why?
To prevent mistakes in content curation, make sure to curate appropriate and excellent content from varied sources, give appropriate credit and perspective, and manually assess the content before sharing it with your audience.

How does content curation stimulate brand-related engagement?
Content curation is an innovative and creative tool to stimulate brand-related engagement by curating high-quality, economically and scientifically relevant content for a specific audience. It helps companies to establish themselves as industry experts and strengthen their market position.

Where does content curation fit in to a digital marketing strategy? How do you decide whether content curation is the right approach for a specific client or brand? Content curation can be a valuable part of digital marketing by providing relevant and authoritative content to the target audience. Brands can use it to position themselves as industry leaders, increase engagement, and provide valuable resources to their audience. However, it's crucial to consider the brand's goals, target audience, and available resources before deciding to use content curation. Content curation should not replace original content creation, but rather complement it and provide additional value to the audience.

What factors make content curation suitable for a specific strategy? Content curation can be a valuable strategy to establish authority and credibility in a specific niche or industry. Factors such as relevance, quality, consistency, diversity, originality, and brand alignment can enhance the effectiveness of content curation and make it suitable for a specific strategy. By considering these factors, one can ensure that curated content is valuable and effective for the target audience.

How important is teamwork in curating content? Please give an example, or two, of how you have inspired colleagues to be highly effective in content curation. Teamwork is also crucial in content curation. Professional expertise from a wide range of fields enriches curation in many aspects.

For example, if we curate studies and reports and want to pass on the content, then several experts from the focus area of these studies and reports check the content in every detail, because even if curated content does not originate from us, we become the sender and must always stand 100 per cent for it.

End of Chapter Tasks

Tutorial Task I

Creative Curation

Choose an article on a business news website and explore in a group discussion how you could repurpose the content in five different ways: a listicle; a thought leadership post contextualised with opinion and a fresh headline; an infographic; a 'community speaks' piece; a series of micro-blog posts that tell a story.

Remember to identify your target market. Explain how you would add value for this audience as a content curator with each piece of content.

You can repeat this process with other types of content. Some examples include: a White Paper on a technical subject on a corporate website; a YouTube video produced by a retailer on how to assemble furniture; an article on a pet food website about dog nutrition.

Task 2

Ethical and Legal Content Curation

Choose a piece of curated content you have received from a brand in your email inbox. Use this check list to help you assess whether the curator has applied best practice in terms of the ethical and legal considerations of content curation:

1   Factual accuracy.
2   Transparent attribution.
3   Image authenticity.
4   Controversial content.
5   Humour.
6   Fair dealing.
7   Adding value.

See the section on 'Ethical and legal content curation' earlier in this chapter for more detail to guide your discussion.

Task 3

You are a content curator for a hotel chain. Choose one content curation tool and analyse whether it is suitable for the hospitality industry. Share your findings in a two-minute mini presentation to your peers. Provide three examples of content curation practices that are enhanced by the use of the tool you picked. Identify three potential risks, pitfalls or challenges associated with your chosen tool.

References

Blumler, J. G. (1979). The role of theory in uses and gratifications studies. *Communication Research*, *6*(1), 9–36.

Castells, M. (2004). *The Network Society* (pp. 3–45). London: Edward Elgar.

Chahal, H., Wirtz, J., & Verma, A. (2020). Social media brand engagement: Dimensions, drivers and consequences. *Journal of Consumer Marketing*, *37*(2), 191–204.

Cohen, H. (2012, December 12). Content curation: 12 ways to add value. Heidi Cohen. Retrieved March 14, 2023, from https://heidicohen.com/content-curation-12-ways-to-add-value/#:~:text=The%20goal%20of%20curating%20content,out%20of%20those%20broadly%20available

Copyright: Detailed information. Intellectual property: Copyright – detailed information – GOV.UK. (n.d.). Retrieved March 14, 2023, from www.gov.uk/topic/intellectual-property/copyright

Gkikas, D. C., Tzafilkou, K., Theodoridis, P. K., Garmpis, A., & Gkikas, M. C. (2022). How do text characteristics impact user engagement in social media posts: Modeling content readability, length, and hashtags number in Facebook. *International Journal of Information Management Data Insights*, *2*(1), 100067.

Habibi, M. R., Laroche, M., & Richard, M. O. (2014). The roles of brand community and community engagement in building brand trust on social media. *Computers in Human Behavior, 37*, 152–161.

Hayes, A. (2023, January 25). Brand equity: Definition, importance, effect on profit margin, and examples. *Investopedia.* Retrieved March 14, 2023, from www.investopedia.com/terms/b/brandequity.asp

Kemp, S. (2023, February 4). Digital 2023: Global Overview Report – DataReportal – Global Digital Insights. DataReportal. Retrieved March 14, 2023, from https://datareportal.com/reports/digital-2023-global-overview-report

Kenton, W. (2022, November 27). What is social capital? Definition, types, and examples. Investopedia. Retrieved March 14, 2023, from www.investopedia.com/terms/s/socialcapital.asp

Lies, J. (2019). Marketing intelligence and big data: Digital marketing techniques on their way to becoming social engineering techniques in marketing. *International Journal of Interactive Multimedia and Artificial Intelligence, 5*, 134–144.

Ndhlovu, T., & Maree, T. (2022). Consumer brand engagement: Refined measurement scales for product and service contexts. *Journal of Business Research, 146*, 228–240.

Rajković, B., Đurić, I., Zarić, V., & Glauben, T. (2021). Gaining trust in the digital age: The potential of social media for increasing the competitiveness of small and medium enterprises. *Sustainability, 13*(4), 1884.

Santos, Z. R., Cheung, C. M., Coelho, P. S., & Rita, P. (2022). Consumer engagement in social media brand communities: A literature review. *International Journal of Information Management, 63*, 102457.

Schivinski, B. (2021). Eliciting brand-related social media engagement: A conditional inference tree framework. *Journal of Business Research, 130*, 594–602.

Sutherland, K. E. (2020). *Strategic Social Media Management: Theory and Practice.* Springer Nature.

Tajfel, H. & Turner, J. (1986). The social identity theory of intergroup behavior. *Social Psychology of Intergroup Relations* (2nd ed.), Nelson-Hall: Stephen Worchel and William G. Austin, Chicago (1986), pp. 7–24.

Trunfio, M., & Rossi, S. (2021). Conceptualising and measuring social media engagement: A systematic literature review. *Italian Journal of Marketing, 2021*, 267–292.

10 Content Marketing and Sponsorship

By Lucas Petermeier, Benjamin Becker, and Prof Christof Backhaus

Learning Outcomes

- To understand the nature and relevance of sponsorship as a marketing instrument, and the role that leveraging sponsorships through content marketing plays throughout the sponsorship lifecycle.
- To understand why community centricity and value generation are crucial in effectively leveraging a sponsorship campaign.
- To understand the steps involved in designing and implementing sponsorship partnerships that effectively deliver value to fans and brand communities.

Nature and Evolution of Sponsorship

Sponsorship has been used as a marketing tool to place brands in the context of an emotional environment for a long time. The sponsorship of Coca-Cola at the Olympic Games, for example, dates back to 1928 (Coca-Cola Company, 2011). Commercial sponsorship can be described as a contractual business relationship between a sponsor and a sponsored property – this can be a person, event, a group of people or an organisation – within which the sponsor provides money and/or non-monetary benefits to the sponsee, who in return offers certain rights allowing the sponsor to associate with the property to achieve business goals (based on Meenaghan, 1983; Renard & Sitz, 2011; Ukman, 2015). The agreed rights and obligations, alongside other aspects such as the duration of the partnership, are codified in a sponsorship contract, which provides the formal basis for a sponsorship engagement.

Over the last five decades, sponsorship has evolved from a niche instrument to one of the most recognisable marketing tools across industries and contexts, and is used at all levels, ranging from local, regional, national to international and global platforms. It was predominantly through sports that sponsorship in the 1970s and 1980s became more widespread (Bruhn, 2017). Since the 1990s, sponsorship has also increasingly been employed in other areas including arts and culture, education, environmental and social initiatives (Dreisbach, 2019).

DOI: 10.4324/9781003346500-10

To communicate their association to sponsees' brands, sponsors in the past mainly relied on logo integration, hospitality, and product placements. Driven, among other aspects, by the growth of sponsor brands seeking to capture audiences' attention and an increasing sensitisation of audiences for commercialisation, such tactics have become less effective (Dreisbach et al., 2021). Therefore, in today's cluttered media landscape much more needs to be done to bring a sponsorship alive and 'make it work' over the course of the relationship: the sponsorship needs to be leveraged and activated, and particularly over the last two decades, sponsorship practice has increasingly recognised this.

The rise of digital communication channels such as social media has led to sponsors and sponsees utilising these new opportunities as well to develop and deploy more integrated and engaging sponsorship strategies. Thereby, the growing interest in sponsorship as a marketing instrument can, alongside that of other indirect or 'below-the-line' forms of communication such as product placements, be seen as part of a general development of brands moving away from traditional advertising and shifting their budgets towards 'integrated communication where the brand becomes part of the programming, part of the sharing, and part of the life experience'. (Cornwell, 2020, p. 4).

Sponsorship and the Case for Content Marketing

Sponsorships primarily drawing on logo placements might still be effective to help in achieving some objectives, such as raising sponsor brand awareness and sponsor memorisation. However, merely presenting a sponsor logo – be it static or moving images, on an LED board or on TV – offers limited opportunities for fan engagement and interaction. Also, while the logo is present and generally visible most of the time during a game or event, it is difficult to add any content that would provide additional value to fans and audiences. Additional challenges of logo-focused sponsorships are limited audience's attention (as usually spectators focus on what is happening on the pitch/stage), and clutter resulting from multiple sponsor logos being visible in a stadium/venue or on screen at the same time (Breuer and Rumpf, 2015; Dreisbach et al., 2021).

To overcome these challenges, sponsors increasingly draw on more comprehensive strategies, leveraging and activating their sponsorship with complementary marketing messaging. Representing a specific form of leveraging, sponsorship activation comprises communication and campaigns that aim at initiating a two-way interaction with the audience (Weeks, Cornwell, & Drennan, 2008).

Effective leveraging and activation go beyond telling emotional brand stories. The following cases show how brands have successfully integrated their sponsoring activities in their overall marketing agenda:

Bacardi and Parookaville Festival. Since 2018, Bacardi has activated their partnership with one of Europe's largest festivals with branded stage, Casa Bacardi. The design followed the desired lifestyle of the brand, a Puerto-Rican style with Caribbean atmosphere, music, and drinks. On-site tactics aimed at engaging the target audience included sweepstake and digital and social activation, which were integrated and in line with all other media channels. Focus of all activities was to reach the target audience in the moment of exuberance with a good fit to the sponsor's products.

SC Johnson and Liverpool Football Club. Liverpool Football Club and SC Johnson teamed up to deliver a collective vision for a healthier world with local and global initiatives focused on three specific areas: sustainability, health, and opportunity. With various in-stadium activities, e.g., plastic upcycling, cleaning and disinfectant stations as well as fan challenges, both parties were able to create and deliver content to activate the fan base (link to online resource: see end of chapter). Within the 'Don't lose your bottle' challenge fans were asked to 'swap out' single use plastic bottles to reusable bottles to keep the oceans clean. (Link to video: https://youtu.be/xi2GCgR11co)

REWE and German Football Association (DFB). REWE leveraged their partnership with the DFB via collecting cards offered around World and European Football Cups. The collecting cards approach not only led to high levels of awareness in a main target audience (i.e., families), but more importantly also significantly increased revenues during campaign duration in the context of the particular UEFA/FIFA Cups.

Apple's partnership with Major League Baseball (MLB) represents an example for a long-term sponsorship engagement where the provision of content to audiences plays a pronounced role. Apple, as part of their partnership with MLB, provides iPad Pro to all MLB teams. A custom, jointly developed app, provides coaching staff access to current and historical baseball performance statistics, drawing on which MLB coaches and staff can work towards improving their players' and teams' performance (CNBC, 2016). Fans are watching those features throughout the media coverage of MLB. Further leveraging the partnership, Apple in June 2022 announced the provision of two live 'Friday Night Baseball' games each week and related value-added content for fans through the Apple TV+ app (Apple, 2022). Under the campaign, the Apple News app provides fans access to personalised MLB highlights and curated MLB-related information. Through Apple Music, content in the form of playlists with batters' walk-up songs of the four 'Friday Night Baseball'-teams and 'classic' baseball-celebrating songs is provided (Apple, 2022). In 2023, the content partnership has been prolonged, allowing fans across 60 country markets to access the content provided over 25 weeks (Apple, 2023).

Often enough, however, brands also fall short in terms of acknowledging the need to integrate sponsorship measures into the broader marketing, and embedding value-enhancing elements into campaigns. Appropriate planning alongside a structured process helps avoid such situations and should lead to more innovative and progressive campaigns that are fan-driven and uniquely tailored to the brands of both sponsor and sponsee. The following four key principles and the sponsorship process were derived from the literature and practical experience in order to help sponsorship practice design and implement sponsorships, which deliver value both for audiences and also for the sponsorship partners involved.

Content-Based Sponsorship Leveraging: Key Principles

Brand platform instead of media platform. A sponsorship property such as a sports or cultural event should not be considered as a media channel in the first place, but rather as a platform to shape your brand mid- and long-term. Sponsorship partners and supporting actors should therefore not focus on reach and CPM too much. Instead, it is important to anchor sponsorship more firmly as an integrative part of your brand management, organisationally supporting the creation of inspiring ideas that lead to audience's engagement and subsequent outcomes.

Cultural instead of company focus. The USP in sports and other types of partnerships is the access for brands to strong values and value-driven communities. To leverage this potential, it is important to change perspectives, starting with the brand audience's or fans' needs and wishes. Embracing their culture and learning to speak their language is the primary focus, rather than the sponsor's own marketing playbook and business goals.

Provide value instead of vying for attention. Based on an analysis of 68 real-life activation campaigns from the German Soccer Bundesliga, Dreisbach et al. (2021) identified value-added elements to be of very high relevance as a design-element of activation campaigns. Specifically, 59 per cent of the campaigns included an element of *financial value* or benefit, 43 per cent offered *symbolic value*, and 22 per cent some kind of *social value*. In an experimental field study, their research further suggests that, while all three types of benefits are effective in terms of driving positive sponsorship outcomes, activations incorporating symbolic and social benefits in particular can elicit positive responses (Dreisbach et al. 2021). In a similar vein, a study of club-generated social media content in the cricket context revealed that social content outperformed information-, entertainment-, and remuneration-based content in terms of eliciting fan engagement (Annamalai et al., 2021).

Individuality instead of 'one size fits all'. Classical approaches with inflexible partnership packages do not fit in advanced sponsorship-leveraging times. The digital world requires programmatic approaches and contractual flexibility to develop joint content strategies. Individualised rights are the basis for co-creation between sponsor and sponsee, and unique ideas that add value for fans through service, product, and entertainment offerings. The better a campaign is embedded within the unique portfolio of touchpoints a sponsee offers to their fans, the higher the likelihood for its acceptance, and fan engagement with the sponsor's offering.

These four key principles of content marketing should be considered throughout the campaign planning and execution during the entire process of the sponsorship.

The Sponsorship Process

To effectively embed sponsorship including a content-based leveraging and activation into the marketing mix, the following step-based approach provides an overview and guideline, summarising the main tasks that need to be completed.

I. Target Definition

As a starting point, it is crucial to formulate targets and define key performance indicators (KPIs). These should be derived drawing on the broader marketing objectives as formulated in the strategic planning process. Formulating a suitable set of targets allows the relevant information needed for planning and decision making to be collected (Homburg et al., 2013). Also, issues that might occur – for example, when fan engagement with activation content is declining – can be identified in good time. Importantly, targets also have a communication function. Informing about how 'things stand' regarding the particular KPIs, signals priorities and desired outcomes to employees involved in partnership management, both on the side of the sponsor, and the sponsee.

As in all target setting, targets should be SMART (specific, measurable, achievable, realistic, timebound). Targets could, for example, relate to achieving brand uplift along the marketing funnel regarding awareness, familiarity, consideration or first choice, creating a certain media or PR value, or achieving an impact on sales. Target definition also creates the foundation for the measurement framework (see 'Measurement' heading in this chapter), which needs to be set up in line with the defined sponsoring targets.

2. Analysis

An effective sponsoring strategy is based on a solid analysis drawing on reliable, timely, and relevant data. While areas to be addressed in the analysis can vary, depending on the individual sponsoring case, in general, the following topics should be analysed:

- **Sponsor Brand**. What does the brand stand for? What are the core brand attributes and values? How is the brand perceived in the market? What are the biggest challenges for the brand? What does the brand's current marketing mix look like? Are there any existing sponsorship activities?
- **Target Group**. Demographics? Interests and passion points? Mindset? Needs, Drivers and barriers to engagement?

- **Market and Competition**. Market environment (macro and micro)? Who are the direct and indirect competitors? How are they positioned in the market? What do their communication and broader marketing-mix activities look like? What (if any) sponsorship activities do they engage in?

Desk research and secondary data approaches are good starting points to compile the information needed for the analysis. General and specialised market and digital audience research companies such as YouGov (https://yougov.co.uk/), GWI (www.gwi.com/) or Nielsen (www.nielsen.com/) provide consumer and industry trend reports, as well as a broad range of tools both paid and free of charge that can be useful in this regard. To address more specific questions and generate deeper insights into a particular target group's demographics, motivations, and behaviours, conducting primary research is advisable. In addition to the established players, also a number of more recently founded providers of market research can provide high-quality data within a brief period of time.

3. Strategy

Based on the condensed results of the analysis, the sponsorship strategy can now be developed. This strategy should answer the question, 'How do we achieve our sponsorship targets in the most effective and efficient way?' and is the foundation for all creative ideation, conception, and also to develop effective sponsorship activations. A good strategy needs to:

- Be clear and 'spot on', also when it comes to language and wordings, allowing all stakeholders to easily understand the strategy.
- Provide guiding principles as 'guardrails' for the implementation.
- Derive tangible actions rather than creating general statements about a possible future.

In the context of sponsoring as a communications channel or content marketing tool, a key part of the sponsoring strategy is to define who to partner with. Therefore, a sponsorship framework should be defined to enable a systematic and informed selection and decision-making process. The framework should take the core aspects, which have been analysed into account, evaluate them according to the targets defined, and should answer the following questions:

- Is there a brand fit between sponsor and sponsee?
- Can the sponsor reach its target group through the sponsoring?
- Is the sponsoring asset (e.g., sports club) or the environment (e.g., respective league) available or blocked by a competitor?

If generating brand awareness through the sponsorship is a target, the specific items to be analysed could, for example, be media reach, PR potential or social media reach and buzz. The strategy should also answer questions about how the brand and the product or service intends to tell unique brand stories that are likely to – in the sense of the preceding chapters of this book – be perceived as providing value to the audience. Often, it can be observed that brands partner, for example, with a particular sport team to address their fans and utilise the 'built-in' reach of the respective partner, but fail to communicate their own role and reason to be there. Oftentimes, in such cases, sponsors are then not perceived as credible partners by the target audience, which leads to lower performance in terms of brand uplift. The last step of the strategy phase is the development of a creative brief for the activations and campaigns planned over the duration of the sponsorship. This brief acts as starting point for campaign ideas to be developed under the ongoing communications umbrella.

4. Concept and Creation

Creativity is the most powerful force in business.

(Bill Bernbach, DDB)

While the preceding steps provide the foundation for a successful sponsorship, the development of the creative core idea and respective messaging is crucial in terms of delivering an impactful sponsorship partnership, including value-oriented content campaigns. With the media and advertising landscape becoming much more complex and dynamic over the last decades, the relative impact of good creative on campaign outcomes has declined; however, creative still represents the most important single driver of sales, as Nielsen Catalina Solutions conclude based on an analysis of nearly 500 advertising campaigns delivered across various media platforms (Nielsen, 2017).

The core idea or creative concept should be based on a strong consumer insight (see analysis and strategy phase) to capture the interest of the target group and motivate them to take action by triggering an emotional response. A well-known example for a creative concept drawing on a consumer insight is the Snickers bar. Based on the consumer insight that it is hard to concentrate and focus on what matters if you are hungry, Snickers developed the slogan 'You're not you when you're hungry' (www.snickers.com/mena/en/our-story). Within the related campaign, Snickers conveyed the message that Snickers is the perfect way to get back to being yourself.

The next step in the sponsoring process is the development of an activation concept based on the sponsorship's overarching objectives, strategy, and core creative idea. This should be followed by a detailed conception of the activation measures including elaboration of the 'reason why' based on the overarching central idea. Activation measures could be, for example, digital such as a social media campaign; on the ground, such as an event or brand/ product integration on-site or a media partnership. Once the activation concept is defined and all activation measures are detailed out, all the necessary branding assets such as a campaign spot, a key visual, social media clips/postings, etc. can be developed and produced.

In the context of sponsorship, also user-generated content campaigns should be considered as an option (see also Chapter 7).

5. Contract Negotiation

As initially stated, the sponsorship contract represents the formal basis for the partnership. While the main characteristics of the sponsorship codified in the contract such as duration and the sponsorship fee provide a framework for the joint communication during the sponsorship period, the contract importantly also contains details regarding the 'gets' and 'gives' for each of the partners, i.e., the sponsoring rights and assets which the sponsor receives in exchange for paying the agreed sponsorship fee. Usually, both parties will align a term sheet as appendix to the main contract to describe all details regarding the rights and assets including visualisations if applicable. Usually, sponsoring rights granted through a sponsoring contract include items from the following categories:

*   IP usage (e.g., logo, title, photos, ...)
*   Content production (with e.g., players)
*   PR activities
*   Product integration
*   Commercial displays
*   Banners and venue signage incl. e.g., perimeter advertising
*   Hospitality and tickets
*   Digital communication/social media
*   CRM (e.g., mailings)

It is advisable to start the contract negotiations as soon as possible after selecting a sponsee based on the sponsoring strategy. It is recommended to complete concept and creation before the final contract signature to be able to adapt the rights package according to the specific needs, and to be able to implement the developed idea and activation measures by utilising the respective rights.

6. Activation and Implementation

Building on the creative concept and the rights defined in the sponsorship contract, a communications plan outlining all ATL (above-the-line, i.e., 'classical' advertising) and BTL (below-the-line) measures is developed. Based on this plan, all activation measures have to be implemented including quality assurance. A very important part of the sponsorship activation is utilising paid media to amplify the built-in reach of the sponsee and generate enough awareness in the desired target group segments (see also Chapter 7). Here, channels like TV, digital (e.g., programmatic advertising, social media) or out-of-home can be used depending on the target group's usage behaviour and the strategic fit, e.g., related to the core idea and the branding assets available.

7. Measurement

The final step within the sponsoring process is success measurement in relation to the defined targets and KPIs. In a sponsorship context, there are two main areas which should be evaluated: within the *sponsoring analysis*, the sponsor tracks the value of the sponsorship and its relation to the sponsorship fee, but it is also possible to monitor competitors or other partners sponsoring activities as a benchmark. The main KPI in this context usually is the media value generated through the respective sponsorship. The sponsorship analysis is a good tool to validate the forecast which is usually provided by the sponsee or a third party such as a sports marketing company. Furthermore, the sponsoring analysis can provide insights into the target group.

Brand analysis: to be able to determine if there is a measurable impact on the brand awareness, perception, consideration/purchase intent or other relevant KPIs through the sponsorship a respective market research should be conducted. Usually there will be two samples, test and comparison group, where the test group has been exposed to the sponsorship, and the comparison group has not. Both groups will be asked different questions about the sponsorship, brand perception and, for example, purchase intent before and after the sponsoring period, to determine whether there has been an uplift in the test group. Based on the results obtained through the sponsoring and the brand analysis it is recommended to combine both into a comprehensive overall sponsorship campaign reporting to be able to interpret all data collected and derive recommendations, e.g., regarding improving the sponsorship or considering termination of the contract, in case the results do not meet predefined targets.

Conclusions

From this chapter, the following conclusions can be drawn:

- 'Content is King' in sponsorship – sponsors need to tell compelling stories and generate value for fans together with the rightsholder.
- The impact of the sponsoring investment strongly depends on the integration of the partnership in the overall marketing activities.

- Sponsoring offers various opportunities for content creation and delivery – the more fans are involved, the higher the chance to create a sustainable impact.
- The four principles outline a pathway to optimising sponsorship activities for fan engagement and impact.
- The sponsorship process guides sponsors and rightsholders through the stages of the partnership to generate value for all: the brand, the rightsholder, as well as fans and brand-related communities.

End of Chapter Questions

1   Explain the nature of sponsorship and its evolution as a marketing instrument.
2   Why is content marketing relevant in the context of sponsorship?
3   Identify a small set of pre-economic and economic marketing KPIs that could serve as the information base for a marketing performance measurement system.
4   Select a sponsorship-leveraging campaign of your choice. For this campaign, design a short fan feedback survey to capture fans' thoughts about and engagement with the campaign. How would you collect the survey data from fans? How would you incentivise fans to participate in the survey?
5   Select a brand of your choice and imagine they are interested in setting up a sponsorship partnership with your favourite sports team (or another property of your choice).

   a   Apply the steps 1 (target definition) and 2 (analysis) as outlined in the sponsorship process.
   b   With reference to step 4 (content and creation), brainstorm core ideas or themes that might be appropriate for content-based activation campaigns to be developed under the agreement.

Case Study – Volkswagen

Background

As one of the largest car manufacturers worldwide, the Volkswagen brand has for more than 70 years made innovative technologies, high quality, and appealing designs accessible to many people. The Volkswagen product range includes bestsellers, the Beetle, the Golf and the all-electric ID. family for the new world of mobility. Today, Volkswagen is present in more than 140 markets, employs more than 170,000 employees, and operates production facilities at 29 locations in 12 countries (www.volkswagen-newsroom.com/en/company-3688).

Campaign Objectives

The aim was to reach a young Polo target group that had previously been unreachable due to ad blockers and ad-avoiding media behaviour. Our goal was to manifest and increase Volkswagen and Polo within the target group in their relevant set and generate an uplift.

Insights:

As a result of the pandemic, life shifted more to the home and consequently also to the digital world. One digital platform whose user and access figures increased steadily during this time and to this day is Twitch. Germany plays an important role here, as the world's second-largest market – after the USA – in terms of viewer numbers. For some time now, gaming and e-sports have been very popular, especially in the young (18–35 years) target group, which is highly represented on Twitch. Thus, Twitch represents a well-suited platform to reach an audience that was ideally suited to the target group for the new VW Polo.

Also highly suited is the game 'Rocket League'. The game principle most closely resembles a car-ball game, in which the players (approx. 100k each month) try to get a somewhat larger ball into the opponent's goal with the help of cars.

Overview of the Campaign

Strategy:

The core of the strategy for Volkswagen Polo was to specifically counteract the 'Joy of Missing-Out' behaviour of the young target group; in other words, their conscious and active decision to avoid unwanted advertising messages. Consequently, Volkswagen had to be present exactly where the target group has shifted its media attention – to gaming – and to do so as authentically and invitingly as possible in order to achieve an efficient and successful media campaign. In this context, it is important to note that numerous car manu-facturers focus on e-sports – a prominent but comparatively small part of the gaming world – by sponsoring teams or leagues.

For example, Twitch, the world's leading interactive live streaming service in gaming, on the other hand, opened a much wider perspective for Volkswagen. Especially because of the young and tech-savvy community, Twitch was the perfect platform to present the new VW Polo to the young target group. After all, the new model from Volkswagen comes with technical features that are only known from the premium segment.

Therefore, the aim was to reach the gaming community with the product promise 'Can do more' and to anchor the new Polo sustainably and positively in the relevant set of young buyers. To fulfil this promise, we developed a community tournament in the popular online game 'Rocket League' together with Twitch – an energetic mixture of arcade football and chaotic driving fun.

Execution:

Under the slogan 'we have to conquer new stadiums' we managed to transfer VW's long-standing engagement in the area of football to the gaming segment within which the tournament is based. 'The New Polo Challenger Series' was something new to VW and Twitch influencers while presenting the 'can do more' promise of the new Polo to viewers and followers. Twitch influencers and gamers were given the chance to take part in a professional, competitive tournament – in a game that is new to them and thus offers new content for their viewers. In addition, they could invite their community to form a team with them and compete against other teams in a professional e-sports format. Furthermore, the winning team could win a new Polo each – for themselves as well as their community. With this approach, we were able to provide a target group that avoids advertising through ad blockers with a unique experience that combines all the things they love in their media behaviour: a) gameplay that they can participate in themselves, b) competition, c) exciting gaming content, d) personal contact with their favourite influencers, and e) the opportunity to win a new car through play. And, by the way, Volkswagen's involvement with the game 'Rocket League' strengthened its own brand positioning as a supporter of German football (among other things, Volkswagen is partner of the German Football Association, DFB).

The Results

Viewers in Germany could not get enough of our industry-first gaming league on Twitch ... and reached a cumulative viewing time of almost 10 years!

The move to not only be part of the gaming community, but to shape gaming itself paid off.

Brand uplift Volkswagen (relevant brand set):

- +3 per cent points within the male target group 18–35 years.
- +4 per cent points within the target group of Rocket League viewers on Twitch (zero measurement in the summer before the tournament/main measurement directly after the campaign).

The media results to prove it are:

- Use of programmatic-non-skippable, 30" prerolls with over 15,8 million impressions, 45,000 clicks (click-through rate of 0.41 per cent), and a view-through rate of over 80 per cent.

- High-reach daily fix placements to flank the live tournament with first impression takeovers (non-skippable, 30" prerolls) and homepage headliners as display brandings with a total of over 4.7 million impressions and over 15,000 clicks, with a click-through rate of 0.32 per cent.

In Total:

- More than 1.13 million live views of Volkswagen branded content with more than 10,000 simultaneous unique live viewers in the final tournament.
- More than five million minutes (equals 9.6 years!) of high-quality Volkswagen branded content watched live.
- The highest number of 'minutes watched' ever achieved for a brand activation in Germany on Twitch!

Takeaways From This Campaign

The campaign has demonstrated how content marketing can be used in sponsorship-related communication. The newly created 'The New Polo Challenger Series' was something new to VW and Twitch influencers while presenting the 'can do more' promise of the new Polo to viewers and followers.

With this approach, we were able to provide a target group that avoids advertising through adblockers with a unique experience that combines all the things they love and value in their media behaviour:

- Gameplay that they can participate in themselves,
- Competition.
- Exciting gaming content.
- Personal contact with their favourite influencers and the opportunity to win a new car through play.

The points mentioned above can be transferred analogously to other markets, since the Twitch platform has a worldwide network and users. Here, for example, a European or world championship could also be considered within the gaming community – which in turn would result in scalable and measurable success within the young an 'unreachable' audience.

PHD Germany | Volkswagen AG

References

Annamalai, B., Yoshida, M., Varshney, S., Pathak, A. A., & Venugopal, P. (2021). Social media content strategy for sport clubs to drive fan engagement. *Journal of Retailing and Consumer Services, 62*, 102648.

Apple (2022). Apple and Major League Baseball to offer "Friday Night Baseball" www.apple.com/newsroom/2022/03/apple-and-major-league-baseball-to-offer-friday-night-baseball

Apple (2023). "Friday Night Baseball" resumes on Apple TV+ on April 7. www.apple.com/newsroom/2023/03/friday-night-baseball-resumes-on-apple-tv-plus-on-april-7/

Breuer, C., & Rumpf, C. (2015). The impact of color and animation on sports viewers' attention to televised sponsorship signage. *Journal of Sport Management, 29*(2), 170–183.

Bruhn, M. (2017). *Sponsoring – Systematische Planung und integrativer Einsatz, 6.* Auflage, Wiesbaden: Springer Gabler.

CNBC (2016). Apple signs multiyear partnership with MLB to supply iPad Pros: WSJ. www.cnbc.com/2016/03/30/apple-signs-multi-year-partnership-with-mlb-to-supply-ipad-pros-wsj.html

Coca-Cola Company (2011). 125 Years of Sharing Happiness – A Short History of The Coca-Cola Company. www.coca-colacompany.com/content/dam/journey/us/en/our-company/history/coca-cola-a-short-history-125-years-booklet.pdf

Cornwell, T. B. (2020). *Sponsorship in Marketing. Effective Partnerships in Sports, Arts and Events.* 2nd edn. London: Routledge.

Dreisbach, J. (2019). *Erfolgsfaktoren der Sponsoringumsetzung und -aktivierung.* Wiesbaden: Springer Gabler.

Dreisbach, J., Woisetschläger, D. M., Backhaus, C., & Cornwell, T. B. (2021). The role of fan benefits in shaping responses to sponsorship activation. *Journal of Business Research, 124,* 780–789.

Homburg, C., Kuester, S. & Krohmer, H. (2013). *Marketing Management: A Contemporary Perspective.* 2nd edn. London: McGraw-Hill Higher Education.

Meenaghan, J. A. (1983). Commercial sponsorship. *European Journal of Marketing, 17*(7), 5–73.

Nielsen (2017). When it comes to advertising effectiveness, what is key? www.nielsen.com/insights/2017/when-it-comes-to-advertising-effectiveness-what-is-key/ Last accessed: April 2nd, 2023.

Renard, N., & Sitz, L. (2011). Maximising sponsorship opportunities: A brand model approach. *Journal of Product & Brand Management, 20*(2), 121–129.

Ukman, L. (2015). *IEG's Guide to Sponsorship: Everything You Need to Know About Sports,* Chicago: IEG.

Weeks, C. S., Cornwell, T. B., & Drennan, J. C. (2008). Leveraging sponsorships on the Internet: Activation, congruence, and articulation. *Psychology & Marketing, 25*(7), 637–654.

Links to Social Media Materials

SC Johnson and Liverpool Football Club. www.scjohnson.com/en/a-more-sustainable-world/liverpool-football-club-and-sc-johnson-take-on-plastic-waste. YouTube video: https://youtu.be/xi2GCgR11co

11 The Dark Side of Content Marketing

By Dr Elaine Mercer-Jones and Dr Kat Rezai

Learning Outcomes

- To develop an in-depth understanding of the ways in which digital content can cause harm to society including, but not limited to, its potential for spreading misinformation, fostering addiction, and affecting mental health.
- To be able to critically assess the effectiveness and ethicality of the digital content disseminated by marketers, social media influencers, and other stakeholders in the content marketing ecosystem.
- To identify frameworks that marketers can utilise to practice ethical content marketing.

Content Marketing Dystopia

Content marketing is a relatively new phenomenon. As such, we are only just discovering what the consequences of this saturation of our media landscape with marketing messages might be. Despite the sensitivity with which brands and companies like to think they act when providing stories and advice, values, entertainment, and relationships, the online world is not always a pleasant and caring place to be, as we will explain below.

A 'dark side' or dystopian view of marketing is not new. In 1998, Hackley and Kitchen described advertising as a 'postmodern communications leviathan', a form of social pollution which, due to its omnipresence in Western culture, poisons our waking lives (Hackley & Kitchen, 1999). In 2015, Mike Proulx of Ad Age declared that 'there is no more social media – only advertising' (Proulx, 2015). Whereas this might have seemed like an extreme statement in 2015, the extent to which social media has become saturated with marketing messages, from branded content, to influencers, advertisements, videos, pop-ups, advergames, and blogs means that the 'communications leviathan' is bigger and more insidious than ever. As we continue scrolling through our social media feed, there is no escape from content marketing. Mara Einstein has also been vocal in their critique of content marketing, whose sole purpose, they argue, is to

DOI: 10.4324/9781003346500-11

find ways to get product in front of people subtly, so they don't realise they are being persuaded to purchase those products, as well as … to push though products to their friends, creating a world where we are in a constant state of buying or selling.

(Einstein, 2016, p. 4)

In addition, for Einstein, any notion of a relationship with a friend, or follower is entirely misleading. These engagements are merely marketing, with content marketing ensuring that 'our relationships … become means of facilitating marketing transactions, or, in the parlance of the market: they have become monetised' (ibid., p .8).

According to Silverman (2015), our fascination with social media means that we are scarcely able to imagine a world without the likes, shares, and follows demanded of us by social media and content marketing, while Williams argues that 'anything innate to humans that can be made into a problem will create a market for the solution' (Williams, 2023, para. 4). The nature of social media, and the content that fills it, is designed to attract our attention, and keep us scrolling. Orlowski reports that a third of US adults, and almost half of those aged 18 to 29, claim to be online 'almost constantly' (Orlowski, 2020, para. 1). The implications of this are manifold. As noted even in the 1990s, consuming more and more, comparing ourselves to celebrities and coveting the looks, lifestyles, and belongings of others does not lead us to happiness (Shankar et al., 2006). Negative aspects of content marketing include those same problems, but now we might also add social media addiction, questions concerning privacy and companies' use of personal information, mental health issues particularly amongst children, lack of digital literacy leading to manipulation and exploitation, excessive unsustainable consumption habits, the spreading of fake news and information regarding health and social issues, to name but a few of the negative consequences associated with content marketing. Some of these issues will be explored below.

Surveillance/Data Misuse and Privacy Issues

Content marketing aspires to be more than just company-focused information – words, pictures, videos which are passively viewed by the consumer. It is interactive, by its very nature requiring a response of some kind. Companies' content marketing is ongoing, and requires continual updates, and a perpetual examination and evaluation of what engages consumers. As a result, consumers are constantly monitored and surveyed (Järvinen & Taiminen, 2016). Time spent on any social media site results in the gathering of data about consumers, which is used to ensure that content is pitched so that it speaks directly to targeted consumers – those most likely to buy who spend their hours scrolling, following, liking, reading posts, and commenting.

This interaction is essential to the gathering of data, which then enables companies to target their messages more closely and clearly (Seymour, 2019). Staying online for longer means that users generate more and more data, which can be harvested and sold to advertisers and content marketers. Seymour discussed the links between gambling addiction and social media addiction, arguing that social media users end up 'constantly distracted, unproductive, anxious, needy and depressed – yet also curiously susceptible to advertising' (Seymour, 2019, para. 3).

Orlowski observes that 'by surveilling nearly all our online activity, social media platforms can now predict our emotions and behaviours. They leverage these insights and auction us to the highest advertising bidder' (Orlowski, 2020, para. 3). Matters of data misuse by marketers are regularly reported. The way some content marketing and social media companies gather and use data is, at times, neither legal nor appropriate. The implications for all of us if companies flout data regulation laws is concerning. For children, however, the implications of all this data gathering and covert surveillance are significant. The way in which data is gathered from children, for example, is open to scrutiny. For instance, 'free' games online might appear at first glance to be harmless entertaining content, but children are lured into these with the promise of 'loot boxes' – virtual rewards and 'special' features that allow them to win more and play for longer. This infinity loop of online gaming is profitable financially for companies, but the harvesting of data, and the loyalty and engagement such content marketing strives for, has darker consequences. For children this includes addictive behaviours, abnormal brain development, lack of social skills, and depression (Anon, 2019; Sherlock & Wagstaff, 2019). *The Financial Times* has described such games and other ubiquitous content marketing techniques as 'online nicotine', whereby companies exploit human weaknesses for commercial gain (Anon, 2019, para. 2). Understanding the attitudes and behaviour of the consumer is required for precisely targeted marketing, for relationships to be developed with the appropriate people. But it also means surveillance and data gathering on a grand and sophisticated scale twenty-four hours a day, seven days a week, often motivated by the need to sell more stuff to more people more of the time.

Self-Surveillance and Correction-Based Content

So far, we have explained how surveillance techniques are embedded within content marketing, raising concerns of privacy issues. But what about how marketing encourages consumers to indulge in self-surveillance? Elias and Gill's (2018) study into beauty apps and content found that young women utilise selfie apps which scan their original selfie, identify potential 'areas of improvement', and then advise them how to remove 'imperfections' using camera filters that are embedded in these beauty apps. In the social media space, young women in particular are constantly marketed to with correction-based content which suggests they can be 'empowered' by improving their self-image through the purchase of various beauty enhancement products (e.g., cosmetic surgery), and body-enhancing products (e.g., waist trainers, slimming drinks, diet medication, protein-shakes, fashion garments). The impact of this sort of content is three-fold: 1) it encourages the consumer to self-scan and critique their own body; 2) it fosters feelings of self-doubt and self-loathing; and 3) it encourages consumers to purchase the product, which they do in hope that they can become 'empowered'. Young women are constantly bombarded with 'body-correction posts' – content marketing tailored to encourage them to use their bodies as continuous 'correction projects'. This is promoted under the guise of the 'Love your Body' (LYB) discourse, as Gill and Elias (2014) explain:

> At the heart of LYB discourses is the production of positive affect. If many media discourses about women's bodies … are characterised by a focus on what is wrong ("dry, lumpy, orange peel skin") or how it can be improved ("get smoother-looking, softer skin"), then LYB discourses constitute a dramatic – apparently counter-hegemonic – interruption. They tell women that they are "sexy at any size", "beautiful just the way you are", and should feel appreciative and confident about their bodies.
>
> (Gill, 2014, pp. 6–7)

The love your body concept is promoted as encouraging consumers to make decisions of their own accord – i.e. 'I love my body, thus I am'. Influencers, discussed in more detail below, play a key role in this, utilising the LYB concept as a means of encouraging their followers to buy the products they are promoting.

Young People and Lack of Digital Literacy

Vloggers, bloggers, influencers who offer the opportunity for direct dialogue with consumers, branded web sites, advergames, social network games, and sponsored endorsements form just some of the ways in which content marketing manifests. Teenagers are especially exposed to these forms of marketing due to their prolonged use of social media, and despite their claims to be digital natives they are especially vulnerable. A Statista survey in 2022 revealed that young people (ages 4–18) in the UK spend an average of 114 minutes a day on TikTok, 91 minutes a day on Snapchat, and 30 minutes a day on Instagram (Ceci, 2023). This equates with up to four hours per day, or an entire day a week, spent using social media, with its rolling feed of advertisement, influencers, advergames, gambling promotions, and exhortations to like, follow, share, and comment. And yet the question remains as to whether young people, especially children, realise the selling intent of much of the marketing activity they see and interact with (Zarouali et al., 2019).

Sweeney et al. (2022) note that content marketing allows commercial messages to be masked, or 'presented in covert form' (Sweeney et al., 2022, p. 55). The concealed nature of much of content marketing means that, for children and more vulnerable members of society at least, they are unable to implement the coping mechanisms available to adults, such as scepticism and critical thinking. They do not know when to adopt measures of self-regulation, or avoidance, to ignore the persuasive attempts of marketers and recognise marketing when they see it. It becomes even harder to tease out marketing messages when that content is interwoven with organic or editorial content. An understanding of the processes behind content marketing means that the consumer can make an attitudinal response, which is to say they can like or dislike it, and from that make an informed evaluation (e.g., 'this game / message / post / is being paid to promote this brand') (Sweeney et al., 2022, p. 56). Inability to understand and recognise processes and patterns such as these means that evaluating what is being viewed in an informed and critical way is impossible. Content marketing can encourage these blurred boundaries, so that young people are often unable to decipher marketing content from non-marketing content (Sweeney, et al., 2022). Being able to recognise commercial and persuasive intent, and from there to make an informed judgement, is a basic right for any individual living in the consumer society. And yet there is, to date, little effort made to regulate and control content marketing, and the amount of it that children are exposed to; little effort made to educate and inform children that what they see and participate in is marketing. Those most unconcerned by these blurred boundaries are often those responsible for the social media platforms themselves, whose profits are driven by marketing and advertising, and who appear reluctant to address these issues unless forced to do so by governments and pressure groups (Murphy & Espinoza, 2023).

There are growing concerns regarding young people's lack of awareness of potentially harmful material embedded in the digital content of their social media feeds. Ofcom (2022) identified children's behaviour online as being increasingly passive: 'children were posting less, watching more and often seeking to avoid actively choosing what they watched, happy to be served a narrow range of content' (Ofcom, 2022, p. 5). The passive behaviour of children is what is most alarming here, as it suggests that children are not consciously aware of the types of content they are being exposed to, and the potential dangers this may bring to them. The following Ofcom findings should be particularly concerning to content marketers:

- Children are being exposed to sexualised or inappropriate content, including marketing content.
- Children have limited understanding of the full range of safety features that can help keep them safe on social media platforms.

- Children are frustrated about their lack of control over the marketing content targeted to them on social media platforms.
- Children are seeing content marketing that encourages high-risk ways to make money, such as cryptocurrency.
- Many older girls had received influencer 'collab' messages, asking them to become a social media influencer.

These findings heighten concerns regarding children's lack of understanding of social media marketing content and its potential dangers. In addition, Orben et al. (2022) report that teenage girls are more likely to experience poor mental health, due to excessive exposure to social media and content marketing over a long period of time. The Royal College of Psychiatrists has raised similar concerns, proclaiming further research and action is needed to protect young people's mental health (Dubicka & Theodosiou, 2020).

The Influence of Influencers

Sweeney reports that 25 per cent of young consumers aged 6 to 16 years stated that social media influencers had the greatest impact on their purchasing choices and behaviour, second only to the influence of friends at 28 per cent (Sweeney, 2022, citing Wunderman Thompson Commerce, 2019). Influencers can seem credible, believable, authentic, and relatable – which can become problematic when content marketing is not understood by young consumers to be the marketing that it is. Furthermore, although consumers make a choice to follow an influencer, in the case of young people this might be due to peer pressure, or the result of an algorithm that means the influencer is offered to them over and over again, rather than the result of an informed choice.

As content creators, in addition to what they might post organically, influencers create posts, or repost information, on behalf of brands and companies. Instagram influencers make a living, generate income or other material reward, by using their social media profiles to promote products and brands to their followers: the term 'influencer' describes a relationship between brands, companies, and their promoters that is entirely commercial. As such, the relationship is based on marketing, and rather that containing anything remotely authentic seeks solely to monetise the advertising potential of followers. While researching their article for *The Guardian* newspaper, Gritters found that many of the influencers they spoke to 'said that they felt tied to a static, inauthentic identity' due to the pressures imposed by companies and brands to present in a particular way (Gritters, 2018, para. 3). This lack of sincerity is at odds with content marketing's often self-proclaimed purpose of offering what is authentic, informative, and genuine.

Leban et al. (2021) argue that ethical conduct of influencers, as an aspect of content marketing, is complex and nuanced. As such it has not been adequately addressed by academics, with only a small number of unethical influencer behaviours scrutinised by marketing scholars. Borchers and Enke (2022) argue that influencers 'often move in ethically grey areas' (Borchers & Enke, 2022, p. 2). They list a range of misdemeanours perpetrated by influencers, including 'blatant sexism' as well as other more commercially related transgressions, such as failing to disclose sponsorships, or purchasing fake followers to increase reach by artificial means whilst simultaneously duping genuine followers with bogus inflated markers of popularity. Influencers stand accused of promoting products of questionable efficacy (diet supplements, waist trainers, skin whitening products, for example), promoting inappropriate products / services to under-aged followers (for example, cosmetic surgery enhancements), and participating in fake advertising collaborations (Borchers & Enke, 2022). Influencers are key players in social media content marketing, not only big stars, but also micro- and nano-influencers, who are able to appear more relatable and authentic and are thus much sought after by brands and companies. The marketing objectives of influencers are clear – to increase awareness, increase sales, and strengthen loyalty though relationship building (Borchers & Enke, 2022). The effect of these online relationships for consumers, especially those who are young and impressionable, is often less than positive, as we shall see below.

Borchers and Enke (2022) name only three problematic areas of influencer behaviour – transparency (lack of disclosure about collaboration with brands and companies), payments (which indicate a lack of independence on behalf of the influencer), and authenticity (whether brands are endorsed simply because the influencer is paid to do so). Other misdemeanours levelled at influencers include the charge of promoting overconsumption and encouraging the purchase of unnecessary items, with all the waste of resources and increased CO_2 emissions that this results in. One might argue, with Borchers and Enke (2022), that influencers – like the rest of us – have a degree of social responsibility to the planet and environment, which is in direct contradiction with their role and purpose as content marketers. This is the case particularly for fashion and beauty influencers, many of whom depend on the speedy change of the fashion and beauty milieu, and actively encourage it for their own pecuniary purposes. Others argue that genuine dialogue with followers is impossible due to management processes and the demands of sponsoring brands (Kent & Taylor, 2002), while the question of how children negotiate sponsored influencer content, and its various impacts on them is an important and regularly cited concern (De Veirman et al., 2017).

In addition, the type of information shared by influencers, via vlogs, blogs, and social media sites has come under question. Marocolo et al. (2021) discuss content marketing in relation to the spread of health-related information. Their specific focus was exercise, health, nutrition, medicine, and physical fitness amongst social media influencers with over 100,000 followers. This number is enough to qualify the influencer for substantial sponsorship and other commercial deals with brands. And yet the information presented by prominent health influencers, at least in the Brazilian context examined by Marocolo et al., demonstrates that not only are these influencers not qualified to claim authority over information they are sharing, but they are actively contributing to the widespread dissemination of misinformation on health matters to their followers. Most shared posts on fitness-based Instagram influencers' accounts held 'an influencer's mere opinion, experience, or marketing, which is frequently not supported by scientific evidence' (Marocolo et al., 2021). In addition, by using images designed to encourage envy and aspiration, and an emphasis on bodily aesthetics, a codependent relationship between influencer and followers often develops.

The marketing content posted by influencers has come under scrutiny in other spheres too. Financial influencers – 'finfluencers' – are increasingly turned to by consumers as authoritative sources for information about money and investments. Rather like the health influencers mentioned above, many of those purporting to educate and inform followers on financial matters lack the knowledge and expertise to advise anyone. Financial influencers promote high-risk investments, with consumers' uptake of these fuelled by the cost-of-living crisis, a desire to retire early, and an inability or unwillingness to pay for the advice of a real expert. Barret described an online world of financial content where unregulated firms and influencers use promotions which 'gamify' investing – making it seem fun and exciting – without explaining the risks involved (Barrett, 2022).

Other content marketing activities that have drawn criticism include the spreading of fake news, for example about vaccines or palm oil (Di Domenico & Visentin, 2020). In addition, the empty 'virtue signalling' engaged in by brands and companies has also been noted as an area of ethical concern. Sodha (2021) argued that companies and brands who are keen to demonstrate a commitment to (for example) LGBT rights in Pride month, or to anti-racism during Black history month, upload positive posts on social media posts in countries where opinion or activity of this kind is encouraged. In countries where human rights abuses are rife, however, no such opinions are forthcoming (Sodha, 2021).

In 2021, the UK's ASA (Advertising Standards Authority) monitored the Instagram accounts of 122 UK-based influencers over a period of three weeks, examining over 24,000 posts. According to the advertising code in the UK, promotional posts and paid-for endorsements must be clearly indicated, usually using the hashtag #ad (Sweeney, 2021). The ASA's findings revealed that nearly a quarter of the posts they reviewed were advertisements, but that only 35 per cent of those were clearly labelled as such. The ASA threatened to 'crack down' on social media influencers as a result of their 'continual flouting of UK marketing laws' (Sweeney, 2021, para. 2). The lack of meaningful punishment available to regulators means that such infringements are, and continue to be, widespread, with marketing content without appropriate labelling or declarations continuing to be posted by influencers.

Self-Esteem Issues

As noted above, children, teens, and young people are those most in thrall to social media and its constant stream of content marketing. Based on survey data obtained from 129 female Instagram users, Sherlock and Wagstaff (2019) found that 'frequency of Instagram use is correlated with depressive symptoms, self-esteem, general and physical appearance anxiety, and body dissatisfaction' (Sherlock and Wagstaff, 2019, p. 482), with social comparison orientation acting as a mediating variable.

Social comparison is exacerbated and driven by the presence of influencers, especially those promoting, fashion, beauty, or fitness. Finely curated posts show only perfection, with the skin, hair, and bodies of influencers flawless and toned, their svelte appearance achieved through products and services available to eager followers, many of whom consider influencers to be 'friends', or at least more 'authentic' and 'relatable' than other forms of marketing and advertising (Sweeney, et al, 2022). Such misconceptions might be good news for companies, but not for the impressionable, self-conscious, and vulnerable young consumers who compare themselves unfavourably to such images for hours at a time. In 2021, a spokesperson for the 5 Rights Foundation, a charitable organisation campaigning for change in digital services to make them more appropriate for children and young people, remarked that 'in pursuit of profit these companies are stealing children's time, self-esteem and mental health'. The world of social media, with its focus on marketing and commerce is, 'human made [and] privately owned, designed to optimise for commercial purposes'. (Gayle, 2021, para. 4).

Sustainability

Finally, for the purposes of this chapter, we might touch upon the implications for sustainability that are presented by the growth of content marketing. Overconsumption is a huge problem in advanced Western economies and since the rise to prominence of neoliberal economics in the 1980s, consuming and consumerism have become normalised in society (Phipps, 2014). Endless marketing of discounted items, Cyber Monday, Black Friday, and other international promotional events, ensure that more and more deals are bombarded directly to us via social media platforms, and the brands and influencers we like or follow.

Content marketing, like most marketing, often encourages consumption, with all the waste and excess that this might involve. Fast fashion influencers encourage the consumption of clothing that is widely recognised as problematic for the environment in terms of its manufacturing, distribution, and disposal, as well as being dogged by questions of exploitation and sweatshop working conditions (Joy et al., 2012; Nguyen et al., 2021).

Increases in consumerism mean that issues concerning the production and disposal of packaging, along with the air miles and fuel usage required to distribute parcels around the world, are important consequences of content marketing and its 24/7 exhortations for us to buy. Content marketing that encourages consumers to constantly seek out new places to visit (e.g., blogs urging readers to visit places around the world, Instagram images of beautiful locations endorsed by or associated with brands and lifestyle choices), has a profound impact on CO_2 emissions, and by implication on climate change, the erosion of the natural world, and the wasting of limited resources (Asdecker, 2022).

Regulation

We have skimmed the surface of the dark side of content marketing. There is much to be done to understand the long-term negative effects of content marketing, when used inappropriately, on societies and individuals, to ascertain what needs to change and what can be done to minimise harms and impacts. There are attempts to regulate content marketing, such as the ASA's insistence that UK influencers ensure that any sponsored posts are marked up with #ad to denote the marketing intention. Protocols like this offer useful starting points for ensuring that the most vulnerable are protected from the most egregious content marketing activities. However, despite high-profile cases of certain celebrity influencers being publicly 'named and shamed' by the ASA for failing to declare advertising/sponsored content, many influencers continue to ignore industry guidelines. Besides, the global, borderless nature of the World Wide Web means that content from other countries can be accessed all over the world, and the ASA, for instance, as a British organisation, cannot regulate US content. According to Stokel-Walker, a third of brands admitted (when surveyed) that they do not disclose paid partnerships with influencers, mainly because Instagram users are less likely to share a post if it is clearly labelled as advertising, or as sponsored content (Stokel-Walker, 2019). Bearing in mind the vast number of influencers and the staggering volume of content created by them, self-regulation, while warranted, might be very difficult to enforce. Organisations such as the ASA therefore need to be equipped with the means to effectively sanction malpractices, which, in turn, need to go far beyond demanding to remove the post, and the offender's name put onto a list that seems to have, in practice, little impact.

Social Media Literacy Education

A complementary strategy that might go some way towards addressing some of the above issues is through investing in social media literacy and education to help empower children to perceive potential dangers in the world of social media and content marketing. Borchers' (2022) study suggests that teenagers' capacity to understand the 'persuasive knowledge' of influencer content is more limited than their understanding of standard branded content. Thus, governments and educators should implement literacy training that focuses on both 'organic' influencer marketing content, as well as generic branded content. Paxton et al.'s (2022) study into the damaging effects of social media on body image emphasised the necessity of social media literacy as an 'intervention' to help reduce the negative impacts in body image – particularly in girls and young women. The need for social media literacy education has also been recognised at a political level. The UK government's Science & Technology Committee (2019) have called for digital literacy education for children, parents, and educators to help protect and safeguard children from potential risks and harm.

Guiding Principles

What can content marketers do themselves to minimise the likelihood for harm to occur, and how can they think about their activities in ways which mean they can operate within a meaningful and practical ethical framework? The TARES test, as posited by Baker & Martinson, (2001) argues that ethical positions could be best understood and applied if they are ordered along the following principles: Truthfulness, Authenticity, Respect, Equity, and Social responsibility. More recently, Borchers and Enke (2022) have proposed a ten-point plan, highlighting key areas of ethical reflection essential to influencers, and directly applicable and relevant to content marketers.

These ten positions are as follows: **autonomy** (the independence of the influencer must be made clear at all times); **transparency** (any sponsorships or other forms of compensation are disclosed to followers in a clear and timely way); **sincerity** (an influencer or purveyor of content marketing should not sell their opinions and should only endorse products or services they approve of. Equally, firms should not collaborate with influencers whose views and outlook they do not fully support). To this they add **truthfulness** (information provided by content marketers should be accurate, and negative elements should not be withheld. This might include elements such as the purchasing of fake followers, or massaging metrics to present content in an artificially positive light); the principle of **caring** (the expectation that vulnerable groups or individuals are not harmed, though this presupposes an understanding of what might constitute harm), standards of **professionalism** (those involved in content marketing ensure a professional standard of content is maintained, including meticulousness in following a brand's instructions, and confidentiality with regard to data protection and data gathering), **reciprocity** (influencer activity should be adequately recompensed, and such recompense should be evident and publicly acknowledged). **Respect** (which emphasises the need for courtesy and politeness in all interactions and relationships), **loyalty** (content should always reflect and support the interests of sponsoring brands), and **social responsibility** (as a role model, and someone watched and copied by many people, there is a need to for companies and brands, and the influencers they sponsor, behave in a way that 'gives something back' or does not encourage irresponsible and damaging behaviour. This includes behaviour that impacts on the environment or presents issues of sustainability) (Borchers and Enke, 2022).

Ethical Theory

Classical ethical theory, which has long been applied in business and marketing contexts, can also provide content marketers with guidance in their ethical decision making. Utilitarianism, deontology, and virtue ethics, applied as a part of Trevino and Nelson's eight-step ethical decision-making framework, are a simple way of considering the rightness of moral actions. Marketing ethics has been defined as 'the systematic study of how moral standards are applied to marketing decisions, behaviours and institutions', whilst ethical marketing might be defined as 'the practices that emphasise transparent, trustworthy and responsible personal and/or organisational marketing policies and actions that exhibit integrity, as well as fairness to consumer and other stakeholders', (Murphy et al., 2017, p. 5).

Utilitarianism, also known as consequentialism, focuses on the outcomes of actions taken, and provides a functional approach to ethical marketing (Tjandra et al., 2020). Utilitarianism is concerned with the minimisation of harms and the maximisation of benefits. Negative utilitarianism aims to reduce harms, positive utilitarianism seeks to maximise benefits. For the utilitarian, the overall purpose is to achieve 'the greater good' for all involved. Trevino and Nelson describe the utilitarian position as follows: 'ethical decisions should maximise benefits for society and minimise harms. What matters is the net balance of good consequences over bad for society overall' (Trevino & Nelson, 2021, p. 40).

At the heart of utilitarianism is the notion that individuals, such as content marketers, influencers, brands, and organisations, are at liberty to pursue their goals, as long as other people are not harmed in any way. Utilitarianism is popular with marketers and businesses due to its focus on the greatest happiness of the greatest number. One of the difficulties in its application, however, lies in identifying all possible stakeholders, from content marketers themselves, to consumers, organisations, influencers, brands, and whole economies. This means it can be hard to gather all the necessary facts before a decision is made. Nonetheless, in its most elementary conception, as a theoretical position that focuses on the consequences of actions rather than the actions themselves, it is persuasive in its simplicity and apparent fairness.

Deontology, on the other hand, is not concerned with consequences, but with actions. For a deontologist, 'ethics is grounded in notions of duty, and it follows from this that some acts are morally obligatory, regardless of their consequences' (Somerville & Wood, 2008, p. 146). This means that a deontological position is one that is focused on doing what is morally right, at the centre of which is the well-being of the individual. For a deontologist, all individuals are equal. The principles of natural law – honesty, promise-keeping, fairness, loyalty, rights to safety and justice, responsibility, compassion, and respect – are central to deontological decision making (Tjandra et al., 2020, p. 607). Furthermore, for a deontologist, an action is only ethical if it can be universalised, i.e., if it can be used in all situations by all stakeholders. Thus, for a deontologist, any action undertaken by content marketers that harms or damages an individual is an action that should not be undertaken. As such, as a stand-alone ethical position, deontology can appear inflexible and uncompromising.

Virtue ethics is concerned with the moral character of individuals, as defined by the community of which they form a part. 'Virtue ethics argues that a person's character must be justified by a relevant moral community, or a community that holds the person to the highest ethical standards' (Tjandra, et al., 2020, p. 608). However, what must be remembered is that individuals belong to several communities: professional communities, perhaps, but also the wider consumer community. A social media influencer, for example, may have a moral responsibility to generate profit for their sponsor. At the same time, they might have a moral responsibility to adhere to the guidelines set down by the ASA, as well as a responsibility to maintain an authentic and sincere dialogue with followers and online community members. Of course, if the values of community members are themselves unethical, for instance when influencers 'forget' to mention that their posts are, in fact, sponsored advertisements mainly because 'everyone else "forgets" too', then our community's ethical standards are open to question. However, behaviour that is based on the principles of virtue ethics should be moderate, truthful, and prudent, and be conducted with integrity, fairness, trust, respect, self-control, truthfulness, and empathy (Ferrell et al., 2015, in Tjandra et al., 2020, p.608).

Importantly, moral responsibility is not limited to the creators and/or disseminators of content marketing messages. Sponsors, marketing agencies, aggregators, platforms, and any stakeholder of the content marketing value chain need to be aware of and play their role in making sure moral principles are adhered to. The key players in the content marketing ecosystem have the potential to drive change by promoting positive practices and setting examples, as well as implementing and enforcing industry standards in their relationships with up- and downstream value chain partners.

An Eight-Step Framework Towards Ethical Content Marketing

How might the three theories outlined above work in harmony to provide a coherent strategy for ethical decision making? Trevino and Nelson have suggested 'eight steps to sound ethical decision making in business' (Trevino & Nelson, 2021, p. 37). Their framework offers a useful structure for guiding content marketers' ethical decision making, and for addressing some of the issues highlighted above.

Step one: gather the facts. Here content marketers might look at the situation that they are faced with, how did it arise, what facts might be gathered to ensure an informed ethical decision?

Step two: define the ethical issues. Here, points of conflict or value might be considered. Are the rights of consumers affected by choices and behaviours? What about the obligations to sponsors, or brands? What questions are there concerning justice, fairness, loyalty, and honesty with respect to those impacted by decisions and actions?

Step three: identify affected parties (stakeholders). Here, one might apply utilitarian and deontological theory. A utilitarian might seek out the harms and benefits that affect different parties because of proposed actions. A deontologist might focus on rights and duties of those involved, from consumers to brands and companies.

Step four: identify consequences. Here, building on step three and drawing strongly on utilitarianism, one would consider who would be harmed by a particular decision, or who might benefit.

Step five: identify the obligations. This step involves the key principles of deontology, requiring an understanding of what duty of care exists between decision maker and affected parties. What rights are involved? This includes contractual rights, such as that which exists between an influencer and a brand, for example, as well as implicit rights, such at the right consumers have to honesty, fairness, and transparency when faced with marketing content.

Step six: consider character and integrity. Drawing on the tenets of virtue ethics, this asks decision makers to reflect on their own values and the values of the community of which they are a part. This might be a professional community such as the Chartered Institute of Marketing, or the Institute of Direct Marketing, or it might be a broader understanding of community, such as a brand's community of followers.

Step seven: think creatively about potential actions. This step exhorts ethical decision makers to stop and think, to weigh up practical alternative courses of action and reflect on the ethical decision-making process so far.

Step eight: check your gut. What decision seem right to you? Despite the reflections occasioned by previous seven steps do your instincts tell you what the correct moral decision might be? (Trevino & Nelson, 2021).

The framework, with its eight sequential steps, combines philosophical arguments and practical reflections. Its application in content marketing-related scenarios might help content creators to make sound ethical decisions, and address some of the less positive elements of content marketing set out earlier in this chapter.

Conclusions

This chapter has described the rise of content marketing as a phenomenon of the 21st century. Such exponential growth has also seen the emergence of elements and practices of content marketing that might be described as its 'dark side'. These include data misuse and issues of surveillance, the lack of honesty amongst certain social media influencers, the growth of self-esteem issues amongst young people, the lack of marketing and advertising literacy surrounding content marketing's 'soft sell' and co-created approach, as well as the impact on the environment of the increase in consumerism occasioned by content marketing's 24/7 exhortations to buy and sell. Greater industry and government regulation might moderate some of these issues, though there are problems in the implementation of any such laws or regulations. Government interventions in social media literacy would also be most welcome. In the meantime, we have suggested some ways of addressing the emerging issues, including Borchers and Enke's (2022) ten-point plan and Trevino and Nelson's (2021) eight steps framework to sound ethical decision making in business.

End of Chapter Questions

1   Outline three arguments explaining the value of content marketing, and three arguments that explain its shortcomings. Consider whether the positives outweigh the negatives.
2   Consider the importance of privacy for content marketers. What might be the consequences for consumers of content marketers' surveillance techniques.
3   Discuss the value of digital literacy for consumers, marketers, and other stakeholders.
4   What themes would you consider appropriate in a social media content marketing literacy programme aimed at young people (consider children aged 5–11, and 12–18).
5   In teams of two or three, argue for and against the following motion: influencer marketing is unethical. Provide examples to justify your arguments.
6   Take five minutes to scroll through your Instagram feed. How many influencer marketing posts do you see in that time. Discuss how and why you are targeted by content marketers and reflect on what this means for you as a consumer.
7   In what ways can content creators be held more accountable for the marketing they produce on social media?
8   Is content marketing compatible with sustainability? Explain your answer with examples of sustainable and unsustainable content marketing activities.

9   Apply Borchers and Enke's (2022) ten-point plan to the content marketing practices of a company of your choice. Is the ten-point plan a reasonable and applicable approach for encouraging content marketers to behave ethically?

References

Anon. (2019, February 3). "Persuasive technologies" prompt child health fears. *Financial Times*.

Asdecker, B. (2022). Travel-related influencer content on Instagram: How social media fuels wanderlust and how to mitigate the effect. *Sustainability*, *14*(2), 855. 10.3390/su14 020855

Baker, S., & Martinson, D. L. (2001). The TARES test: Five principles for ethical persuasion. *Journal of Mass Media Ethics*, *16*(2–3), 148–175. 10.1080/08900523.2001.9679610

Barrett, C. (2022, December 9). Beware influencers plugging the financial advice gap. *The Guardian*.

Borchers, N. S. (2022). Between skepticism and identification: A systematic mapping of adolescents' persuasion knowledge of influencer marketing. *Journal of Current Issues & Research in Advertising*, *43*(3), 274–300. 10.1080/10641734.2022.2066230

Borchers, N. S., & Enke, N. (2022). "I've never seen a client say: 'Tell the influencer not to label this as sponsored'": An exploration into influencer industry ethics. *Public Relations Review*, *48*(5), 102235. 10.1016/j.pubrev.2022.102235

Ceci, L. (2023, February 16). UK children daily time on selected social media apps 2022. Statista.

De Veirman, M., Cauberghe, V., & Hudders, L. (2017). Marketing through Instagram influencers: The impact of number of followers and product divergence on brand attitude. *International Journal of Advertising*, *36*(5), 798–828. 10.1080/02650487.2017.1348035

Di Domenico, G., & Visentin, M. (2020). Fake news or true lies? Reflections about problematic contents in marketing. *International Journal of Market Research*, *62*(4), 409–417. 10.1177/1470785320934719

Dubicka, B., & Theodosiou. (2020). Technology use and the mental health of children and young people, The Royal College of Psychiatrists.

Einstein, M. (2016). *Black Ops Advertising: Native Ads, Content Marketing and the Covert World of the Digital Sell* (1st ed.). OR Books.

Elias, A. S., & Gill, R. (2018). Beauty surveillance: The digital self-monitoring cultures of neoliberalism. *European Journal of Cultural Studies*, *21*(1), 59–77.

Ferrell, O. C., Fraedrich, J., & Ferrell, L. (2015). *Business Ethics: Ethical Decision Making and Cases* (10th ed.). Cengage Learning.

Gayle, D. (2021, September 14). Facebook aware of Instagram's harmful effect on teenage girls, leak reveals. *The Guardian*.

Gill, R., & Elias, A. S. (2014). 'Awaken your incredible': Love your body discourses and postfeminist contradictions. *International Journal of Media & Cultural Politics*, *10*(2), 179–188.

Gritters, J. (2018, December 3). The psychological toll of becoming an Instagram influencer, *The Guardian*.

Hackley, C. E., & Kitchen, P. J. (1999). Ethical perspectives on the postmodern communications leviathan. *Journal of Business Ethics*, *20*(1), 15.

Järvinen, J., & Taiminen, H. (2016). Harnessing marketing automation for B2B content marketing. *Industrial Marketing Management*, *54*, 164–175. 10.1016/j.indmarman.2015.07.002

Joy, A., Sherry, J. F., Venkatesh, A., Wang, J., & Chan, R. (2012). Fast fashion, sustainability, and the ethical appeal of luxury brands. *Fashion Theory, 16*(3), 273–295. 10.2752/175174112X13340749707123

Kent, M. L., & Taylor, M. (2002). Toward a dialogic theory of public relations. *Public Relations Review, 28*(1), 21–37. 10.1016/S0363-8111(02)00108-X

Leban, M., Thomsen, T. U., von Wallpach, S., & Voyer, B. G. (2021). Constructing personas: How high-net-worth social media influencers reconcile ethicality and living a luxury lifestyle. *Journal of Business Ethics, 169*(2), 225–239. 10.1007/s10551-020-04485-6

Leite, L. H. R. (2021). Is social media spreading misinformation on exercise and health in Brazil? *International Journal of Environmental Research and Public Health, 18*(22), 11914. 10.3390/ijerph182211914

Marocolo, M., Meireles, A., de Souza, H. L. R., Mota, G. R., Oranchuk, D. J., Arriel, R. A., & Murphy, H., & Espinoza, J. (2023, January 5). Meta fined almost €400mn over EY privacy rule violations. *Financial Times.*

Murphy, P., Laczniak, G. R., & Harris, F. (2017). *Ethics in Marketing: International Cases and Perspectives* (2nd ed.). Routledge.

Nguyen, H. T., Le, D. M. D., Ho, T. T. M., & Nguyen, P. M. (2021). Enhancing sustainability in the contemporary model of CSR: A case of fast fashion industry in developing countries. *Social Responsibility Journal, 17*(4), 578–591. 10.1108/SRJ-03-2019-0108

Ofcom. (2022). *Children Media Lives: A Report for Ofcom.* www.ofcom.org.uk/__data/assets/pdf_file/0021/234552/childrens-media-lives-2022-summary-report.pdf (last accessed 20/01/2023)

Orben, A., Przybylski, A. K., Blakemore, S.-J., & Kievit, R. A. (2022). Windows of developmental sensitivity to social media. *Nature Communications, 13*(1), 1649. 10.1038/s41467-022-29296-3

Orlowski, J. (2020, July 27). We need to rethink social media before it's too late. We've accepted a Faustian bargain. *The Guardian.*

Paxton, S. J., McLean, S. A., & Rodgers, R. F. (2022). "My critical filter buffers your app filter": Social media literacy as a protective factor for body image. *Body Image, 40,* 158–164. 10.1016/j.bodyim.2021.12.009

Phipps, A. (2014). *The Politics of the Body: Gender in a Neoliberal and Neoconservative Age.* Polity Press.

Proulx, M. (2015, April 2). *There is no more social media – just advertising.* https://Adage.Com/Article/Digitalnext/Social-Media-Advertising/297841

Science & Technology Committee, H. of C. (2019). *Impact of social media and screen-use on young people's health (HC 822).*

Seymour, R. (2019, July 16). The machine always wins: What drives our addiction to social media – podcast. *The Guardian.*

Shankar, A., Whittaker, J., & Fitchett, J. A. (2006). Heaven knows I'm miserable now. *Marketing Theory, 6*(4), 485–505.

Sherlock, M., & Wagstaff, D. L. (2019). Exploring the relationship between frequency of Instagram use, exposure to idealized images, and psychological well-being in women. *Psychology of Popular Media Culture, 8*(4), 482–490. 10.1037/ppm0000182

Silverman, J. (2015, February 26). 'Pics or it didn't happen' – the mantra of the Instagram era. *The Guardian.*

Sodha, S. (2021, November 7). Social media fuels narcissists' worst desires, making reasoned debate near impossible. *The Guardian.*

Somerville, I., & Wood, E. (2008). Business ethics, public relations and corporate social responsibility. In *The Public Relations Handbook* (p. 143160). Routledge.

Stokel-Walker, C. (2019, February 3). Instagram: Beware of bad influencers … *The Guardian*.

Sweeney, E., Lawlor, M.-A., & Brady, M. (2022). Teenagers' moral advertising literacy in an influencer marketing context. *International Journal of Advertising, 41*(1), 54–77. 10.1080/02650487.2021.1964227

Sweeney, M. (2021, March). UK social media influencers warned over ad rules breaches. *The Guardian*.

Sweeney, M. (2022, September 26). TikTok could face £27m fine for failing to protect children's privacy. *The Guardian*.

Tjandra, N. C., Aroean, L., & Prabandari, Y. S. (2020). Public evaluation of the ethics of tobacco marketing in Indonesia: Symbiotic ethical approach. *Qualitative Market Research: An International Journal, 23*(4), 603–626. 10.1108/QMR-01-2020-0011

Trevino, L. K., & Nelson, A. K. (2021). *Managing Business Ethics: Straight Talk About How To Do It Right* (8th ed.). John Wiley & Sons.

Williams, Z. (2023, January 8). Young people don't hate their bodies because they are weak – but because capitalism demands it. *The Guardian*.

Zarouali, B., de Pauw, P., Ponnet, K., Walrave, M., Poels, K., Cauberghe, V., & Hudders, L. (2019). Considering children's advertising literacy from a methodological point of view: Past practices and future recommendations. *Journal of Current Issues & Research in Advertising, 40*(2), 196–213. 10.1080/10641734.2018.1503109

12 Contemporary and Emerging Content Marketing Trends

By Dr Simone Kurtzke

Learning Outcomes

- To recognise the key contemporary and emerging marketing trends and discuss their impact on content marketing.
- To identify current and emerging forms of the metaverse and the role of virtual content marketing within it.
- To develop an in-depth understanding of the role of AI in content marketing and how it can be applied in practice.

Metaverse and Virtual Content Marketing

In 2020, the term 'metaverse', first used in the 1992 science fiction novel *Snow Crash* by Neal Stephenson, started gaining popularity in the tech community. Interest in the metaverse significantly increased in 2021 after Mark Zuckerberg rebranded Facebook to Meta on 28 October of that year, announcing his intention to create the next version of the internet as an immersive world built in virtual reality (Kim, 2021). A Google Trends search conducted in January 2023 (see Figure 12.1) shows that the term has been actively searched for since 2021 peaking after Zuckerberg's announcement, although consumer interest has declined since.

Figure 12.1 Metaverse Google Trends search Jan 2023.

DOI: 10.4324/9781003346500-12

This may not be surprising as, while the metaverse is generally considered the next phase of the internet that will allow omni-connected, immersive experiences, the technology and infrastructure are still being developed and a separate metaversal world beyond the real world is expected to take another 10–15 years (Kim, 2021). In addition, several large tech firms including Meta and Microsoft are investing millions of dollars in building a digital experience consistent with the notion of the metaverse. However, it is not yet clear if and how a shared version will exist because, similar to the internet, the metaverse cannot be owned by one corporation (IAB, 2022; Kim, 2021). Despite this, it is generally agreed that early forms of metaverse technologies and ecosystems already exist, and mass consumer adoption is expected to be achieved by 2030, with McKinsey predicting global annual metaverse-related spending to reach $5 trillion by then (Alcántara & Coffee, 2022; Wagner & Cozmiuc, 2022). While no singular definition of the metaverse exists and a fully realised version has yet to emerge, for the purpose of this chapter, we will consider current metaversal experiences and associated content marketing opportunities that brands should be aware of.

The Metaverse as Virtual Worlds

An early forerunner of the metaverse is generally agreed to be *Second Life*, a free-to-use centralised virtual world populated by real humans represented as avatars, filled with user-generated content (Giang Barrera & Shah, 2023; Virgilio, 2022). *Second Life* launched in 2003 and, while it borrowed its architecture and aesthetics from video game simulations such as *The Sims*, it was not a game but intentionally designed as an alternative virtual world where users could live fantasy lives with new virtual identities in virtual communities of their choosing (Brown, 2022; Virgilio, 2022). In 2006, Adidas became the first brand to set up a virtual shop in *Second Life* where users could buy virtual trainers with 100 Linden dollars (the *Second Life* currency) to give their avatars additional bounce when moving in the world (Bannister, 2006). While *Second Life* continues to exist today averaging around 200,000 daily active users, this early metaverse never broke through to mainstream success and did not grow beyond a million users, with media attention dying down after the late 2000s (Gent, 2021; Virgilio, 2022). The key innovation of *Second Life* was to provide a shared, three-dimensional online experience in the form of a persistent digital world, populated by multiple participants and easily accessible from a web browser. The legacy of *Second Life* can be found in two other proto-metaverse experiences brands should be aware of and are subsequently discussed: gaming-based virtual worlds, and blockchain-based virtual worlds.

Gaming-Based Virtual Worlds

Online gaming platforms are currently the closest approximation of an immersive experience in a persistent digital world, typically accessible without purchasing additional hardware (such as a VR headset). The gaming industry has seen significant growth in recent years, further fuelled by the Covid-19 pandemic and its lockdowns, and is predicted to be worth $321 billion by 2026 (PwC, 2022). While video games are played across all age demographics and almost 82 per cent of all internet users worldwide are also gamers (Statista, 2022, 2023), the three games most closely associated with metaversal experiences (Fortnite, Roblox, and Minecraft) have a primarily young audience and are also more likely to skew male (Melcher, 2022). Key to the success of these proto-metaverses is that they double up as virtual hangouts, where gaming is a vehicle for socialising and the virtual world surrounding it provides a meeting place. These proto-metaverses thus can be understood as an equivalent to a shopping mall or town square in the pre-internet age, and have been called the new IRL ('in real life', internet slang for 'reality') where young people hang out and spend much of their leisure time (Nielsen, 2020; Perry, 2022). Gaming-based virtual worlds tend to be governed and owned by a single corporation, typically a game publisher. They often feature the ability for users to make customisable avatars of themselves, as well as tools to create user-generated content, further increasing engagement (IAB, 2022). In what follows, we supply a brief comparison of the three most popular platforms before introducing key opportunities for brands in these immersive content environments. The overview is based on information from Iqbal (2023), Dean (2022), and Pilipović (2023), and should be treated as an approximation as it has not directly been provided by the companies themselves.

Table 12.1 Comparison of the three most popular online games

	Fortnite	*Roblox*	*Minecraft*
Owner	Epic Games	Roblox Corporation	Microsoft
Launch Year	2017	2006	2011
Monthly Active Users	83 million	202 million	141 million
Age	18–24 (62.7%), 25–34 (22.5%) 35–44 (12.7%), 45–54 (2%), 55+ (0.01%)	Under 9 (25%), 9–12 (29%), 13–16 (13%), 17–24 (16%), 25+ (14%)	Average player age is 24; many younger players; no precise age breakdown exists

(Continued)

Table 12.1 (Continued)

	Fortnite	Roblox	Minecraft
Gender	90% male, 10% female	51% male, 44% female, 5% unknown	Skews male, e.g., ages 3–12: 54% male, 32% female, 14% unknown; ages 6–8: 68% male, 29% female, 3% unknown; no precise gender breakdown exists
Geography	Available in nearly 100 countries, with the highest popularity (measured in revenue) in the U.S., followed by France, the UK, Canada, and Brazil	U.S. and Canada (28%), Europe (27%), APAC (16.7%), others (28%)	Top five countries (measured by daily usage recorded): U.S. (21.21%), Brazil (6.17%), Russia (5.59%), UK (5.06%), Germany (4.60%)
Accessed via	PC, PS4, PS5, Xbox One, Xbox X|S, Android, Nintendo Switch	Desktop and mobile	PC, PS3, PS4, PS5, Xbox One, Xbox X|S, Android, iOS, Nintendo Switch

Numerous opportunities for content marketing are currently available for brands on proto-metaverses like Roblox and Fortnite – less so on Minecraft, which restricted promotional use in 2016 (IPG Media Lab, 2016). In general, brands on the first two platforms are allowed to create any virtual content they want, but they must compete for the players' attention with exceptionally well-liked alternatives to the in-game experience. As a result, the focus must be on action, enjoyment, and reward, and brand virtual content must add value to, and integrate with the virtual experience, as opposed to interrupting it (IAB, 2022). Tools for content creation are typically available in the game (for example, Fortnite Creative), and branded content competes with user-generated content and other professionally sourced content. For brands wishing to undertake virtual content marketing in these proto-metaverses, we outline three of the most common approaches as follows:

- **Creation of virtual items**: One of the easiest ways to get started with virtual content marketing is through the creation of virtual items such as clothing and accessories for avatars. Since an avatar is the embodied self of a consumer in the metaverse, it is part of their identity and a key site for self-representation and expression of personality (Giang Barrera & Shah, 2023; Kim, 2021). It is thus no surprise that fashion brands are at the forefront of metaverse content marketing. One example is Balenciaga, who in 2021 brought digital fashion to Fortnite including outfits and accessories such as a backpack and a designer pickaxe (www.youtube.com/watch?v=_gKiVi3tmqI). Another example is retailer Hot Topic, who in late 2022 launched a collection of ten branded, Halloween-themed virtual clothing items for sale in the Roblox Avatar Store and continues to maintain a shop front selling virtual items (www.roblox.com/groups/15966394/Hot-Topic#!/store)

- **Creation of virtual content for existing games**: A second option for content marketing in gaming-based virtual worlds is to create virtual content for existing games or experiences. For example, in 2022, food brand McCain launched the game 'Farms of the Future' within LiveTopia, one of the top ten Roblox experiences, to promote its new Regen Fries (www.youtube.com/watch?v=4t3vngvJOCY). Another example is fashion brand Burberry, who in 2022 collaborated with Minecraft to create a bespoke in-game adventure as downloadable content (DLC). The map also featured 15 Burberry skins (customisation options), including avatar outfits and armour (www.youtube.com/watch?v=b4wGLnd9Lzk).

- **Creation of stand-alone game or experience**: The most involved virtual content marketing brands can undertake is the creation of a stand-alone immersive content experience. Examples include Gucci, who in 2021 created Gucci Garden, its first Gucci-themed immersive experience on Roblox, followed by Gucci Town in 2022, its permanent digital destination in the virtual world. The experience also features Gucci Shop, a boutique where visitors can purchase digital Gucci items to collect or to dress their avatars (www.youtube.com/watch?v=ezJFu15N3w0). Gillette, in 2021, created a custom-built battle map in Fortnite (www.fortnite.com/creative/island-codes/gillette-bed-battles-0457-9793-6848) and in 2022 launched the Gillette Cup, an in-game two-day tournament with a cash prize of $25,000.

Gaming-based virtual worlds are currently the most established metaversal experiences, benefiting from large pre-existing audiences that brands can engage with using virtual content marketing. There have also been attempts to create non-gaming metaverses as separate virtual worlds with a real digital economy and distributed ownership. These systems are enabled by blockchain technology and fuelled by cryptocurrency and non-fungible tokens (NFTs). NFTs represent the digital ownership of a unique (digital or physical) asset such as a piece of art, music, a collectable, or an estate, and they can be sold in marketplaces (Guidi & Michienzi, 2022; Yencha, 2023). Blockchain-based virtual worlds have not presently achieved mainstream breakthrough, and research has shown that concepts such as NFTs are significantly less popular than media coverage suggests, with less than a quarter of internet users understanding what NFTs are (DataReportal, 2022). It has also been suggested that half of the supposed value of NFT trades may be based on scams. In 2022, one of the largest cryptocurrency exchanges, FTX, was declared bankrupt with customers losing large amounts of money, and its CEO being accused of manipulating the markets (DataReportal, 2022; Flitter & Yaffe-Bellany, 2023). We thus recommend that brands interested in virtual content marketing in the metaverse start with gaming-based worlds rather than those based on blockchain technology; however, the latter are briefly explored in the next section for the sake of completeness.

Blockchain-Based Virtual Worlds

Blockchain-based virtual worlds are social platforms made up of numerous land parcels that are owned by players, businesses, and investors rather than one company. These decentralised proto-metaverses are user-governed and their aim is to ultimately become the property of the participants. This is facilitated by blockchain technology which allows for the use of crypto-currency to buy and sell digital assets known as NFTs in marketplaces (Gadekallu et al., 2022; Güven & Ercan, 2022). The best known of these virtual worlds is *Decentraland*, a community-owned platform based on the Ethereum blockchain where anyone owning or renting land has the freedom to build anything they like. Users can develop and monetise experiences, for example by creating interactive objects and mini games on their land parcel. Blockchain-based virtual worlds are socioeconomic digital environments, where users truly own what they purchase and where they can generate real income (Guidi & Michienzi, 2022; Yencha, 2023). As these worlds are not centrally owned, and function as a space both for leisure and for making money, they are seen by some as a better representation of the future meta-verse. That's because the blockchain technology underpinning them can provide a complete economic system that connects the virtual world with the real world (Gadekallu et al., 2022; Guidi & Michienzi, 2022).

Before investing in virtual content marketing in blockchain-based virtual worlds, brands should be aware that current user data for these proto-metaverses suggests low adoption; for example, in October 2022, it was re-ported that *Decentraland* had only 38 daily active users in the preceding 24 hours, while competitor *The Sandbox* had 522 daily active users in that same time (Thompson, 2022). Brands have nevertheless undertaken virtual content marketing in these proto-metaverses. In late 2021, sports brand Under Armour created the first branded virtual sneaker, called Genesis Curry Flow, that could be worn across blockchain-based worlds including *Decentraland* and *The Sandbox*. The Genesis Curry Flow was released in a limited edition of 2,974 NFTs at the cost of $333 each and sold out in 10 minutes (IAB, 2022). In March 2022, the first metaverse fashion week was hosted in *Decentraland*, and brands participating included Dolce & Gabbana and Tommy Hilfiger, with the event attracting 108,000 users (Lifestyle Asia, 2022). A user video of the showcase is available online (www.youtube.com/watch?v=yuaeVgZfZII).

The Metaverse as Extended Reality (XR)

A key concept of the future metaverse is that of extended reality (XR), where users are located within a fully embodied version of the internet, as opposed to looking at it on a screen. The ultimate aim is the coexistence of a permanent physical-virtual reality (IAB, 2022; Lee et al., 2021). Consumers increasingly demand more tactile and immersive capabilities from their digital interfaces, and this is only possible with XR technologies of virtual reality (VR), augmented reality (AR), and mixed reality (MR) (Gadekallu et al., 2022; Giang Barrera & Shah, 2023). This metaverse is a digitally replicated environment that consumers can fully experience as an immersive virtual world through their digital avatars, which serve as the users' virtual representations and have the same legal standing as their real-world counterparts (Gadekallu et al., 2022; Lee et al., 2021). Current technologies to experience a version of XR are typically through a VR-enabled immersive device, such as a headset or even a full-body haptic bodysuit (Gadekallu et al., 2022). While VR and AR are relatively well understood, there is no commonly agreed definition of MR as it is on a spectrum between the physical world and the digital world, incorporating elements of both VR and AR (Lee et al., 2021; Microsoft, 2023). The figure underneath demonstrates the relationship between the overarching concept of XR, and its components of AR, VR, and MR, as utilised in this chapter.

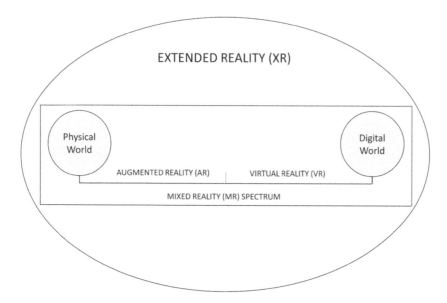

Figure 12.2 Metaverse as Extended Reality (XR).

While the vision of the metaverse that blends physical and digital worlds, powered by XR and an immersive internet is yet to be realised, some of the building blocks are already in place. In what follows, we will first provide a brief overview of the key concepts involved (drawing on Lee et al., 2021; Microsoft, 2023; and Wagner & Cozmiuc, 2022), so that brands are aware of XR technologies already available. We will then give examples of existing virtual content marketing efforts in this space.

Table 12.2 Overview of XR technologies

	Augmented Reality	*Virtual Reality*	*Mixed Reality*
Definition	A technology that projects virtual objects in real physical environments in the real world.	A technology that fully immerses a user in a computer-generated simulation.	A technology that immerses a user in a physical reality blended with a computer-generated simulation.
Key features	User remains present in physical reality. Low immersion. User sees virtual objects as overlay onto physical reality but cannot interact with them.	User experiences a digital reality separate from physical reality. Full immersion. User can interact with and manipulate virtual objects.	User can be present both personally and digitally in the physical world, as an avatar. Partial immersion. User can interact with and manipulate both physical and virtual objects.
Accessed via	Head mounted device (e.g., headset, glasses) Handheld device (e.g., smartphone)	Headset Haptic clothing (e.g., gloves, suit)	Head mounted device (e.g., headset, glasses)
Example devices	iPhone, iPad	Meta Quest	Microsoft HoloLens
Example applications	Pokémon GO IKEA Place	Meta Horizon Worlds The Elder Scrolls V: Skyrim VR	Microsoft Mesh

Brands' involvement with virtual content marketing in XR has to date mostly involved AR-accessed experiences, as these are more easily accessible to consumers without purchasing additional equipment. Examples of XR brand content experiences are provided underneath.

• **AR campaign**: Modelo beer in 2019 created an AR campaign to turn outdoor billboards of the brand into moving art pieces to celebrate Dia de Los Muertos, a celebration of life that honours the dead in Mexican culture (www.youtube.com/watch?v=tkB5fQfOCVs).

- **AR app**: Treasury Wine Estates, a premium wine brand, has created a free Living Wine Labels AR app that unlocks additional virtual content on its labels for consumers to watch (for example, zombies breaking out of *The Walking Dead* themed bottles, www.youtube.com/watch?v=mLOnqndJ-FQ, or, crime stories narrated on its 19 Crimes brand, www.youtube.com/watch?v=jtlXtcA1eo4).
- **Virtual try-on**: AR-based virtual content marketing is increasingly popular in the fashion industry. For example, brands such as Gucci, Burberry, and Prada offer virtual try-on, which uses AR to allow consumers to overlay clothing or accessories over a live image from their camera (www.youtube.com/watch?v=C3nZumsSisg). In 2022, British Vogue presented a Snapchat experience to Cannes Lions where attendees could try on digital clothing from brands including Versace and Dior (www.youtube.com/watch?v=i1NaIITVriw).
- **VR experience**: Wendy's, a fast-food chain of restaurants, in 2022 opened Wendyverse, a branded VR experience located in Meta's Horizon World platform. Consumers can visit various areas and play different games within the world, with a focus on creating fun experiences for consumers with virtual goods (www.youtube.com/watch?v=lWLejP1DzQw0).

Opportunities for virtual content marketing on the metaverse will continue to unfold at pace and beyond the chapter of this book, both on current and emerging platforms. While Meta's VR *Horizon Worlds* has struggled to make an impact, with under 200,000 monthly active users reported in October 2022 (Moyer, 2022), Epic Games, owner of popular proto-metaverse *Fortnite* introduced earlier, is emerging as a key player. In 2022, the company made a significant investment in metaverse infrastructure and also joined forces with LEGO with the purpose of building a children-focused metaverse (Peters, 2022; Tassi, 2022). At the business end, a prototype metaverse built on Microsoft Mesh called Global Collaboration Village was launched at the 2023 World Economic Forum meeting in Davos (Herskowitz, 2023). While a fully realised metaverse may still be a decade away, brands must be aware of the shift in consumer behaviour and the opportunities for virtual content marketing now, in order to have a competitive advantage in this next phase of the internet.

Artificial Intelligence in Content Marketing

Gartner, a global information technology research and consultancy company, predicted in 2015 that by 2018, 20 per cent of business content would be generated by machines (Pemberton Levy, 2015). In the 2020s, artificial intelligence (AI) for content marketing has significantly advanced, extending to generative AI able to create original content across text, images, and video (Rose, 2022). The use of AI in marketing is not limited to content marketing but rather, the technology is a critical influencing factor disrupting all areas of marketing and business (Chintalapati & Pandey, 2022; Vlačić et al., 2021). While there are many different definitions of AI, in this chapter, we follow Haenlein and Kaplan's (2019, p. 5) who define it as 'a system's ability to correctly read external input, to learn from such data, and to use those learnings to fulfil specific goals and tasks through flexible adaptation'. It is worth noting that AI is utilised as a catch-all phrase for a wide range of activities and concepts including machine learning, service robots, automation, big data, neural networks, natural language processing (NLP), and the Internet of Things (IoT). The fundamental premise of AI underlying these concepts is that different kinds of computers, using software and algorithms, can facilitate or carry out tasks that previously required human cognitive abilities (Mustak et al., 2021).

Machine Learning versus Generative AI

Before exploring the role of AI in content marketing, it is important to first distinguish machine learning (ML), an AI technology that has been used for some time in areas including personalised social media content and advertising based on consumers' own data and profiles (Ma & Sun, 2020), from generative AI, a technology that has progressed rapidly in the 2020s and is highly disruptive as it could supplement or replace human content creation across all categories (Galloway, 2022). ML was until recently the key technology commonly understood and used by companies as their main application of AI in marketing. ML is a subfield of AI that involves training algorithms to learn patterns in large data sets and independently make 'intelligent' decisions based these data. Generative AI, in contrast, is a type of AI that is able to generate new information rather than merely make decisions based on existing data (Galloway, 2022; Ma & Sun, 2020). In the context of content marketing, the new information generated can be in the form of text, images, audio, or other types of media, also called synthetic media (Synthesia, n.d.). For example, generative AI can be used to create realistic images, human-sounding voices, as well as new ideas and concepts. Both ML and generative AI can make decisions autonomously and without human intervention. In technical terms, ML algorithms are used to make predictions based on patterns in the data, while generative AI algorithms are used to create new content based on a set of rules or a model of the data (Galloway, 2022; Ma & Sun, 2020). Consumers tend not to be aware of the existence of AI and intelligent agents despite the widespread use of AI-driven personalised engagement marketing. In the digital environment, each individual has a different customer journey, created by automated systems (Kumar et al., 2019; Ma & Sun, 2020). The use of AI in marketing thus has social and ethical implications for brands (Hancock et al., 2020), which are outlined in a later section.

AI Content Personalisation using Machine Learning

The original and first application of AI agents using ML in content marketing lies in content personalisation and optimisation, that is, predicting which content is most likely to be effective in generating user engagement or action, aligned with marketing objectives. For example, automated bidding algorithms analyse a consumer's online profile in milliseconds to determine the best bid for delivering a digital advert, chatbots engage in conversations based on customers' input, ML powers recommendations engines on e-commerce websites (e.g., Amazon) and content platforms (e.g., Netflix). It can also be used to analyse billions of images and customer sentiment on social media to draw insights for future content success (Ma & Sun, 2020; Mustak et al., 2021). In e-commerce, AI agents can optimise content to positively influence consumer purchase behaviour. For example, travel booking website Expedia used AI to train its ML models to identify and highlight the most attractive hotel images in its data set. It was then able to predict images that increased click-through and purchases (Campbell et al., 2020). Beauty brands utilise chatbots to facilitate online buying. The chatbot can interact with consumers through a small box on-screen while they are exploring the website, making personalised product and service recommendations. Research has shown that such 'beauty chatbots', particularly if programmed to have friend-like characteristics, positively impact purchase behaviours in Gen Z women (Ameen et al., 2022).

The use of ML in content marketing is now a necessity for brands due to the significant explosion of content in the digital environment. This has led to a paradox of choice where consumers are overwhelmed by digital content options and choice leading to information overload, making AI essential to narrow and curate content in a personalised relevant way (Kumar et al., 2019). Thus, AI-powered content marketing can be understood with the broader concept of relationship management, where ML facilitates personalised brand relationships at scale and meets customer expectations for an experience tailored uniquely to their own preference (Chandra et al., 2022; Hopkinson & Singhal, 2018). Key use cases of AI content personalisation that brands should consider in their content marketing are summarised below.

- **Customised digital ads**. Ads can be tailored to consumers' online behaviour patterns based on automatic analysis of user signals (e.g., ads on social media platforms based on user interest and past interactions). For example, *The Economist* digital publication used AI-driven programmatic advertising to drill down into specific reading habits and preferences of its audience segment of 'reluctant readers' to better match message and targeting, resulting in 3.6 million new readers.

- **Automatic email marketing**. ML is used to send personalised messages and content triggered by consumers' actions (e.g., 'cart abandonment' emails where a discount offer message is sent if customers do not complete an online purchase). It can also utilise consumers' interest data as a basis for personalisation. For example, the American Marketing Association increased monthly engagement rate of their e-newsletter by 42 per cent after using AI to generate individualised subject lines based on interest data of each of their 100,000 subscribers.
- **Use of chatbots**. AI chatbots can answer real-time queries and provide tailored deals, recommendations, and interactions based on consumers' input and behaviours. For example, beauty brand Sephora started using chatbots in 2016 to help consumers narrow down product preferences and offer relevant options, resulting in positively influencing purchase decisions through personalised product recommendations.
- **Personalised content recommendations**. ML is used to personalise newsfeeds and apps, serving digital content (e.g., images, videos, articles) tailored to consumers' characteristics, networks, queries, predicted journey paths, and any other relevant user signals. For example, Starbucks' App keeps track of consumers' purchase habits, including where and at what time of the day it was made. It then provides personalised content and marketing messages based on this data, including recommendations when a customer approaches a nearby store, and special deals to increase the customer's average order value.

While these marketing technologies are at different stages of maturity, some are widespread. ML and personalisation algorithms underpin much of the digital consumption environment are a key feature of contemporary digital communications. In 2022, it was reported that 80 per cent of companies worldwide use chatbots (ServiceBell, 2022). With the acceleration of intelligent, human-like bots and their efficacy in supporting a personalised customer experience cheaply and at scale (Chandra et al., 2022), brands should seriously consider friendly AI agents as a key tool in their personalised content marketing toolkit. This is particularly relevant as the dawn of synthetic and generative AI is likely to transform chatbots from a relatively 'dumb' (ML) technology to one that is increasingly intelligent and human-like.

AI Content Creation using Generative AI

The rapidly emerging area of generative AI in content marketing originates from what is called synthetic content (also called synthetic media), used to describe 'video, image, text, or voice that has been fully or partially generated using artificial intelligence algorithms' (Synthesia, n.d.). The year 2022 has been called by some the year of generative AI as the technology achieved mass awareness following the launch of ChatGPT. This is a chatbot created by OpenAI and was initially released for free use on 30 November 2022, reaching a million users in only 5 days (Olsen, 2022). A Google Trends search conducted in January 2023 illustrates that consumer interest in AI technology generally and in ChatGPT specifically continues to rise, and the ChatGPT tool as well as OpenAI's image creation tool, DALL-E 2, are used to showcase synthetic content marketing in practice in a later section.

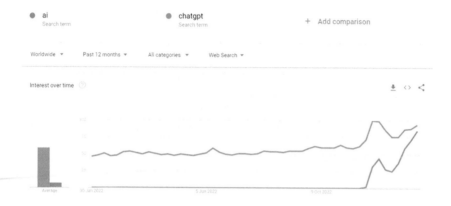

Figure 12.3 AI Content Creation using Generative AI.

As a currently emerging area, synthetic media and generative AI are likely to continue receiving significant attention as its disruptive potential affects not only business and creative sectors but society as a whole (Larsen & Narayan, 2023).

For brands, it is therefore critical to understand both the current state of synthetic media, as well as the benefits and risks such as ethical implications, to give them the tools to prepare for the future. Generative AI is accelerating at a fast pace, and synthetic content is likely to become increasingly widespread and accepted, with major implications on both the creation and consumption of digital content and thus content marketing (Riparbelli, 2023).

Synthetic media is already used every day, both by content creators and Fortune 500 companies, and this is likely to rapidly increase; for example, Jasper, one of the best-known AI copywriters and content generators, is used by over 100,000 marketers and in October 2022 raised $125 m of investment to further accelerate growth (Jasper, n.d.; Larsen & Narayan, 2023). The following list provides examples of synthetic content that marketers should be aware of, and in a later section we provide a selection of specific AI content creation tools currently available.

- **Synthetic text**: Generative AI tools can create large amounts of high-quality text, assist with research and translations, create copy for social media and email marketing and more, all in a short period of time. ChatGPT is one of the best-known examples of AI-generated text. It is a third-generation language model that leverages deep learning to produce various text-based content, including articles, blog posts, essays, stories, legal documents, news reports, etc.
- **Synthetic images**: Images including photos and art can be created synthetically. For example, Dall-E 2 is an image generation system by OpenAI that can create images based on text input. Realistic-looking pictures of people can also be created and a website to illustrate this and quickly generate synthetic photos can be found at https://thispersondoesnotexist.com/.
- **Synthetic audio**: Generative AI can produce audio (e.g., music) and voice (including in different languages). AI simulations of real people's voices are increasingly popular, and it is difficult to detect the difference between human and synthetic voices. It is possible to both clone your own voice or that of a celebrity, or, to generate entirely new voices. In addition, text to speech technology can instantly convert text into realistic-sounding voices.
- **Synthetic video**: Video is a significant contemporary content marketing trend as outlined earlier in this chapter. Synthetic video content can now be produced with a fraction of the time and without the need for cameras, actors, microphones, or audio, while still appearing 'authentic'. Similar to synthetic images, AI-generated video can be created just from text prompts (an example product demo can be found here: www.youtube.com/watch?v=6DSjn9QDGll). While most synthetic media companies are startups, Meta (formerly Facebook) in September 2022 launched its own synthetic video tool, Make-A-Video (https://makeavideo.studio/).

While the above gives an indication of more standard synthetic content types, brands should also be aware that synthetic media applications may extend to areas including AI influencers (for example, lilmiquela, www.instagram.com/lilmiquela/), and deepfakes, where generative AI can be used to swap out faces. Examples of the latter include a deepfake video of actor Morgan Freeman, www.youtube.com/watch?v=oxXpB9pSETo, and a deepfake TikTok account of Tom Cruise, www.tiktok.com/@deeptomcruise. Ethical implications of AI-generated content are discussed in a later section.

AI Content Creation in Practice

Author's disclaimer: Some of the following text is generated by ChatGPT, an AI language model and is to be considered as machine-generated content. This has been intentionally included to demonstrate the power of generative AI in content marketing. All content created by ChatGPT has been checked for accuracy and AI text is labelled with #ai for full transparency.

What is ChatGPT?

#ai

ChatGPT is a machine learning model that uses natural language processing (NLP) to generate human-like text. It is trained on large amounts of text data and can be used to generate text on a wide range of topics.

In simple terms, it's a computer program that can write text in a way that resembles human writing. It can be used for a variety of applications, such as writing articles, composing emails, generating responses to customer inquiries, or even writing poetry or fiction.

It can be integrated with other software to make the process of text generation more efficient; it can also be fine-tuned to perform specific tasks like answering customer service inquiries or creating product descriptions.

ChatGPT is considered as a state-of-the-art model and it can provide a high level of fluency and coherence in the generated text; however, like any other AI model, it is not perfect, and the generated text may require human editing and proofreading before being used in any context.

What is DALL-E 2?

#ai

DALL-E 2 is a follow-up to the DALL-E, which is an AI-powered image and text generator developed by OpenAI. DALL-E 2 is an improvement on the original DALL-E, and it is capable of generating a wide range of images and text. It can generate images from textual prompts, such as 'Generate an image of a cat wearing a top hat' or 'Generate a picture of a beach at sunset', and text from images, such as 'Generate a caption for this image of a dog playing with a ball'.

DALL-E 2 can also generate images and text that don't match the prompts exactly, but that are related to them in some way. For example, if you prompt DALL-E 2 to generate an image of a cat wearing a top hat, it might generate an image of a cat wearing a fedora instead.

DALL-E 2 is based on a transformer architecture and uses a combination of unsupervised and supervised learning. It has been trained on a large dataset of images and text, so it can generate images and text that are highly realistic and diverse. DALL-E 2 is considered a state-of-the-art model. It can be used for various applications, like generating images for social media, creating illustrations for books, and even for creating assets for video games. However, as with any AI model, it is not perfect and it's important to review and edit the generated content before using it.

The Role and Use of Prompts

#ai

A prompt is a sentence or a set of instructions that you give AI such as ChatGPT to generate content. It's like asking a question or giving a task for ChatGPT to complete. The prompt can be as simple as 'Write a sentence' or as complex as 'Write a descriptive paragraph about a beach vacation'. It's basically the starting point for ChatGPT to generate the text you desire.

Here are some tips for writing effective prompts to use ChatGPT for marketing:

- **Be specific**: Use clear and specific language to ensure that ChatGPT understands the context and can provide accurate responses. For example, instead of saying 'Write an article about our product', you could say 'Write a 1000-word article that explains the features and benefits of our product'.
- **Use action verbs**: Use action verbs to prompt ChatGPT to take specific actions, such as 'generate a tweet about our new product' or 'write a blog post about the benefits of our service'.
- **Provide context**: Provide enough context for ChatGPT to understand the topic and the audience. For example, if you're writing a prompt for a blog post about a new product, provide information about the product, the target audience, and the goals of the post.
- **Keep it simple**: Avoid using jargon or overly complex language, as this can make it difficult for ChatGPT to understand the prompt and provide a relevant response.
- **Be creative**: Experiment with different prompts and formats to see what works best for your marketing needs.
- **Use examples**: Provide examples of the type of content you are looking for or use examples to train the model on the type of text you want it to generate.
- **Provide constraints**: If needed, provide constraints like length, tone, and language to guide ChatGPT to generate the desired output.

By following these tips, you can ensure that the text generated by ChatGPT is relevant, accurate, and effective for your marketing needs. But remember, even though ChatGPT is a powerful tool for content generation, it's not perfect. Always fact-check and edit the generated text before using it in any marketing materials.

AI Content Example: Blog Post

Prompt: As a boxing coach employed at a new Edinburgh-based boxing gym with a monthly club membership, write a 500-word blog post that explains the benefits of boxing for mental well-being including examples, to encourage potential customers to try out a taster session taking place the third Saturday of each month.

Content generated (ChatGPT):

#ai

Boxing for mental well-being

Boxing is much more than just a physical activity – it can also have a significant impact on mental well-being. At our new Edinburgh-based boxing gym, we believe that the benefits of boxing can be life-changing for anyone who gives it a try.

One of the biggest benefits of boxing is the release of endorphins, which are chemicals in the brain that act as natural painkillers and mood elevators. When you're hitting a punching bag or sparring with a partner, your brain is flooded with endorphins, which can help to reduce stress and anxiety, and improve overall mood.

Another benefit of boxing is the sense of accomplishment and self-esteem that comes from learning and mastering new skills. Whether you're a beginner or an experienced boxer, there's always something new to learn and improve upon, and the sense of accomplishment that comes from mastering a new technique or combination can be incredibly empowering.

Boxing also requires intense focus and concentration, which can help to improve cognitive function and mental clarity. When you're in the ring, you need to be completely present and focused in order to succeed. This focus and concentration can also carry over into other areas of life, making you more productive and efficient in everything you do.

Additionally, boxing is a great way to build self-discipline and self-control. The discipline and control required to train for a fight and stay in shape can help to improve overall self-control and willpower.

Boxing also provides a great way to channel and release pent-up anger and aggression in a healthy and constructive way. Hitting a punching bag can be a great outlet for frustrations and can help to reduce feelings of anger and aggression.

Overall, boxing can be incredibly beneficial for mental well-being. It can reduce stress and anxiety, improve mood, increase self-esteem, boost cognitive function and mental clarity, build self-discipline and self-control, and provide a healthy outlet for anger and aggression.

We invite you to come and experience the benefits of boxing for yourself at our new Edinburgh-based gym. We will be holding a taster session on the third Saturday of each month, where you can come and try boxing for yourself, meet our coaches and get a feel for the gym. We believe that once you try it, you'll be hooked! So why not come and give it a try and see how it can change your life for the better.

In conclusion, boxing is not just a physical activity, it also has a positive impact on mental well-being. It can help to reduce stress, anxiety and improve overall mood, cognitive function, self-discipline, self-control, and provide a healthy outlet for anger and aggression. We encourage you to join our taster session on the third Saturday of each month and experience the benefits of boxing for yourself.

AI Content Example: Email

Prompt: As a personal trainer, write an email to a male client who has stalled with his fitness and weight-loss goals, suggesting three things they can do to get back on track and start exercising again.

Content generated (ChatGPT):

#ai

Subject: Let's Get Back on Track

Dear [Client],

I hope this email finds you well. I've noticed that you've been a little absent from our sessions recently and I wanted to check in and see how you're doing. I understand that life can sometimes get in the way of our fitness goals, but I want to remind you that you're capable of achieving them.

Here are three things you can do to get back on track and start exercising again:

1   Set realistic and specific goals: Instead of setting a general goal of losing weight, set a specific goal of losing x pounds in x weeks. This will give you something specific to work towards and make it more likely that you'll achieve it.
2   Find an accountability partner: Whether it's a friend, family member, or a trainer, having someone to hold you accountable can be a great motivation to stick to your exercise routine.
3   Mix up your routine: If you've been doing the same workout for a while, your body may have adapted to it and you may have hit a plateau. Mixing up your routine can help keep your body challenged and prevent boredom.

I'd love to help you with any of these suggestions and create a personalised plan that will help you reach your goals. Let's schedule a session soon and get back on track together.

Best, [Your Name]

AI Content Example: Social Media

Prompt: As a fitness studio owner, write three separate social media posts including hashtags promoting a monthly subscription offer of £9.99 if you sign up during January including a call-to-action, one for Twitter, one for Instagram, and one for Facebook.

Content generated (ChatGPT):

#ai

Twitter: 'Start the year off strong with our January subscription deal! Sign up for just £9.99/month and get access to all of our classes. #NewYearNewYou #FitnessGoals #MonthlyDeal'

Instagram: 'Don't miss out on our January subscription offer! For just £9.99/month, join our community and reach your fitness goals. Hit the link in our bio to sign up. #GymMotivation #WorkoutDeals #NewYearNewYou'

Facebook: 'Welcome to the new year! Kickstart your fitness journey with our January subscription offer. Sign up for only £9.99/month and gain access to all of our classes. Limited time offer, click the link to join now. #FitnessChallenge #NewYearNewYou #MonthlySubscription'

AI Content Example: Images

Prompt: A logo for a boxing club for young people.

Content generated (DALL-E 2):

#ai

Figure 12.4 A logo for a boxing club for young people.

Prompt: Two black and white boxing gloves raised for a fight.

Content generated (DALL-E 2):

#ai

Figure 12.5 Two black and white boxing gloves raised for a fight.

Prompt: A black and white illustration of a trendy gym.

Content generated (DALL-E 2):

#ai

Figure 12.6 A black and white illustration of a trendy gym.

Prompt: A black and white illustration of a personal trainer encouraging a client in the gym ·

Content generated (DALL-E 2):

#ai

Figure 12.7 A black and white illustration of a personal trainer encouraging a client in the gym.

AI Content Creation Tools

The table below is a curation of current (2023) generative AI content creation tools brands can use in their content marketing. The list can also be found online on https://ai.digitalmarketing.scot/.

Text and Writing

Table 12.3 Generative AI content creation tools for text and writing

Name	Brief Description (from Website)	URL
ChatGPT	We've trained a model called ChatGPT which interacts in a conversational way … … it is a sibling model to InstructGPT, which is trained to follow an instruction in a prompt and provide a detailed response.	https://chat.openai.com/
Creaitor.ai	Creaitor will help you write content in a more powerful, emotionally expressive way.	www.creaitor.ai/
Frase	Frase AI helps you research, write, and optimise high-quality SEO content in minutes instead of hours.	www.frase.io/
HyperWrite	HyperWrite helps you write with confidence and get your work done faster from idea to final draft.	https://hyperwriteai.com/
Jasper	Jasper is the AI Content Generator that helps you and your team break through creative blocks to create amazing, original content 10X faster.	www.jasper.ai/
Persado	The Persado Motivation AI Platform interprets the intent of a message, uses AI and machine learning models, and together with an unparalleled decision engine, generates the precise language that motivates each individual to engage and act.	www.persado.com/
Rytr	Rytr is an AI writing assistant that helps you create high-quality content, in just a few seconds, at a fraction of the cost!	https://rytr.me/
WordHero	With WordHero's AI technology, you can create original blog posts, social media content, emails, and more – in just seconds.	https://wordhero.co/
wordtune	Say exactly what you mean through clear, compelling, and authentic writing.	www.wordtune.com/
Writesonic	Create SEO-optimised and plagiarism-free content for your blogs, ads, emails, and website 10X faster.	https://writesonic.com/

Images

Table 12.4 Generative AI content creation tools for images

Name	Brief Description (from Website)	URL
Astria	Tailor-made AI image generation	www.astria.ai/
Cleanup.pictures	Remove unwanted objects from photos, people, text, and defects from any picture for free. Cleanup.pictures is an advanced editing tool based on Artificial Intelligence that is much better than other clone stamp tools.	https://cleanup.pictures/
craiyon	Free online AI image generator from text.	www.craiyon.com/
DALL·E 2	DALL·E 2 is a new AI system that can create realistic images and art from a description in natural language.	https://openai.com/dall-e-2/
designify	Pick any image to create AI-powered designs by automatically removing backgrounds, enhancing colours, adjusting smart shadows, and so much more.	www.designify.com/
Hotpot	Hotpot helps you create amazing graphics, pictures, and text. AI tools like AI Art Generator spark creativity and automate drudgery while easy-to-edit templates empower anyone to create device mockups, social media posts, marketing images, app icons, and other work graphics.	https://hotpot.ai/
ImagetoCartoon	Image to Cartoon is an online AI cartooniser that converts your face to cartoon style. Make cartoon avatar, characters in a single click.	https://imagetocartoon.com/
Looka	Use Looka's AI-powered platform to design a logo and build a brand you love.	https://looka.com/
Magic Studio	Magic Studio helps you automatically edit and create images, using AI.	https://magicstudio.com/
Playground	Playground AI is a free-to-use online AI image creator. Use it to create art, social media posts, presentations, posters, videos, logos and more.	https://playgroundai.com/

Audio and Voice

Table 12.5 Generative AI content creation tools for audio and voice

Name	Brief Description (from Website)	URL
Amper	Amper is an AI music composition company that develops tools for content creators of all kinds.	www.ampermusic.com/
Big Speak	Big Speak allows you to generate realistic-sounding audio from text. We use a mix of machine-learning algorithms to bring you the best voice generation technology.	https://bigspeak.ai/
boomy	Make generative music with Artificial Intelligence.	https://boomy.com/
Coqui	Direct emotive, generative AI voices for video games, post-production, dubbing and much more.	https://coqui.ai/
Harmonai	We are a community-driven organisation releasing open-source generative audio tools to make music production more accessible and fun for everyone.	www.harmonai.org/
Mubert	Human x AI Generative Music. For your video content, podcasts, and apps.	https://mubert.com/
Murf	Make studio-quality voice-overs in minutes. Use Murf's lifelike AI voices for podcasts, videos, and all your professional presentations.	https://murf.ai/
Play.ht	Generate realistic Text to Speech (TTS) audio using our online AI Voice Generator and the best synthetic voices. Instantly convert text into natural-sounding speech and download as MP3 and WAV audio files.	https://play.ht/
Resemble AI	Resemble's AI voice generator lets you create human-like voice-overs in seconds.	www.resemble.ai/
Soundraw	Royalty-free music, AI-generated for you. Simply choose the mood, the genre, and the length. Our AI will generate beautiful songs for you.	https://soundraw.io/
Speechelo	Instantly generate voice from text 100 per cent human-sounding voiceover with only three clicks! In less than 10 seconds you'll have your AI voice-over generated.	https://speechelo.com/
WellSaid	With WellSaid, you and your team can create a compelling realistic AI voice-over for all your digital content.	https://wellsaidlabs.com/

Video

Table 12.6 Generative AI content creation tools for video

Name	Brief Description (from Website)	URL
Colossyan	Create videos with AI actors – stop spending your time on studios. Leave professional video editing to Colossyan Creator without any training or advanced skills. Simply type in your text and have a video ready in 70+ languages within minutes.	www.colossyan.com/
Dubverse	Using text to speech (TTS), advanced machine translation and generative AI, Dubverse Platform delivers ready-to-publish videos 10x faster than manual dubbing.	https://dubverse.ai/
Elai	Create AI videos from just text. Build customised AI videos with a presenter in minutes without using a camera, studio, and a greenscreen.	https://elai.io/
Fliki	Turn text into videos with AI voices. Create videos from scripts or blog posts using realistic voices in two minutes!	https://fliki.ai/
Make-A-Video	Make-A-Video is a state-of-the-art AI system that generates videos from text.	https://makeavideo.studio/
Opus	Text to Video generation using AI. Computational Production – everything from scenes, assets, characters, dialogue and visual effects. Original content.	https://opus.ai/
Rephrase.ai	We create digital avatars of real humans to produce hyper-personalised videos at scale, helping businesses communicate with their stakeholders effectively.	www.rephrase.ai/
Runway	With 30+ AI Magic Tools, real-time video editing, collaboration, and more, Runway is your next-generation content-creation suite. Right inside your browser.	https://runwayml.com/
Synthesia	Create videos from plain text in minutes. Synthesia is the #1 rated AI video creation platform. Thousands of companies use it to create videos in 120 languages, saving up to 80 per cent of their time and budget.	www.synthesia.io/
Tavus	Meet Tavus, the programmatic personalised video tool made for top-performing product, marketing, and sales teams that want to transform how they build relationships. Record once and discover the power of Tavus as our AI automatically generates personalised videos for audiences large and small.	www.tavus.io/

Ethical Implications of AI-Generated Content

#ai

As a marketer, using ChatGPT or other AI-generated content can be a powerful tool for creating engaging and relevant content for your audience. However, it's important to keep in mind the ethical considerations that come with using this technology. Here are some ethical considerations that marketers should be aware of when using ChatGPT, and tips on what to do.

- **Transparency**: It's important to be transparent with consumers about the origin of the content and to clearly label it as being generated by AI. Misrepresenting AI-generated content as human-generated content can be considered as a form of deception and can affect the trust and credibility of the company. Always use a disclaimer or a label that clearly states that the content is generated by AI and be transparent with the audience.
- **Bias**: ChatGPT is trained on large amounts of text data, which may include biases. Therefore, it's important to be aware of the potential biases in the training data, and to take steps to mitigate these biases in the generated content. One way to do this is by using a diverse set of data to train the model and by reviewing the generated content for any biases.
- **Misinformation**: The generated text may not always be accurate or credible. Therefore, it's important to fact-check and verify any information before using it in marketing materials. Before using any generated text, always review it for accuracy and credibility.
- **Job displacement**: The use of AI in content generation could lead to job displacement for human writers and content creators. It's important to consider the impact of AI on employment and to ensure that the use of AI is done in an ethical and responsible way. One way to do this is by using AI to augment human work, rather than replace it.
- **Privacy**: The use of ChatGPT or other AI-generated content also raises privacy concerns, particularly when it comes to the use of personal data used to train the model. It's important to make sure that the data used to train the model is collected in an ethical manner, with the appropriate consent and in compliance with data protection regulations.

In conclusion, using ChatGPT or other AI-generated content can be a powerful tool for creating engaging and relevant content for your audience. However, it's important to keep in mind the ethical considerations that come with using this technology. By being transparent, aware of biases, fact-checking information, considering the impact on employment, and protecting privacy, you can ensure that the use of ChatGPT is done in an ethical and responsible way.

#human

While the above section on AI content's ethical implications was written by AI and thus is in itself synthetic, it identifies key areas of ethical issues brands need to be aware of. Three of these are explored in more detail below.

- **Trust and credibility**: The first issue concerns trust and credibility in relation to the use of synthetic content. Brands should be transparent when using synthetic media in their content marketing. For example, chatbots should clearly state that they are non-human agents, and synthetic images and video should have a digital watermark or imprint. While this area is currently still developing, promising initiatives include the Content Authenticity Initiative, a cross-industry project to help develop technology and standards to preserve trust online, including in the area of synthetic content (Content Authenticity Initiative, n.d.). Some tool providers (for example DALL-E 2) already include digital watermarks in their AI-generated content. It is also predicted that with time, consumers will become more used to synthetic media and society overall will adapt the more people are exposed to such content, in a way similar to their understanding of social media images being enhanced using filters (Riparbelli, 2023).

- **Privacy and bias**: A second area relates to privacy and fairness, including bias. Regarding consumer privacy, both machine learning AI and generative AI rely on data to make it work. That is, personalisation itself is only possible through consumer data being provided. For individual-level AI-powered content personalisation to be successful, consumer data and individual digital activity (previous purchases, reviews, ratings, comments, etc.) are required (Chandra et al., 2022). Brands in their use of AI thus must ensure that consumers' privacy rights are protected (Mariani et al., 2022). When it comes to bias, a key consideration is that an AI algorithm is not neutral or objective but rather, will reproduce the biases and prejudices found in the data it was originally trained on (De Bruyn et al., 2020). For example, research has shown that women are less likely to be targeted with ads that are less profitable, such as job postings in IT, because the AI algorithm optimises for cost-effectiveness, and targeting women costs more in online targeted advertising. This creates gender biases in the advertising of professional opportunities relating to IT (Lambrecht & Tucker, 2019). Similarly, when using generative AI image tool DALL-E 2 for the purpose of content creation in this chapter, the author tested two prompts that were exactly the same, with the only difference being gender. The resulting 'women' image incorporated pink colour, and the 'men' image featured an angry and aggressive face, as illustrated in Figure 12.8.

Prompt: A logo for a new boxing gym for women

Content generated (DALL-E 2):

#ai

Figure 12.8 A logo for a new boxing gym for women.

Prompt: A logo for a new boxing gym for men

Content generated (DALL-E 2):

#ai

Figure 12.9 A logo for a new boxing gym for men.

- **Unemployment and displacement**: The final ethical implication of AI-generated content relates to the potential impact on employment. Human creators face existential risks from AI models' growing capacity to produce high-quality and valuable content across all categories as this content is more and more human-like (Tuomi, 2023). Images and other visual content in particular are increasingly important in content marketing as they provide a lasting and powerful impression, stay in the mind for longer, and are easier to process than other types of content (Mayahi & Vidrih, 2022). The explosion of short form video in particular is ripe for human displacement. A five-minute-video can now be created in a browser, by typing words in any language, choosing an avatar (based on a real person), and then synthesising a voice (either your own or a synthetic one). All of this can be accomplished in a few minutes as opposed to the traditional, lengthy, and costly video production process (Riparbelli, 2023). While there is thus a risk that future content creation will requires less and less human input, there are also potential opportunities. Those on a budget, for example entrepreneurs or SMEs, may be empowered to do more of their own content marketing in-house (Tuomi, 2023). In addition, the future of marketing overall will require greater personalisation in real-time and at scale. This will only be possible with a strong human-machine partnership, with generative AI amplifying human creativity, not replacing it (Schaefer, 2022).

Case Study – Škoda and Decentraland

Background

ŠKODA is the first car brand in Germany to advertise on the growing platform 'Decentraland', one of the most important metaverses of the moment. There, a floating 3D model of the ŠKODA ENYAQ COUPÉ iV is ready to be discovered.

Campaign objectives

The aim was to reach the so-called 'early adopters', a very exclusive target group that had previously been difficult to reach due to ad blockers and ad-avoiding media behaviour. Our goal was to manifest and increase ŠKODA within the target group in their relevant set and generate an uplift.

Overview of the campaign

Strategy

The core of the strategy for ŠKODA was to specifically counteract the 'Joy of Missing-Out' behaviour of the young target group (20–39 years); in other words, their conscious and active decision to avoid unwanted advertising messages.

If we take a closer look: TV has been replaced by streaming. Ad blockers prevent targeting on YouTube and in digital in general.

In addition, the advertising pressure in the automotive industry is extremely high, which makes it even more difficult to stand out from the crowd.

We were looking for a place where early adopters gathered and where advertising was still what it was on television many years ago: something special that was met with curiosity – instead of rejection. And we found this new land. In the metaverse Decentraland, more than 1.5 million active users can take part in events such as the 'Metaverse Fashion Week' or attend concerts by artists such as Deadmau5 and Jason Derulo. Representing a symbiosis of real and virtual reality, the metaverse opens completely new possibilities for both individuals and brands.

Here, 75 per cent of the users exactly meet the requirements of our target group. Moreover, there is still no car brand that advertises on the metaverse from Germany.

It became clear: in order to communicate with early adopters, brands sometimes have to behave like early adopters themselves.

And since the users in the metaverse still behave like explorers and look at the virtual environment much more attentively, we decided on virtual OOH.

Execution

The Decentraland is divided into 90,601 'parcels', where each parcel can be compared to a type of land. Virtual land is immaterial land that exists in virtual worlds. Just like physical land, it is also sold as plots and can be bought in the currency of the respective country.

To attract the attention of visitors to Decentraland, landowners design their land majestically into the 3D environment. Accordingly, we took advantage of this for the presentation of the new ENYAQ COUPÉ IV.

More precisely, we used floating 3D graphics of the new ENYAQ COUPÉ IV so that users can view the model from all sides.

The playout on a total of 120 OOH surfaces is based on the principle of reverse proxy, that is, when a user approaches one of the 120 properties on which the screens are located, her/his IP address is identified, and the location can be determined. Of course, compliant with GDPR.

As soon as the location has been determined, the metaverse request is forwarded to the ad server, which then decides whether the creative should be delivered – or not. If the user's location does not match the campaign criterion, a) the screen is not included on the property, or b) a fallback image or another campaign's creative is delivered on the screen.

The Results

A real pioneer campaign with an impressive floating 3D model that users looked at with great interest from all sides.

In this context, it is important to know: anyone who wants to explore the metaverse must first create a 'wallet' such as MetaMask. The whole thing does not cost any money, it is only necessary for the further process.

Accordingly, a 'cost per wallet reached' is currently the best key figure for evaluating measures in the metaverse, as this is the quasi equivalent of the Facebook/Instagram login or the web3 cookie.

The first results of the campaign, which is still ongoing, have exceeded expectations:

In figures, we have already reached around ten thousand wallets in the term of nine days.
More impressive, however, is the length of time: users spend more than 42 seconds in the visible, perceptible area of the ŠKODA 3-D OOH installation. An accompanied research study is also in place to gather further insights in this totally new advertising space. Stay tuned.

met[ads] Co-Founder Lukas Flöer:
With our partnership-based and innovative implementation for Skoda, we created a scalable immersive format for the first time – which was characterised by the unique floating integration of the 3D model of the Enyaq – which was activated at over 120 locations in the Decentraland, so that the marketing part of content marketing was not neglected. We were able to generate not only relevant reach in the metaverse, but also valuable insights into the socio-demographics of the users reached.

References

Alcántara, A.-M., & Coffee, P. (2022). Metaverse spending to total $5 trillion in 2030, McKinsey predicts. *The Wall Street Journal*. www.wsj.com/articles/metaverse-spending-to-total-5-trillion-in-2030-mckinsey-predicts-11655254794

Ameen, N., Cheah, J. H., & Kumar, S. (2022). It's all part of the customer journey: The impact of augmented reality, chatbots, and social media on the body image and self-esteem of Generation Z female consumers. *Psychology and Marketing*, *39*(11), 2110–2129. 10.1002/mar.21715

Bannister, L. (2006). Adidas targets avatars with shop in Second Life. Campaign.

Brown, S. (2022). What *Second Life* and Roblox can teach us about the metaverse. https://mitsloan.mit.edu/ideas-made-to-matter/what-second-life-and-roblox-can-teach-us-about-metaverse

Campbell, C., Sands, S., Ferraro, C., Tsao, H. Y. (Jody), & Mavrommatis, A. (2020). From data to action: How marketers can leverage AI. *Business Horizons*, *63*(2), 227–243. 10.1016/j.bushor.2019.12.002

Chandra, S., Verma, S., Lim, W. M., Kumar, S., & Donthu, N. (2022). Personalization in personalized marketing: Trends and ways forward. *Psychology and Marketing*, *39*(8), 1529–1562. 10.1002/mar.21670

Chintalapati, S., & Pandey, S. K. (2022). Artificial intelligence in marketing: A systematic literature review. *International Journal of Market Research*, *64*(1), 38–68. 10.1177/14707853211018428

Content Authenticity Initiative (n.d.). https://contentauthenticity.org/

Costa-Sánchez, C. (2017). Online video marketing strategies. Typology by business sector. *Communication and Society*, *30*(1), 17–38. 10.15581/003.30.1.17-38

DataReportal. (2022). Digital futures: What 2023 holds. www.youtube.com/watch?v=3RnJpUhwa1U

De Bruyn, A., Viswanathan, V., Beh, Y. S., Brock, J. K. U., & von Wangenheim, F. (2020). Artificial intelligence and marketing: Pitfalls and opportunities. *Journal of Interactive Marketing*, *51*, 91–105. 10.1016/j.intmar.2020.04.007

Dean, B. (2022). Roblox user and growth stats 2022. https://backlinko.com/roblox-users

Flitter, E., & Yaffe-Bellany, D. (2023). FTX founder gamed markets, crypto rivals say. *New York Times*. www.nytimes.com/2023/01/18/business/ftx-sbf-crypto-markets.html

Gadekallu, T. R., Huynh-The, T., Wang, W., Yenduri, G., Ranaweera, P., Pham, Q.-V., da Costa, D. B., & Liyanage, M. (2022). Blockchain for the metaverse: A review. 1–17. http://arxiv.org/abs/2203.09738

Galloway, S. (2022). AI. www.profgalloway.com/ai/

Gent, E. (2021). What can the metaverse learn from *Second Life*? *IEEE Spectrum*. https://spectrum.ieee.org/metaverse-second-life

Giang Barrera, K., & Shah, D. (2023). Marketing in the Metaverse: Conceptual understanding, framework, and research agenda. *Journal of Business Research*, *155*(PA), 113420. 10.1016/j.jbusres.2022.113420

Google. (2022). Shortform and longform videos. https://support.google.com/google-ads/answer/2382886

Guidi, B., & Michienzi, A. (2022). Social games and blockchain: Exploring the metaverse of Decentraland. *Proceedings – 2022 IEEE 42nd International Conference on Distributed Computing Systems Workshops, ICDCSW 2022*, 199–204. 10.1109/ICDCSW56584.2022.00045

Güven, İ., & Ercan, T. (2022). *Determining Factors of Virtual Land Value: The Case of Decentraland*, 518–537. International Technology and Design Symposium.

Haenlein, M., & Kaplan, A. (2019). A brief history of artificial intelligence: On the past, present, and future of artificial intelligence. *California Management Review*, *61*(4), 5–14. 10.1177/0008125619864925

Hancock, J. T., Naaman, M., & Levy, K. (2020). AI-Mediated communication: Definition, research agenda, and ethical considerations. *Journal of Computer-Mediated Communication*, *25*(1), 89–100. 10.1093/jcmc/zmz022

Herskowitz, N. (2023). Microsoft Mesh: Creating connections at the World Economic Forum 2023. www.microsoft.com/en-us/microsoft-365/blog/2023/01/16/microsoft-mesh-creating-connections-at-the-world-economic-forum-2023/

Hopkinson, P. J., & Singhal, A. (2018). Exploring the use of AI to manage customers' relationships. July. www.researchgate.net/publication/324647995

IAB (2022). Metaverse for Brands Guide (Issue November).

IPG Media Lab. (2016). Microsoft restricts brand advertising in popular game Minecraft. https://medium.com/ipg-media-lab/microsoft-restricts-brand-advertising-in-popular-game-minecraft-e66b594a113c

Iqbal, M. (2023). Fortnite usage and revenue statistics. www.businessofapps.com/data/fortnite-statistics/

Jasper. (n.d.). www.jasper.ai/

Kim, J. (2021). Advertising in the metaverse: Research agenda. *Journal of Interactive Advertising*, *21*(3), 141–144. 10.1080/15252019.2021.2001273

Kumar, V., Rajan, B., Venkatesan, R., & Lecinski, J. (2019). Understanding the role of artificial intelligence in personalized engagement marketing. *California Management Review*, *61*(4), 135–155. 10.1177/0008125619859317

Lambrecht, A., & Tucker, C. (2019). Algorithmic bias? An empirical study of apparent gender-based discrimination in the display of stem career ads. *Management Science*, *65*(7), 2966–2981. 10.1287/mnsc.2018.3093

Larsen, B., & Narayan, J. (2023). Generative AI: A game-changer that society and industry need to be ready for. World Economic Forum.

Lee, L.-H., Braud, T., Zhou, P., Wang, L., Xu, D., Lin, Z., Kumar, A., Bermejo, C., & Hui, P. (2021). All one needs to know about metaverse: A complete survey on technological singularity, virtual ecosystem, and research agenda. *14*(8), 1–66. http://arxiv.org/abs/2110.05352

Lifestyle Asia. (2022). Decentraland to host the second edition of Metaverse Fashion Week in March 2023. www.lifestyleasia.com/ind/style/fashion/metaverse-fashion-week-2023-on-decentraland-details/

Ma, L., & Sun, B. (2020). Machine learning and AI in marketing – Connecting computing power to human insights. *International Journal of Research in Marketing, 37*(3), 481–504. 10.1016/j.ijresmar.2020.04.005

Mariani, M. M., Perez-Vega, R., & Wirtz, J. (2022). AI in marketing, consumer research and psychology: A systematic literature review and research agenda. *Psychology and Marketing, 39*(4), 755–776. 10.1002/mar.21619

Mayahi, S., & Vidrih, M. (2022). The impact of Generative AI on the future of visual content marketing. June. http://arxiv.org/abs/2211.12660

Melcher, N. (2022). Deep dive: Early metaverse players – Data on demographics, socializing, playing, & spending. https://newzoo.com/insights/articles/deep-dive-metaverse-gamers-data-on-metaverse-demographics-socializing-playing-spending-2

Microsoft. (2023). What is mixed reality? https://learn.microsoft.com/en-us/windows/mixed-reality/discover/mixed-reality

Moyer, E. (2022). Meta's "Horizon Worlds" Virtual Land isn't grabbing users, report says. Cnet. www.cnet.com/tech/metas-horizon-worlds-virtual-land-isnt-grabbing-users-report-says/

Mustak, M., Salminen, J., Plé, L., & Wirtz, J. (2021). Artificial intelligence in marketing: Topic modeling, scientometric analysis, and research agenda. *Journal of Business Research, 124*(November 2020), 389–404. 10.1016/j.jbusres.2020.10.044

Nielsen. (2020). Fortnite is the New IRL: Why brands must plan for a rise in virtual gatherings. www.nielsen.com/insights/2020/fortnite-is-the-new-irl-why-brands-must-plan-for-a-rise-in-virtual-gatherings/

Olsen, P. (2022). Google faces a serious threat from ChatGPT. *The Washington Post.* www.washingtonpost.com/business/energy/google-faces-a-serious-threat-from-chatgpt/2022/12/07/363d2440-75f5-11ed-a199-927b334b939f_story.html

Pemberton Levy, H. (2015). Gartner predicts our digital future. www.gartner.com/smarterwithgartner/gartner-predicts-our-digital-future

Perry, A. (2022). The "real" metaverse already exists and it's called "Fortnite." Mashable. https://mashable.com/article/fortnite-is-the-real-metaverse

Peters, J. (2022). Tim Sweeney wants Epic to help build a metaverse that's actually positive. www.theverge.com/2022/12/15/23511494/tim-sweeney-epic-games-metaverses-positive-dystopian

Pilipović, Š. (2023). Minecraft statistics. https://levvvel.com/minecraft-statistics/

PwC (2022). *Perspectives from the Global Entertainment & Media Outlook 2022–2026.* www.pwc.com/gx/en/industries/tmt/media/outlook/outlook-perspectives.html

Riparbelli, V. (2023). The future of (synthetic) media. www.synthesia.io/post/the-future-of-synthetic-media

Rose, R. (2022). ChatGPT: The future of AI in content is in your hands. https://contentmarketinginstitute.com/articles/chatgpt-ai-content-future

Schaefer, M. (2022). Why ChatGPT will profoundly transform every marketing career, starting now. https://businessesgrow.com/2022/12/08/chatgpt/

ServiceBell (2022). 53 Chatbot statistics for 2022: Usage, demographics, trends. www.servicebell.com/post/chatbot-statistics

Statista (2022). U.S. video gaming audiences 2022, by age group. www.statista.com/statistics/189582/age-of-us-video-game-players/

Statista (2023). Global gaming penetration 2022, by age and gender. www.statista.com/statistics/326420/console-gamers-gender/

Synthesia. (n.d.). What is synthetic media? www.synthesia.io/glossary/synthetic-media

Tassi, P. (2022). Fortnite's Epic Games makes a metaverse investment to scale up even further. www.forbes.com/sites/paultassi/2022/09/23/fortnites-epic-games-makes-a-metaverse-investment-to-scale-up-even-further/

Thompson, C. (2022). It's lonely in the metaverse: DappRadar data suggests Decentraland has 38 'daily active' users in $1.3B Ecosystem. *Coindesk*. www.coindesk.com/web3/2022/10/07/its-lonely-in-the-metaverse-decentralands-38-daily-active-users-in-a-13b-ecosystem/

Tuomi, A. (2023). *AI-Generated Content, Creative Freelance Work and Hospitality and Tourism Marketing*. Springer Nature Switzerland. 10.1007/978-3-031-25752-0

Virgilio, D. (2022). What comparisons between second life and the metaverse miss. https://slate.com/technology/2022/02/second-life-metaverse-facebook-comparisons.html

Vlačić, B., Corbo, L., Costa e Silva, S., & Dabić, M. (2021). The evolving role of artificial intelligence in marketing: A review and research agenda. *Journal of Business Research*, *128*(January 2021), 187–203. 10.1016/j.jbusres.2021.01.055

Wagner, R., & Cozmiuc, D. (2022). Extended reality in marketing—A multiple case study on Internet of Things platforms. *Information (Switzerland)*, *13*(6), 1–25. 10.3390/info13060278

Yencha, C. (2023). Spatial heterogeneity and non-fungible token sales: Evidence from Decentraland LAND sales. *Finance Research Letters, August 2022*, 103628. 10.1016/j.frl.2023.103628

YPulse. (2022). 5 successful brand experiences in the metaverse. www.ypulse.com/article/2022/11/01/5-successful-brand-experiences-in-the-metaverse/

Book Summary - 12 Guiding Principles of Content Marketing

By Dr Agata Krowinska

Summarising the chapters of this book, the following 12 guiding principles provide a roadmap to marketers who seek to implement content marketing into their marketing practice.

1 Content Marketing can only be successful if content is in some way of value to the targeted audience. To increase the likelihood for this to occur, the audience must be clearly defined so that content can be created to match or fit with the target group's interests. Importantly, content marketing is not the same as advertising – therefore, its focus should be on the benefits that campaigns with each individual piece of content offer. Content signals brand personality and values, and thus shapes stakeholders' views of its sender. It is thus crucial that marketers create a clear branding guide for employees and external partners involved in content creation and delivery to ensure quality and consistency of their content marketing outputs.

2 Planning is an essential element of developing a content marketing strategy. Marketers should not engage in producing and distributing any content without having defined SMART objectives. Also, content to be shared with their audiences must be created and delivered strategically and be an integrated part of the overall marketing plan. Planning also includes selecting a set of appropriate metrics to monitor and evaluate content performance.

3 Content creation requires creativity. Effective content marketing puts content ideation at its core, developing creative outputs that respond to the brief. As consistently developing innovative and creative ideas is challenging, tools such as reflective diaries or brainstorming sessions can be useful to foster creativity.

4 One pathway towards effective content marketing practice is through the provision of value through informative content. Elicitation of value through informative content can help organisations stimulate positive customer engagement behaviours on social media, have a positive impact on brand perceptions, improve brand health, and help raise brand awareness. Content creators should evaluate the educational value of their content and ensure that the content's main topic is related to the brand

DOI: 10.4324/9781003346500-13

values and ethos. Expert knowledge or areas of expertise an organisation or individual can draw on are a very good basis for the creation of informative content.

5   Providing audiences with content that has entertainment benefits can stimulate brand-related interactions and help brands communicate their personality. Branded entertainment content should always focus on providing entertainment while the branded message should only be embedded very subtly. Where appropriate, brands can use humour in their content marketing practice; this can help the message to become more relatable and engaging. Given the visual nature of most social media platforms, it is important to use high quality visuals as they can also foster engagement and improve a brand's reputation.

6   Also, embedding social value in content marketing can positively impact consumer satisfaction, trust, brand reputation, and loyalty. Marketers can create social value through digital content that stimulates interactions between brands and consumers as well as other consumers in the social media settings. Relational content helps brands to foster socialisation, improve brand experience, and build strong and long-lasting relationships with targeted audiences. The more interactions marketers can stimulate via content, the greater the chances for building strong online brand communities – which should be a goal of any digital marketer.

7   Brands should engage in activities that embrace co-creation and inspire the creation of user-generated content (UGC). UGC is particularly suited to stimulate engagement and increase reach. People tend to trust other people over brands, therefore, UGC content can be a great way to improve trust and convince users. However, marketers need to clearly define their UGC campaigns so that the developed content corresponds with brand values and marketing goals. It is crucial for marketers to always acknowledge UGC creators and thank them in an appropriate form for their content.

8   Using social media influencers to create or disseminate content is a great way to generate user engagement, increase trust, and boost online reach. As there are many types of influencers, organisations need to make sure that they select the influencer who is appropriate for their content marketing goals. When deciding about which influencers to collaborate with, marketers should be guided by the following criteria: influencer's reach, engagement rate, authenticity, trustworthiness, content and audience quality, and values.

9   To effectively engage online audiences, brands should aim to post content regularly. However, constant creation of new content can be costly and time consuming. Rather than solely focusing on own content, marketers can also embrace content curation and adapt existing content from third party sources to the brand's messaging. When engaging in content curation, it is crucial for the marketer to make sure that the curated

content comes from a reputable source, and that it is relevant to the target audience.

10 Content marketing can be of particular value when used in conjunction with sponsorship and as a means of leveraging the sponsor-sponsee relationship throughout contract duration. Also here, the provision of value to fans and brand-related communities is key; whereby symbolic, and social benefits have been identified as particularly effective in terms of driving positive audience responses. A focus on mid- to long-term brand shaping, assuming a fan- and audiences-based perspective, a co-creative approach, and integrating sponsorship and leveraging within the broader marketing mix are additional important principles for content marketing in sponsorship contexts.

11 Marketers should practice ethical content marketing. This includes aspects such as ensuring to disclose sponsorships or compensations schemes, maintaining sincerity and honesty in their practice, and always fact-check every piece of content to make sure that the dissented information is accurate. Furthermore, the marketer should avoid harm to vulnerable groups, maintain professional standards, adequately recompense influencers, be respectful, loyal, and socially responsible.

12 As the digital environment is under the state of constant development, content creators need to make sure that they stay up to date with the latest trends and technological advancements. AI-generated content can be a powerful tool for creating engaging and relevant content for the target audience. Similarly, embracing the augmented reality and virtual reality formats can help to effectively engage key audiences and spark third-party publication.

Index

References to figures appear in *italic* type; and those in **bold** type refer to tables.